Catherine Labouré

Catherine Labouré

VISIONARY OF THE MIRACULOUS MEDAL

René Laurentin

Translated by Paul Inwood

BOOKS & MEDIA
Boston

Library of Congress Cataloging-in-Publication Data

Laurentin, Rene.

[Vie de Catherine Laboure. English]

Catherine Laboure : visionary of the miraculous medal / Rene Laurentin ; translated by Paul Inwood.

p. cm.

Originally published: The life of Catherine Laboure, 1806–1876. 1983.

Includes bibliographical references.

ISBN 0-8198-1578-0 (pbk.)

1. Laboure, Catherine, Saint, 1806–1876. 2. Christian saints—France—Biography. I. Title.

BX4700.L2L3813 2006

282.092—dc22

2005028082

Cover design by Rosana Usselmann

Cover and interior photos from the private collection of Father René Laurentin. Used with permission.

All rights reserved. No part of this book may be reproduced or transmitted in any form or by any means, electronic or mechanical, including photocopying, recording, or by any information storage and retrieval system without permission in writing from the publisher.

"P" and PAULINE are registered trademarks of the Daughters of St. Paul.

Originally published as *Vie de Catherine Labouré*, Copyright © Descée de Brouwer, Paris 6, 1980.

English translation © 1983 Sisters of Charity of St. Vincent de Paul, London NW7 1EH

First North American edition 2006

Published by Pauline Books & Media, 50 Saint Paul's Avenue, Boston, MA 02130-3491. www.pauline.org.

Printed in the U.S.A.

Pauline Books & Media is the publishing house of the Daughters of St. Paul, an international congregation of women religious serving the Church with the communications media.

1 2 3 4 5 6 7 8 9   11 10 09 08 07 06

*The author dedicates this book
to John Paul II,
pilgrim to the Rue du Bac on May 31, 1980,
as a celebration of the 150th anniversary
in the white light of pure truth.*

 Contents

Preface ix

Acknowledgments xii

Editor's Note xiv

Chapter I
Childhood and Bereavement (1806–1818) 1

Chapter II
Vocation 6

Chapter III
Seminary 24

Chapter IV
First Steps at the Enghien Hospice 51

Chapter V
Time of Fruition 71

Chapter VI
The War and the Commune (July 1870–June 1871) 123

Chapter VII
Declining Years–Ascending Life (1871–1876) 150

CHAPTER VIII
Catherine's Death (December 31, 1876) *186*

CHAPTER IX
Catherine's Sanctity *200*

Calendar *253*
    Abbreviations Used in the Notes *275*
    Notes to the Calendar *276*

Notes *279*

 Preface

On December 31, 1876, Sr. Catherine Labouré died at Reuilly in the house where she had served for forty-six years. She was 70 years old and had scarcely ever talked about herself. Robust at her work, she was a former Burgundy farm woman who had been put in charge of the sisters' chicken run and garden; and she had always given pride of place to ministering to the poor in the spirit of St. Vincent—a work of service carried out with few words but with no less efficiency and warmth for all that. For a long time after her death, her memory lingered on in the heads of the old folk at the hospice as "the sister who said," after giving them their food, "have you got enough?"

There did not seem to be anything else remarkable about her. Nevertheless, it was rumored that the "Henhouse Sister" was not as ordinary as she looked. It might well have been she who had seen the Blessed Virgin in the chapel at the Rue du Bac in 1830 and had been responsible for starting the Miraculous Medal—over a thousand million copies of it had found their way all around the world: it was a sign of so many conversions and cures.

Those who had asked her about this had been rewarded for their pains. To some, she had replied, "You've got the right idea," in such a natural and neutral tone of voice that it sowed doubt in the mind of the questioner. To others, she had said, "Get along with you!" and went straight back to concentrating on her work as if nothing else existed for her. Yet again, she sometimes seemed not to hear anything. People thought that she was a bit deaf toward the end of her life.

But as soon as she was dead, the secret was revealed. A great multitude of people came flocking to Reuilly, just as they were to do two years later to Bernadette's coffin in Nevers—but Bernadette had been famous in her lifetime. People rushed to see Catherine, to touch her, to beg for her intercession before the coffin was closed. The burial was more like a carnival than a day of mourning. There was singing, lanterns, flag-waving—all on the spur of the moment. Popular hymns replaced funeral chants.

The sisters had wanted to keep Catherine's mortal remains as a treasure. The wife of Marshal MacMahon, President of the Republic, had obtained authorization for Catherine to be interred in a vault under the house—which then became a place of pilgrimage for the next fifty-seven years until, for the purposes of the canonization process, she was exhumed, her body intact and her eyes still blue.

Who was this Catherine? Her simplicity was disconcerting, like Bernadette's. But unlike the visionary of Lourdes, exposed to the public from the time of her youth, Catherine's anonymity provoked no welter of documentary studies.

She was neither talkative nor demonstrative—in fact, she was typical of the peasants of the Auxois region where she came from and more especially typical of her family, the Labourés, whose most common profession was actually one of manual laborer. People who are good with their hands are not often so good with words. Catherine's parents and friends were not very forthcoming on the subject of Catherine herself. Also, they were not the storytelling sort. She herself was sufficiently taken up with the sheer hard business of living (as well as being an "interior" kind of person) not to feel the need to bring the foundations of her early life into view. "The Servant of God never spoke about herself, nor about her parents," testified Sr. Cosnard at the canonization process.[a]

Catherine's secret only had the effect of accentuating the discreetness that one often finds in peasant circles as a defense against the curious, so the historian often finds himself or herself in a fog. There is little in the way of picturesque or touching scenes, let alone large frescoes or dramatic episodes. A certain gray tint covers everything. Catherine's shining light appears at first to be rather lackluster, devoid of contrasts, like mountain mists where the sun filters dimly through.

To be able to write the story of her life, let alone to read it, one needs to have a love of the earth, of the monotony of the everyday, of the bread of the poor, of confidences only hinted at. The saint's biographer is reduced to digging in the thick book of everyday life (which today forms a principal part of historical research) and evaluating a few vague indications, monosyllabic grunts and long silences, all of which leave one guessing at the quality of what lies hidden underneath. In this particular case, the chronicler has to work through the medium of x-ray photographs, rather than ordinary ones; as a "seer" rather than as a storyteller. But it is thus that he or she is not disappointed and runs no risk of being disappointed, for the biographer uncovers the flames beneath the ashes. He or she reaches down into the most essential, the most marvelous thing in the eyes of God—the sanctity of the poor.

Having finished this work and re-reading these last introductory phrases, the author can now say just how much the impression of fog which gave rise to them has been dissipated by dint of work. The discovery of new archives—principally family archives—and the analysis of a plethora of neglected documents have revealed a whole galaxy of hitherto unknown facts. At last we know that the apparitions of the Virgin were not a blurred and undefined phenomenon; that there were three apparitions of the Virgin, all in 1830 on precise dates and so on. We are now able to follow in Catherine's footsteps, tracing her life from one day to the next, similar to what could already be done for Bernadette of Lourdes. No doubt Catherine has succeeded in keeping her secret. But with some of the mystery blown away, it has become a transparent secret, accessible to all those who have received that evangelical virtue which was so beloved of St. Vincent—the simplicity that gives a true sight of God.

Catherine's gift to us—and especially to St. Vincent's two "families"—is the daily example of a wonderful love of the poor. It is hope, joy, but also patience at times of sore trial; it is a communion with the cross borne each day and the art of bearing that cross without ever loading it on to others but rather lightening their burdens. It is a transparent contact with God, our Lord, and our Lady. Like our Lady, Catherine freely agreed to be a "handmaid." Catherine's gift flows naturally from a fresh springing up of the values of the Gospel, a hundred and fifty years ago—a wellspring that remains always available for those who thirst.

 # Acknowledgments

THE AUTHORS PRESENT THEIR GRATITUDE on the part of history and of our Lady herself to all those who have helped in the realization of this book:

Fr. Superior General of the Congregation of the Mission and the Company of the Sisters of Charity, and the Provincial Superior, whose encouragement has been invaluable;

Sr. L. Rogé, Superior General of the Sisters of Charity and her Council, whose support has been the epitome of efficiency;

Those Sisters of Charity who worked under a cloak of anonymity and with a humility analogous to that of Catherine to bring to fruition a project so demanding that, for a long time, seemed impossible.

The nieces and nephews of Catherine Labouré, who gave us access to family archives and family traditions:

Mme. de Loisy, née Christiane Labouré;
Mademoiselle Madeleine Labouré;
Mme. Garelli-Duhamel;
Mme. Guillou;

Mr. Jean Guitton of the Académie Française, who insisted that this work be undertaken and has been unstinting in his encouragement;

Msgr. . . . Archivist of the Congregation for the causes of canonization of saints;

The archivists of the Vincentians and the Sisters of Charity;

The archivists of the Bollandists who hold the memoirs of Fr. Coste;

Monsignor the Comte de Paris, who has allowed us access to the Archives de la Maison de France to consult the files relative to the house at Enghien/Reuilly where Catherine lived;

Maître Lurat, whose talents as a researcher have enabled us to trace missing persons and documents;

Canon Marilier, archivist of the see of Dijon;

Mademoiselle Françoise Vignier, keeper of the departmental archives at Dijon;

Fr. Albert Colomber;

Dean Richard;

Sr. Anne-Suzanne de Jésus, who provided us with invaluable information and revised the chapters of Catherine's Burgundian childhood;

Abbé Ploix, who helped us with files in the historical archives of the archdiocese of Paris;

Fr. Ph. Roche, CM, who worked on the groundwork of this study;

Fr. J. Gonthier, CM, who has checked through the entire book;

Doctors Jean Laurentin and Anne Retel, who helped in interpreting Catherine's medical history;

Mme. Courtin, who produced the morphological analysis of Catherine's face;

Dr. Ermaine, who provided prosopological expertise;

Mr. A. Legrand, expert on the Holy Shroud, for help concerning relics and fragments of Catherine's body;

Fr. Mayaud, SJ, who cleared up certain chronological problems relating to the aurora borealis;

Mr. de Guibert, who agreed to produce not only the French narrative volume but its accompanying documentary-evidence volume in the face of the technical demands that they would make and without balking at commercial considerations;

Mr. Hoeltzel, who designed the French edition of the books;

Fr. Angelo Zangari, CM, whose unique collection of thousands of Miraculous Medals and numismatic competence have provided a singular contribution;

The historians who went before us, bringing their contributions in their different ways according to their various temperaments: Aladel, Le Gillou, Chevalier, Villette, Crapez, Misermont, as also Fr. Coste, whose critical scruples have helped us to ask ourselves all the necessary questions without shrinking and have compelled us to throw all possible light on the subject in producing the answers and the accompanying evidence.

Editor's Note

THIS BOOK IS PRINCIPALLY a narrative account of Catherine's life, translated from the French. In the French edition, there is also a second volume of Preuves—documentary evidence arrayed on a vast scale, often very fascinating for the serious scholar. The numbered references throughout the text of this English translation relate to the corresponding notes in this second French volume (published by Desclée de Brouwer, Paris, 1980).

Additionally, there are many source references in the French original within the body of the text. To make the English text easier to read, these have been converted into a second series of references, using small letters *a* to *z*, then *aa* to *zz*, followed by *aaa*, etc. These notes can be found at the end of the book.

Using the same principal, references to the Calendar can be found separately, also at the end of the book.

In this book the term *Sister(s) of Charity* is used throughout—in full, Sister(s) of Charity of St. Vincent de Paul. In many English-speaking countries they are known today as Daughters of Charity.

The word *seminary* (*séminaire*) is used in place of such terms as novitiate, house of studies, and house of formation. Novices are referred to as *seminary sisters*. With two easily recognizable exceptions, the word *seminary* is not used in this book to denote a male house of formation. However, *seminarian* does have its usual meaning of student for the priesthood.

The Christian names and surnames of sisters are used indiscriminately throughout the French original; thus Sr. Angélique Tanguy may be referred to as Sr. Angélique or as Sr. Tanguy.

xiv

CHAPTER I

Childhood and Bereavement

(1806–1818)

ON OCTOBER 9, 1815, THE EMPEROR NAPOLÉON was on his way to St. Helena, which he and his little band of disciples would reach on the fifteenth. In France, the Restoration was in the process of settling in and getting its second wind, while great dreams of revolution and glory dissolved like wracks of cloud over ruined fields.

Orphan girl

On the same day in Fain les Moutiers, a Burgundy village of scarcely two hundred inhabitants,[1] a little girl was crying. Her name was *Catherine* Labouré, but she answered to the name of *Zoe,* the saint's name on whose feastday she had been born.[2] She was not the only one crying, but the eighth of ten children who had just lost their mother, Madeleine Gontard.[3] Aged 46, Madeleine had come from a comfortable background and become a farmer's wife by her marriage to Pierre Labouré.[4] Death had come suddenly and the house had been in mourning since 5:00 A.M. The neighbors offered their condolences and help to farmer Pierre Labouré who, up until the previous month, had been the local mayor. The main room of the farmhouse was filled with muffled whisperings. Everybody prayed with the new lease of prayer-life, which had sprung up in the wake of the devotional secrecy that had held sway during the Revolution—a memory still uncomfortably close. Great pity was felt on account of the youngest children: Catherine, 9 years old;[5] Tonine, age 7; and Auguste, age 5, crippled as the result of an accident.[6]

That night the doors were not locked. Shadows seemed to come and go in turns to pray around the bed where the dead woman lay, her face like ivory.[7] General disorder and pressing needs made it clear after her death exactly what Madeleine had done in her life and what she would no longer do, what had worn her down and destroyed her bit by bit. Brought up in a well-heeled, almost worry-free background, she had given way under the weight of the farm: the land, the animals, the farmworkers, the children. She had had seventeen children in less than twenty years,[8] and ten of them had survived;[9] in an era of high infant mortality, only the survivors counted. Figures for deaths were something to be mitigated as much as possible. Madeleine was so stretched that she was not even able to teach the youngest children to read. For a long time Catherine was ashamed that she could not sign her own name. As for the youngest, little Auguste, his puny condition seemed to testify to the exhausted state that his mother had reached by the time she was in her forties. Entrusted to a servant girl in the ramshackle carriage that was bringing the family back from Senailly, he fell out on the road and was unconscious when picked up. He remained in a coma for several days and was crippled for the rest of his life,[10] clear-headed enough to be deeply embarrassed by it and temperamental as a way of hiding his anguish.

What was to be done with this little collection of humanity? The farmer conjured up solutions with a peasant-like patience. The two little girls, Catherine and Tonine, were to be looked after by one of their father's sisters, Marguerite, who was married to Antoine Jeanrot, a vinegar merchant at St. Rémy,[11] five miles northeast of Fain. Marie-Louise,[12] aged 20, the second child of the ten and the eldest of the girls, had a much rougher deal. Up to that point she had been lodging in Langres with one of her mother's sisters[13] who was married to an army officer and who had no children of her own. Marie-Louise returned home and valiantly took on the load that had crushed her mother. As for her father, he thought himself lucky to have resigned the previous month from the *mairie* where he had succeeded his cousin Nicholas Labouré.[14]

Twenty-three years of marriage

Pierre's life was in pieces after twenty-three years of marriage during which were born more children than he could manage to keep at home.

It was on June 4, 1793, two days after the proclamation of the Terror, that Pierre Labouré had married Louise Madeleine Gontard of Senailly in the canton of Montbard, near Semur–the region of St.

Bernard of Clairvaux and St. Jeanne de Chantal. How was the marriage celebrated? Did these two Christians have to find a priest in secret? Or did they, in this time of crisis, return to the ancient usage whereby the union of two baptized persons is in itself a sacrament? (At the same time that it set up the "canonical form" as a requirement for the validity of a marriage, the Council of Trent had preserved this primitive law for cases where the ministry of a priest could not be had.) There is a complete blank on this subject both in the family's written archives and in memories handed down orally.[15]

Pierre had been born in 1767. At the age of 20 or thereabouts, he had started studying to be a priest,[16] but the Revolution closed down the seminaries. Realistically, he went back to the land, following the family tradition, while preserving his Christian opinions during the troubles. When he was 25, he met Madeleine Gontard. She was 23 and lived at Senailly where the Gontards were, like the Labourés at Fain, one of the leading families of the area. She had been educated, like him—but, contrary to what has been said in the past as a result of confusing her with her daughter-in-law, Antoinette Gontard,[17] she was not a teacher. After their marriage, Pierre went to live at Senailly with Madeleine in his mother-in-law's house.[18]

Then Hubert, Pierre's father,[19] a great huntsman, began to founder under the onset of old age. The family farm was too much for his 72 years. He took legal steps to divide his estate among his children, choosing Pierre to take the running of the farm in hand. This took place in difficult conditions, as the farm remained undivided and the father reserved to himself an active interest in it until his death.

Time and patience resolved the complicated situation. On February 9, 1809—perhaps with the help of Hubert, now in his eighties and with his health failing—Pierre bought out[20] the share of his brother Jacques (a landowner at Vassy) and his brother Charles (in the army) for the sum of 9,400 livres, with an additional payment of 850 livres to his unmarried sister Claudine. Hubert died the following year, 1810.

So the last five Labouré children to survive were born at the farm in Fain. This beautiful house, with its gateway opening on to the square and the communal well, had the largest dovecote in the village. Pierre was well known for having held a civil officer's post at Senailly and presiding over marriage ceremonies during the Revolution, and so he became mayor of Fain in 1811.[21] But before that, for Catherine's birth on May 2, 1806, at 6:00 P.M., he had not brought the baby to the *mairie* (whose door was opposite the farm entrance) but the registers to the house! There the mother, having just gotten her breath back, signed on the dotted line at 6:15! (This only happened with her two younger daughters born at Fain, Catherine and Tonine.[22]) But she did not attend the baptism, celebrated the next day in the church at Fain by a Benedictine, Dom Georges Mamert, parish priest at Moutiers.[23]

Before their mother's death, the older children, who showed no taste for working the land, had already begun to leave home. In 1811, Hubert, aged 17, went to join Napoléon's army, where he made his career. Catherine's other brothers all became tradesmen in Paris: Jacques (1796–1855), a wine merchant; Antoine (1797–1864), a pharmacist; Charles (1800–1878), a restaurateur; Joseph (1803–1880), a bottle merchant (he was the inventor of a type of beer bottle with a patent stopper, known as a *cannette*); and Pierre-Charles (1805–1889), an employee and later a merchant. Several of them came home to end their days in Burgundy in the bosom of the family.[24]

In the autumn of 1815, Catherine left the farm where she had been born. Hand in hand with Tonine, she walked along paths where great trees were already turning purple and gold. She felt herself doubly an orphan because her mother's death was taking her away from her father, and this separation was not insignificant. Her father meant a lot to her, as she was the elder of the two girls who had remained at home until then.[25] Her life continued to be orientated toward the paternal farm like a compass toward the North Pole.

As for the void left by her mother, Catherine herself found a solution. There was a statue of Mary in the dead woman's bedroom. "Zoe" was not tall enough to reach it. Full of tears, she climbed on a chair and embraced our Lady, asking her to replace the mother she had just lost. She thought she was alone, but the servant girl, who did not miss much, saw her and later told Tonine about it.[26]

These tears were the first and the last. Catherine was now strong. The new mother she had chosen taught her not to groan and rely on others, but to take her own life in hand.

For the time being, her exile to St. Rémy was the ordeal to be faced. The place was pleasantly situated beside the river Brenne. The large house, with its tiled roof and its main doorway full of the comings and goings of vinegar merchant's customers, was welcoming; but the garden wall cut off the view toward the river—a dangerous place and out-of-bounds. The house was a lively one, with two boy cousins and four girl cousins, from 10 to 18 years of age, all of them older than the two little girls. But Aunt Jeanrot, who had enough on her hands with this large family and the demands of the vinegar business, mostly left the two little ones in the care of the servant girl.[27] No doubt she had overestimated her own capabilities when she had suggested taking on the two orphans.

Return home (January 1818)

After two years, Pierre—who had only reluctantly agreed to the separation while distracted by grief—was missing Catherine (his favorite among the three girls) too much, and summoned her back home.[28] For Catherine, this was a celebration from all points of view, for she was also coming home to make her First Communion, fixed for January 25, 1818.[29] She was filled with fervor, her purely human pleasure at coming back home nourishing a joyous outburst of feeling toward God. She had a taste for work and she had initiative.

It was the solution to a problem for Marie-Louise, Catherine's older sister, who initiated her into the work involved in running the house.[30] At the time her mother died, Marie-Louise had been on the point of offering herself as a postulant to the Sisters of Charity at Langres, the town where she had grown up. For her, returning to Fain had been a constricting exile. Catherine's enterprising personality and her good relationship with her father had the effect of freeing Marie-Louise. By the following May 5, she had returned to Langres to begin her postulancy at the house of the Sisters of Charity.[31]

Catherine/Zoe, only just 12, had paved the way for this departure. When it was discussed, she had looked joyfully at her younger sister Tonine (9½) saying, "The two of us will run the house between us."[32]

Catherine's seeking refuge in Mary had not been like the reaction of a child who is cold and looks for someone to snuggle up against. It was as a free, responsible daughter that she tied this knot in the night of faith. At 12 years old, she was mature enough to take on the burden that had crushed her mother, and became her father's right hand.

 CHAPTER II

Vocation

A twelve-year-old "farmer's wife"

THIS, THEN, WAS HOW CATHERINE became a farm woman. She took on the role of *mater familias* and mistress of the house.

The farm, with its roof of red-gray tiles,[1] formed a rectangle of buildings, almost enclosed like a cloiser.[2] A gateway opened on to the street. The buildings were topped by the famous dovecote–so wide[3] that it was almost squat–which proclaimed the Labourés to be "one of the foremost families in the area."[4] People would look twice at it before crossing the threshold of the former mayor.

"Didn't you ever go to play with Zoe?" a girl from Fain of the same age as Catherine was asked. "Oh, no," she replied. "The Labourés were of a higher social standing than us. You couldn't go to see them just like that, without a good reason. They were big landowners. It was one of the best houses in Fain."[5]

Fain may have been a small place, but Catherine's father was the leading man in it by virtue both of his education and his high reputation.

Huysmans has painted a picture of Catherine as "a former servant-girl from a farm."[6] This was not the case at all. He adds that the Virgin selected someone who was "unpolished and narrow in outlook." Is this true? What *is* true is that Catherine was unable to read and write until she was 20, later than Bernadette of Lourdes. But, like Bernadette, she had a breadth of vision and the natural richness of human resource so often found in the poor; and these enabled her to live to the full without having to wait for education to catch up with her. As the eldest, Bernadette would eventually have all the duties of an "heiress" according to the customs of the Bigorre.[7] The title of "heiress" was ironic for

Bernadette, whose parents had nothing to leave but debts...but Catherine's parents owned land and they cultivated it.

As an orphan, Catherine had been elevated to being mistress of the house while still a child.[8] This was a position that many women did not reach until their fifties—or never at all: some went to the grave still under the yoke of an all-powerful mother-in-law. At the age of 12, Catherine was queen of this great farm that seemed closed to the world like a castle keep—at least from an architectural point of view. She was a hard-working queen, but in authority over the workers and over the servant girl.[9]

Her kingdom was the farmyard, the outhouses, the garden, and, above all, the farmhouse. Her father was king in this realm when he returned from the fields. His utterances were rare but decisive.[10] First and foremost, they guaranteed Catherine's authority over the living quarters as well as kitchen. This queen, realizing that she was nothing except by virtue of her king, kept quiet when he was there. Her domain was also to be found in the bakehouse,[11] the orchard, the cowshed, the henhouse,[12] and the dovecote with its 1,121 pigeonholes,[13] a home for between 600 and 800 pigeons.[14] Catherine loved its murmuring, cooing inhabitants, who beat their wings all around her trying to catch the flying grains that she threw in abundance. In retrospect, the imagery of witnesses gave the flying birds the form of a crown or halo.[15]

A day in Catherine's life

As mistress of the house, Catherine was always the first up in the morning.[16] All through the year she had to wake before anyone else. Her eyes would open as the night sky paled and the horizon began to turn blue or mauve through the windows that looked out on a plateau of woodland mixed with pastures. She loved the dawn,[17] especially in winter when the nights were longer than her own tiredness and she used to lie beneath the eiderdown, watching for the first gleam of daylight.

In midsummer, it was a different story. Catherine started at 4:00 A.M. and the days were never too long for the work that had to be done. Waking up, she had to fight against fatigue and stiffness to pick up the threads again. When it was like this, the daybreak seemed almost aggressive, as if following hard on the heels of any twinges of self-pity. "It's between the two of us, my God...and my work!"

The principal daily task of a farmer's wife is providing food.[18] Three meals: "breakfast" in the morning—well named, as it really did "break the fast" of the night—consisted of soup, together with the dispensing of snacks for the laborers to take with them into the fields.[19] Midday dinner weighed heavily in summer when it had to be carried out to the reapers.[20] Supper required more in the way of cooking, but was always the same thing: vegetable stew with lumps of bacon in it.[21]

A farmer's wife was both mistress of the house and a servant. She gave herself more than anyone else. She did not eat at the same table as the men, but in a corner next to the fireplace.[22] She did not join in conversation. Catherine had been formed in a hierarchical world, schooled in respect and silence; but she had also been taught to take time in working things out so that plans might be fulfilled and the impossible made possible whenever necessary.

Looking after the animals dictated the rhythm of the day. Milking cows, morning and evening, is hard work for the hands and sometimes even more so for a bent back. Catherine would give out fodder and herd the animals to the communal drinking trough. She gave the pigs their soup, thickened with all the rubbish and leftovers. She collected the eggs from the henhouse. All day long she would go back and forth to the well—fortunately not too far away—to fetch water, which she used as economically as possible.[23]

During the long winter evenings smaller jobs continued without respite.[24] Sitting up around the fire by candlelight would take place in different houses in turn—and often in the Labourés' house, which had a large main room and a bakehouse.[25] It was the latter that would provide a refuge when it was freezing cold. The furthermost parts of the room stayed warm with an intense heat, helped by the thick layers of red bricks. Meeting together in this way would save wood and also provide an opportunity for socializing: news, reminiscences, tales of horror or delight. The prayer that brought the evening to a close added an extra dimension to mere human communication, producing an aura of freedom, felt deep inside, through rite and tradition.

A week in Catherine's life

Interwoven with the daily round were other regular activities that must be mentioned.

Each week, Catherine kneaded flour and yeast and heated up the oven with seven or eight bundles of wood. When the heat had gotten well into the stonework, Catherine would remove ashes and cinders with a scraper, gather glowing embers into charcoal extinguishers, and then take up the long wooden shovels to load, in good order, seven or eight large round loaves of soft, white dough. Then it was a question of waiting while getting on with another chore. At the end of an hour or so, Catherine would pull out the loaves, swollen and baking hot under their hard, brown crusts. How she must have fretted the first few times in case the magical transformation did not work![26]

Thursday was market day at Montbard (10 miles away),[27] for the Moutiers market had vanished from that town, savagely deprived of its sumptuous abbey by the Revolution. One of Catherine's duties was to go in a light cart with butter and eggs and sometimes with vegetables and fruit. The poultry yard, dairy, and garden were the means of covering the running expenses of the household.[28]

Each week there was also the usual washing to do: routine and boring.

A year in Catherine's life at Fain

The "great wash" was something quite different and happened two or three times a year. This was the day when pride of place was given to the large amount of linen handed on from generation to generation (for, with slow changes on the "crop of rotation principle," it did not wear very much). The great wash was a real event. Out of chests and trunks came absolute mountains of sheets. Neighbors would come and lend a hand. It was a festival—but a harsh one!

At the bottom of a huge copper kettle, Catherine would lay out bundles of vine-twigs. These were covered by a sheet and then on top of that a layer of wood-ash (beware of any eggshells mixed in with this—they stain!). The ash would be covered with another sheet and on top of that Catherine would place the laundry, which had been soaking in cold water since the day before. Then the operations could commence. A large pan of water would be boiling fast over the fire. With small jugs, Catherine would pour steaming water on the laundry and let it sink in. Then, tirelessly, she would catch the water underneath that had slowly filtered through and pour it in on top again. In this way the wash would get concentrated. But you could not go on too long in this way or the mixture would end up by attacking the skin on your hands and even the linen itself. Catherine was learning to leave well enough alone. When the ash had done its work, the laundry would be taken in a wheelbarrow to the communal washing place opposite the house and down the street. The washerwomen would have to maneuver the laundry down several steps. Then, on their knees in the cistern, they would rinse and beat it with a paddle, all the time keeping an eye on the weather and the wind, which would determine how long the sheets would take to dry. After drying would come ironing and putting away in cupboards, now full to the brim with spotless linen, perfumed with iris bulbs or lavender.[29]

Each year at the beginning of winter, a pig would be slaughtered. On a big farm like the Labourés', they might even slaughter two, perhaps doing so again on Shrove Tuesday if necessary. The animal would have been fattened up to about 300 pounds in weight. This was a different kind of festival, more joyful than washing day: a riot of black puddings, grilled steaks, potted minced pork, and so on—for perishable meat had to be eaten or given away very quickly. Those living on the farm and those who came to help might, at times like this, eat twelve or thirteen meat dishes. Solid stomachs could in this way make up for a previous deficiency of protein. It was thirsty work, and, although the Labourés had no vines, several bottles (and much good humor) would always be found—or just happen to turn up!

The important thing was what was *not* eaten on this day: ham and bacon[30] were cured straight away. For the rest of the year this would provide a meat diet, for fresh meat was rare. It was only under Napoléon III that the Auxois region was turned into a meat-producing area.

Beef was sometimes available in profusion, but through misfortune. When a cow had an accident or grew old, it was shared out among the neighbors, who would do the same thing when it happened to them.[31] Losses thus became festivals simply in order that nothing should be wasted. Disaster was transformed into plenty and into sharing with others.

So Catherine took to herself innumerable rites, recipes, and traditions which, year by year, she made a better job of. You took no chances with animals (the cow that will not give milk because its calf has been taken away from it), nor with people (those women in town who haggle to the bitter end over butter or eggs), nor with the weather. It was an era opening on to eternity through the everlasting returning to the ascendant of the cycle of feasts.[32]

Each year, Catherine was better able to work out the liturgical cycle: from Advent to Easter, and then on to the interminable series of "green Sundays" after Pentecost—the time when the most work took place. At the passing of the year, on November 2 (the feast of All

Souls), the priest would come to the church where the whole village would be assembled. He went through individual absolutions for the dead so that it took all afternoon. It seemed interminable, but no family was happy until it had had its proper share. The days got shorter. The coming of night was like going back into the womb. Nothing to do but dream, talk, and sleep at great length. It was the season for death, which thus entered the cycle of life.

Catherine's secret

Catherine knew how to defend her domain and how to give what she ought to everyone, according to one's rank and needs, starting with her father and then her sickly little brother, who was the object of her most tender care.[33] The two best looked after were Pierre, because he was the master, and Auguste, because his misery cried out to the heavens. After them came brothers, sisters, and servants. Last of all, Catherine herself.

She did not grumble over her initial mistakes, but rectified them without fuss and learned a lesson from everything. She had not been to school—but this was her school. Where on earth did she get the strength, at the age of 12, to master this crushing toil? Her life was filled from the first light of dawn, when she made up the fire, till the evening, when the dying flames lightened the shadows enough to finish off the day's work—things that could be done without having to see very well, such as washing up and clearing things away. Catherine kept everything in order.

In fact, she managed so well that the servant girl became superfluous. Indeed, interference from an adult who was not too keen to accept the authority of a mere child brought more hindrance than help. "Rest" was when the work was going well and you were making something out of it, with Tonine, active and helpful, at your side. At the age of 14, Catherine got rid of her servant at the first opportunity and won her bet: things went better than before.[34]

Was it love for the land that kept her at it? Certainly she loved the fruitful land, the dawn that woke her each morning, and the tasks that filled her life after the emptiness of St. Rémy. But all that was only on the surface.

Could it have been the lure of making a profit—the peasant's passion for making savings at any price? Catherine certainly managed all the complex intertwinings of her work with great ingenuity. If she had not, it would have meant ruin—something of which townsfolk did not have the slightest conception. One had to be able to take the unforeseen in stride: animal and plant disease, bad weather, accidents. But Catherine loved people and things more than money, however necessary. She knew that her small closed-circuit management of the interior running of the farm was only one element in the domestic finances, the essential part of which rested in the hands of her father.

Catherine's secret is concealed in her time spent off the farm. She disappeared each day for a fair amount of time. It was not to see a young man. Her love was hidden in the church at Fain, close to the farm and a little farther up on the other side of the street. It was a church without a priest, for clergy had dissolved away during the Revolution. Fain had to depend on a traveling priest who went from one mission church to another, celebrating marriages and funerals, but only rarely Sunday Mass.[35] On the Sundays when there was Mass, Catherine and her family occupied a special pew in the Lady chapel, known as the Labouré chapel as the family had paid for its restoration.[36]

It was not the honor of sitting in a church warden's pew that attracted Catherine to the church. She came on her own during the week and prayed for long periods on the cold flagstones.[37] (It is said that this sowed the seeds of her arthritis.[38]) Her prayers in the church gave meaning to everything else.

"Praying doesn't get the work done," said the neighbors.[39] But the work did get done. Catherine was a spirited and healthy girl. She managed her work so efficiently that she had time for prayer as well. "It's a waste of time," said the village gossips occasionally. Catherine's piety did not increase her reputation in their eyes, but she did not care.

Her time was not her neighbor's time, stuck as they were in their daily round. Catherine lived out her daily tasks, but as it were in another time scale, one which gave meaning to the undefined repetitions and to the people with whom she came into contact and for whom it would be better if she met them halfway—in fact, it was a meaning that would not fade away.

For Catherine lived with God, in faith and love; in the communion of saints as well, as a courageous fellow countrywoman. At St. Rémy her aunt had shown her the statue of her patron saint, St. Catherine of Alexandria, full of wisdom and light, strong when facing her persecutors.[40] Catherine/Zoe was familiar with the saints whose reassuring silhouettes adorned the walls of the church at Fain as at St. Rémy.[41] But this was even more true when it came to the Virgin Mary. Catherine encountered her each time she went into the church at Fain: first of all in the porch, with the child in her arms,[42] then inside the church, with her hands held out in a gesture of welcome.[43]

The tabernacle was empty[44] in this priestless church, but the Lord's presence permeated his house and could be sensed in the depths of the heart. It was a joy for Catherine. She found that she wanted to plunge herself into it over and over again. It was here that she found the strength to be a good servant. Here, too, was her dream for the future, as Tonine very soon guessed. Her little sister had noticed how Catherine had become "all mystic," as she put it, "since her First Communion":[45] no doubt in the sense that her compatriot St. Bernard was described as *mire contemplativus,* astonishingly contemplative, in the earliest biographies of him.[46]

The stream of prayer that seemed to have been dried up by the Revolution flowed again in Catherine, as in others of her contemporaries unknown to her: St. John Mary Vianney, Jeanne Jugan, Jeanne-Antide Thouret, Mother Javouhey, Madeleine-Sophie Barat, and so on. Prayer sprang up from within her, unstemmable. She spent long periods in the church at Fain, whose tragic emptiness only intensified the silence and a call.

This was an intense experience, and the unlettered girl expressed it in trenchant fashion later on (when she had learned to write):

> What a lot of religion there is in the district! One Mass on a Sunday—and even then it's only a binating priest from a neighboring district who says it. Vespers are sung by the schoolmaster and so there is no Benediction. To go to confession, you have to search out a confessor. Go and see if what little religion there is, is still safe.[47/a]

To make up for not being able to meet the Lord in the Eucharist, Catherine found him in her heart—the heart of a baptized Christian. More especially, she encountered him in the poor whom she made welcome and the sick that she visited—another charming facet of her life that has come down to us, a life at once austere and filled with light.

It was most often to Moutiers that Catherine went for Sunday Mass,[48] for the traveling priest only came to Fain on rare occasions. Tonine went to Mass with her. However, this was not enough for Catherine; she sometimes went to Moutiers for Mass during the week[49]—a good two to three miles each way. The road goes uphill for about a mile and then drops sharply. At this point Catherine would see the church tower on her left and a sense of great joy would take hold of her: the joy of another meeting. For the return journey, she felt herself strengthened for the climb back to her daily chores.[50] The paths she was called to follow were not easy ones.

One of her former contemporaries, an elderly woman of 88, witnessed that Catherine was not a prey to distractions: "Those Labouré girls were so pious that they didn't take part in fun and games with the other girls."[51] Prematurely absorbed by responsibility, matured ahead of time by the harsh tasks of the farm, Catherine was not much of a "partyer."[52] But it would be a hagiographical excess to exaggerate what her nephew Philippe called "her serious, modest, and sober personality."[53] Another of her contemporaries, a "little girl of her age," whose name has not come down to us, tells us that she was quite capable of having a good time when her parents took her to the festivities in her cousins' house at Cormarin.[54]

St. Robert's Day

These festivities took place on St. Robert's Day (April 29) when it fell on a Sunday, or, if it did not, on the first Sunday following at the beginning of May.[55] Cormarin was some ten miles from Fain and was reached by small, winding, climbing trackways. It was not actually a village but a little hamlet with no church, so the festivities included the minimum of religious observances: patronal Mass in the neighboring village, but no vespers. On a more basic level, it was the biggest day in the life of the village—really quite something! In the widest part of the one and only street, at a point pompously referred to as "the square," a "rotunda" was put up in front of St. Robert's statue.[56] This was where games and other attractions took place. The feast was something else again. Every household that had invited family and friends prepared a lavish meal, with brawn and galantine, numerous meat dishes—rabbit cooked in white wine, chicken in "ivory" sauce (the recipe still exists) and, to finish up with, all kinds of pastries; the whole thing washed down with generous servings of Burgundy wine. After this there would be games in the square for the men and the children, while the women did the washing-up and got ready the next stage in the culinary indulgence, for the evening meal was not skimped and the merrymaking went on until the following day.

A little Cormarin girl, when over 80 and with a halo of white hair, gave this account in 1896:

> Catherine was not pretty, but she was kind and good, always good-natured and gentle with her companions, even when they teased her as children are wont to do. And if she saw anyone getting cross with somebody else, she would try and make peace between them. If a poor person came up, she would give away all her own delicacies.... At the patronal Mass, Catherine Labouré prayed like an angel...never turning her head to left or to right.[57]

Nourishment through fasting

At the age of 14, Catherine began to fast on Fridays and Saturdays all year long.[58] Tonine noticed this and was afraid that it would do Catherine no good. She tried unsuccessfully to dissuade her and so threatened to tell their father. Catherine was not impressed: "Go on, then: tell him!"

Provoked into action, Tonine was as good as her word. Her father backed her up, but Catherine had already decided for herself. Fasting was something between her and God. She found it a source of strength. It was nobody else's business—not even her father's—so long as the work was done.... So she carried on.

All this was quite free from any tinge of resentment. Her father was her father, God was God. This difference of opinion did not even affect her good relations with Tonine, who continued helping her with a stout heart and much shrewdness.

Vocation

About the same time, Catherine confided in Tonine—and only in her—that her life was going in the direction of a religious vocation,[59] but she did not know how or where. It was not in order to "be like Marie-Louise," but a very personal plan between her and God.[60] Tonine was understanding and she gave her sister help and support as she went along this path. It had to remain a secret between the two girls because their father had already done his duty by the good Lord in this regard. He had not indulged in recriminations when Marie-Louise had left, though her presence had been very necessary for the farm. He had given away his daughter and her dowry. This was fine, but it was quite enough.[61]

When Catherine went to weekday Mass at Moutiers, it was in the chapel of the Sisters of St. Vincent de Paul,[62] who ran a little school and looked after the elderly. At that time the Sister Servant (which is the name given to the sister in charge, according to the custom of the Sisters of Charity) was a Sr. Soucial,[63] who came from the Landes area where St. Vincent de Paul had also originated. She had been in the community at Châtillon when the Revolution had suddenly started and her community had been broken up. There was no other choice than to "go back into the world" like her companions. She had set off for her native region but had gotten sidetracked. At Moutiers, the sisters had welcomed her with open arms and had her admitted to the community through the action of a cooperative revolutionary functionary. In this way, she had continued to minister to the poor in lay dress, just like the first "daughters" of St. Vincent. Having come by accident, Sr. Soucial stayed for the rest of her life, until she was 80. She left behind the memory of an intense love for the poor. She used to try and ensure that she was able to minister *personally* to the most unfortunate people possible, following the counsels of St. Vincent. "No affliction, however hideous" seemed to change the affectionate smile she reserved for the sick. It may well be on the model of Sr. Soucial–the closest point of reference–that Catherine had already conceived her vocation. Marie-Louise's entering the Sisters of Charity was not really a guiding factor. Catherine's vocation sprang from inside herself; it remained unformed and undefined, but it was this that pushed her into discovering for herself alone what prayer, fasting, and visiting the sick entailed.[64]

A dream

Then one night this call took on the form of a dream. In it Catherine found herself in the church at Fain, in her usual place in the Labouré chapel. She was praying when an old priest came in. He was wearing vestments and proceeded to celebrate Mass on the white altar with its gilded ornamental moldings. What struck her was the way he looked when he turned around for the *Dominus vobiscum*. At the *Ite, missa est* he signaled her to draw nearer, but she was seized with fear. She backed away, mesmerized by him, unable to look away from his eyes. It was something that she would remember for the rest of her life. Leaving the church, she went to visit a sick person (still dreaming). The old priest found her there and said, "My daughter, it's good to care for the sick. You may be running away from me now, but one day you'll be happy to come to me. God has designs on you. Don't forget it!" Still fearful, Catherine moved away from him again, but with a sense of warmth in her heart. "She was walking on air." As she entered the porch of the paternal homestead, she woke up.[65]

It was nothing but a dream,[66] but it gave Catherine a renewed impulse. Her realm, the farmhouse, had become a temporary resting place, even a place of exile. She did her work even better than before, but as if she were not doing it at all. Her real life had overtaken her daily life, which in spirit she had already left behind. She thought about things, sketching out plans for the future. To enter with the sisters, she would at least have to know how to read and write.[67] She had been told that this was a condition for being admitted. Moreover, she felt humiliated by her lack of education.

With the sole object of concealing her ignorance, she paid out thirty gold francs—her savings—to a smooth talker who in fact had quite a job teaching her to sign her name.[68] But this was not enough. It was time to learn reading, writing, and arithmetic—on paper, not just in the head, even though a peasant woman's head, helped by a ten-finger abacus, was a formidable calculating machine![69]

First stay at Châtillon (1824–1826)

Catherine was 18, and Antoinette Gontard, a first cousin on her mother's side, suggested taking on her education at Châtillon where she ran a well-known boarding school.[70]

Tonine was 16, strong enough to take on the house and as helpful as ever. Their father was very hesitant about the whole thing. His daughter's good sense and devotion worried him, and he was frightened at the prospect of losing her.[71] But at the same time he was not proud of his younger children's ignorance when the older had had such a good start in life.[72] So Catherine had her way.

At Châtillon[73] she was delighted to find that she could attend Mass without having to go very far to find a church with the Blessed Sacrament reserved and a priest available. This was the Abbé Gailhac, parish priest and dean, in his eighties (he lived from 1743 to 1828).[74] Catherine ventured to confide in him regarding her dream. The priest knew the Sisters of Charity well and he was struck by the description of the old man: the beard, the black skullcap, and the ministry to the poor. "My girl," he said, "I think this priest must have been none other than St. Vincent."

A little while after, Catherine went to the sisters' house in the Rue de la Juiverie, escorted by her cousin. In the parlor, what a surprise! A portrait hanging there was the priest that she had seen in her dream. "But that's our father, St. Vincent de Paul," the sisters explained to her.[75]

Sometimes people ask how it was that Catherine never saw the genuine portrait in the sisters' house at Moutiers. The answer is that this painting, full of life and attributed to François of Tours, was at that time hanging in one of the sisters' private community rooms.[76]

Catherine had now settled on her decision, but what to do next? One had to have parental consent to enter the postulancy and, in this case, there would be no question of it being forthcoming.[77] She would have to wait, but she was in a great hurry and her coming-of-age was two and a half years away! At her age, with such a burning desire, two and a half years seemed like eternity.

Furthermore, Catherine was not feeling too comfortable at her cousin's. She was 18, but at the same academic level as the little ones, and her farm woman's ways clashed with those of the young ladies. Her cousin and companions good-naturedly encouraged her to imitate their own good manners. But all this toiletry, buttons and bows, and general "refinement" were not to her taste, and the condescension of her companions wounded her pride and occasionally even disrupted her usual uprightness and simplicity.[78]

Drama

Faced with two unpalatable choices, she preferred the one that was straight and hard: going back home. Her stay at Châtillon had been a relatively short one,[79] but it had not been a waste of time.

Back at Fain, Catherine was able to sign the register in a firm hand on July 16, 1826, at the baptism of her goddaughter: Catherine Zoe Suriot.[80] It was most probably on this occasion that she wore for the first time the purple silk dress that would form part of her "trousseau." Her father had it made for her, as she was now of marriageable age. A bolt from the blue would fix everything. In the meantime, there was the life of the farm: "calves and cows, pigs and hatchings." Catherine, unshakeable and taciturn, did not sulk at all the work nor think any less of it. Her vocation was bearing hard on her.

As far as Tonine was concerned, everything was going well. She had bravely taken on the role of "farmer's wife." But the sky seemed black for Catherine's father and it would have been foolish to have provoked the storm before having legal right on her side. Patiently, Catherine waited for her coming-of-age.

She was 21 on May 2, 1827, and she announced her decision.[81] Her father disagreed violently.[82] He had already given one daughter to God and had always said that he would not give another. Moreover, Catherine was useful: she was normal and had a joyful disposition, she did not remain aloof from festivities in the surrounding villages—Senailly, Cormarin....[83] Her hand had been asked in marriage.[84] She would surely end up being tempted by a handsome young man or a good offer! He laid out all the arguments, but alas for Pierre Labouré. Catherine knew what she wanted—and what God wanted for her.

Exile in Paris (1828–1829)

In the spring of 1828, her father changed his mind. His fifth son, Charles, had set up a wine and bottle business in Paris at the Rue de l'Echiquier, and his wife had also been running a restaurant there for a workmen's company, but she had died on February 21, 1828, two years after their wedding. Charles needed help, so what better than that Catherine should go and help him? The capital would wake up a young girl's ideas and the restaurant would develop her "courting" talents.

Catherine felt that this was adding insult to injury. Not content with refusing to accept her vocation, her father was "expelling" her and breaking all the ties that meant so much to her. It was only a sense of duty and her own ability that enabled Catherine to persevere with this new task, working at the side of her widowed brother whose wounds were only just beginning to heal.[85] Charles was pleased with his sister and wanted her to stay "to keep his house in order." He tried to marry her off locally,[86] for this Burgundy lass of 22 was not without her attractions. However, she felt almost as if advances from suitors or the lighthearted remarks and propositions she encountered in the restaurant had no connection with her. Even the distractions afforded in the suburb and her own culinary triumphs with the restaurant's customers left her unmoved.

Charles was not persistent and soon the opportunity arose when Catherine could be freed. Charles remarried on February 3, 1829.[87] Two women in the same house would be one too many.

Catherine seized the opportunity with both hands. She wrote to her sister-in-law at Châtillon,[88] who had been very touched by what

Catherine had to go through; and then to Marie-Louise who, the previous year, had been nominated Sister Servant of the Sisters of Charity at Castelsarrasin (in the *département* of Tarn-et-Garonne).[89] Her reply was almost ablaze with happiness and enthusiasm:

> What does it mean to be a Sister of Charity? It's giving oneself to God without reserve in order to serve, in the poor, his suffering limbs.... If at this moment there were someone powerful enough to offer me not just a kingdom but the whole universe as my possession, I would consider it as no more than the dust on my shoes, as I am quite convinced that in possessing the universe I would not find the happiness and the contentment that I experience in my vocation....[90]

A sudden scruple stems her outpouring: "It is not our custom to urge anyone to enter our community."

But she quickly forgives herself this "moment of weakness," and the letter ends with a restatement of her desire that Catherine might be one of those who one day will be called.... "Better to serve the good Lord than the world."[91]

Later on (April 24, 1834), this letter would rebound on Marie-Louise in circumstances that we will deal with below. For the moment, she advised Catherine to go back to Châtillon.

> I would really like you to spend some time with our dear sister-in-law, as she has proposed to you, in order to acquire a little education, which is very necessary no matter what the circumstances may be. You will learn to speak French a little better than people do in our village, you will devote yourself to writing, arithmetic, and, above all, to piety, to religious fervor, and the love of the poor.[92]

Second stay at Châtillon[93]

Her cousin's large house at the foot of the St. Vorles hill had changed since Catherine's previous visit. On December 15, 1828, Jeanne-Antoinette Gontard had become her sister-in-law through marriage to her eldest brother Hubert, now a police sub-lieutenant, who had been in Charles X's bodyguard in Paris in 1824. The young married couple was good at pleading Catherine's cause to her father, who was not very proud of the irresolvable situation he had landed himself in through his own spitefulness. He took advantage of the possibility of an honorable compromise.

So Catherine found herself once more in the less-than-appealing boarding school, but she spent more and more time with the Sisters of

Charity. This time, she encountered a new sister: Victoire Séjole, who was immediately filled with an instinctive liking for Catherine, based on a discreet admiration. It was this, which, for the rest of her life, whenever she spoke about Catherine, provoked her to remark: "Never have I known a soul so guileless and so pure."[94]

Catherine and Sr. Séjole had much in common: they were both of good peasant stock, close in age (22 and 27), and both had elder sisters in the Sisters of Charity. Above all, they both had a love for the Blessed Virgin and for the poor. Sr. Séjole came from Pont-du-Château in the *département* of Puy-de-Dôme, where she had been born in 1801. She entered the Sisters of Charity in August 1824. When Catherine had been in Châtillon the first time, Sr. Séjole had been at Saconnex in Switzerland, but the climate had affected her health and she had been transferred to Burgundy in 1827.

Sr. Séjole understood how uncomfortable a peasant woman would feel when surrounded by the refined life of the boarding school. She pressed Sr. Cany, superior since 1814: "Admit her. She is all guilelessness and piety and not at home among these blue-stockings. She is a good village girl, as St. Vincent likes them to be."[95]

Sr. Cany hesitated, for Catherine had almost no education. "Let her take time to learn then, seeing as her sister-in-law happens to run the most highly-esteemed boarding school in the whole region!"

"But it is not her kind of environment," Sr. Séjole pursued. "She is getting nothing out of it. Take her on here and I will teach her everything necessary!"

Sr. Cany was finally convinced and the bargaining began. Catherine was overjoyed at hearing the news, but she did not want to go against the then-prevailing custom and enter without a dowry. She took it on herself to talk about it in confidence with her brother and sister-in-law. Pierre Labouré would be immovable on the subject. His daughter could do what she pleased, but—great heavens above!—he would not provide a second dowry! No matter; brother and sister-in-law would supply it. They were well off, both wage earners, he as an officer, she as the headmistress of a reputable boarding school.

Postulancy

At the beginning of January 1830, the motherhouse received a recommendation in favor from Sr. Cany. There, the Council of the Sisters of Charity took it up on January 14 in the following terms:

> Our Sr. Cany has proposed Mademoiselle Labouré, sister of the superior at Castelsarrasin. She is 23 and very suitable for our way of life: very devout, of good character, with a strong constitution, a love of work, and a most cheerful disposition. She receives Communion regularly once a week. Concerning moral character and honesty, her family is intact but financially not well endowed. We are strongly urged to admit her.

The principal person behind the "strong urging" was Sr. Séjole, and the allusion to lack of financial means paved the way for a smaller dowry, according to the then-prevailing custom.

A favorable reply from Paris arrived on January 22. Catherine said joyous good-byes to her friendly but over-refined schoolmates and stepped with a full heart through the gates at the house in the Rue de la Juiverie. Sr. Séjole was delighted to train Catherine in the prayer life and the general life of the community. She introduced her to the "soup pot for the sick poor." This charitable work had been suppressed at the beginning of the Revolution as having "aristocratic" connotations, but it was quickly found necessary to reestablish it, responding as it did to the most urgent needs. In this way, Catherine learned about human misery and the service of others on a grand scale. Twice a week, on Sundays and Thursdays, about 1:00 P.M., a huge amount of soup would be prepared, and the poor would flock to it, some armed with earthenware pots, others with saucepans or other receptacles, to take soup with them to give to their sick.[96]

An old servant of the house, Mariette by name, admired Catherine's prayer habits. Each day at 3:00 P.M. she would go to the chapel and recite the act prescribed by the Rule:

> I adore thee, Jesus Christ, my Savior, dying on the cross for love of me.
> I thank thee, that thou didst die to redeem me. Eternal Father...accept his divine sacrifice.... It is indeed the very death of God that I offer.[b]

Those words, "the death of God," would take on strange overtones in the days to come when God and his ministers were so much under attack.

Right at the start of her postulancy, Catherine received a letter posted on January 22, 1830, from her elder sister, who was still Sister Servant at Castelsarrasin. Marie-Louise was "very edified by the latest letter" from Catherine (which unfortunately she did not preserve for us) and encouraged her with unflagging enthusiasm.[97]

Departure

By mid-April the ordeal of postulancy was over.[98] Catherine had come out of it well. Now it was time for packing the trousseau, and the following items were crammed into a trunk:

4 pairs of sheets, used
12 towels, used
Linen for making chemises and 11 chemises already made
5 dresses: 4 calico and 1 of violet silk
4 skirts, including 1 calico
4 shawls
1 white woolen underslip
3 of black wool, [including] 1 in very bad condition
13 small shawls of violet silk
1 piece of cotton
30 headbands [...]
11 pocket handkerchiefs
3 pairs of "pockets" [used instead of handbags at that time]
3 pairs of stockings
1 corset
1 black dress[99]

Catherine also brought with her the dowry offered by Hubert and her sister-in-law, amounting to 693 francs.[100] They went to the inn to take the coach. The heavy vehicle made a glorious exit from the village by the "Paris Gate," built in the form of a triumphal arch. Sr. Hinault, aged 70, who had for a long time been Sister Servant at Châtillon, accompanied Catherine on the journey.[101] Her destination was the community of elderly sisters in the Rue du Bac, a journey of 200 miles or so. The countryside seemed to be bursting with new greenery and flowers. It was an Eastertide of light and sprouting seeds.[102]

Chapter III
Seminary

Arrival

WEDNESDAY, APRIL 21, 1830!... HORSES' hooves clattered over the paving stones of Paris, bearing in their wake the dull sound of iron-shod wheels like a kind of thunder, at once far away and near at hand.

For Catherine, there was nothing novel about the French capital, but what a change from the first time she had been there! Two years previously she had experienced coercion and exile: she had been removed far from a rejecting father, far from the dream that "St. Vincent" had woken in her. Now her father was reconciled with her, and St. Vincent's house was open to her! The obstacles had crumbled like the walls of Jericho! Despite being overwhelmed by the confusion all around, despite her tiredness, Catherine savored the taste of a victory resulting from a faith that can move mountains.

For her, Paris would no longer mean the restaurant,[2] the bottles, the workmen's coarse banter. From now on it would mean prayer, silence, and ministering to the sick and the poor. Her dream was becoming a reality. Catherine had been told that the period of formation would be tough, but she was ready for anything that might arise. Nothing would be too much for her now that she was following the call in her heart.

The coach reached its terminus amid the hullabaloo of coachmen and neighing horses. Some sisters from the motherhouse were there, dressed like those at Châtillon: the same family, the same warmth; and the two travelers, one very old and one young, received the same welcome.

Settling in at the Rue du Bac[3]

They got into a cart together, with their luggage and clothes. The sound of wheels rang under the entrance of 132 Rue du Bac and then again fifty yards farther on under another arch, finally coming to a halt in a rectangular courtyard. On the right, a building with a clock; on the left, the seminary with its bell which would call Catherine to her prayers.

It was toward the latter that Catherine was led: the Hôtel de Châtillon, a strange place in which to quarter a novitiate. The house had been designed in the seventeenth century to emphasize the prestige of the La Ballière family, and the windows were inordinately high. There was a garden on the other side of the building from the courtyard where Catherine arrived. From it a double staircase in stone with sumptuous wrought-iron balustrades led upward to a flight of steps entering the first floor where the Superior General's quarters were located. The seminary sisters were underneath on the ground floor, at a lower level that gave the impression of being in a basement. They were cramped for space, as there were 112 of them at meals and prayers.[4] At night they would climb up to the dormitories in the attic on the second floor, which communicated under the eves with the chapel, lower than it is today. In the chapel, too, it was warmly overcrowded. On the right of the impressively large double staircase (i.e., on the east side, in a sort of courtyard where the missions office would later grow up) there was a henhouse and a stable to remind Catherine of the farm where she had been born.[5]

Catherine changed out of her peasant costume—*cannette* and skirt with petticoat—and donned the coif and *fichu* [a sort of shawl] of the seminary sisters. Here, style of clothing was not important. St. Vincent had wanted the sisters to be dressed like people in the world—not fashionable society but ordinary people. In the nature of things, the habit had evolved in the direction of a religious outfit. Catherine was quite surprised at the differences in color and quality of cloth between one sister and another, which had not been the case at Châtillon. Some appeared ladylike in stockings and shoes, sporting outsized *cornettes*, bedecked with generous collars and hemstitching, set off with ribbon trimmings and even going so far as wearing *beaverette* or sheep-cloth aprons; other sisters had preserved their appearance as women "of the people," closer to St. Vincent's intentions.[6] All this was the result of a realizing of standards, against which it was vain to struggle at this period of "Restoration." Indeed, this very word had overtones of flabbiness and a certain complacency—it was a nostalgic return to an arid past.

But Catherine's heart was on fire. She looked at everything with a fresh eye, as if it were the Promised Land. Her eye did not yet dwell on lapses of this kind.

The young farm woman who had had to fight for time to pray in the midst of a constricting and leisureless existence was now able to taste freedom of heart and spirit, for here God and prayer took first place. She did not miss all the duties that had occupied her life. This vacuum did not worry her—on the contrary, it fanned the flame within her.

On her arrival, a piece of news was giving rise to much expectation: the following Sunday the relics of St. Vincent were to be solemnly transferred from Notre Dame to St. Lazare—the Archbishop had decided to give them back to the Vincentians. He would lead the procession; and the King himself—a remote and almost mythical person—would be there. The seminary would take part in the procession. Once again, St. Vincent was indicating to Catherine that she should approach him; and this time she did not flee or even back away. Her whole being surged forward to this encounter: a festal occasion to which lots of ordinary people were expected to come.

People and places

As she waited for this great day, Catherine began to get to know the important people of the house. Most of them had managed to escape the Revolution.

The Superior General of the Vincentians and the Sisters of Charity was Fr. Salhorgne (aged 72),[7] elected a year previously. He lived at 95 Rue de Sévres, the motherhouse of the Congregation of the Mission, 300 yards away. His task was slowly to rebuild this Company of which, immediately after the Revolution, there was nothing left but "fourteen old men, venerable remnants of the former edifice erected by the Founder," to use Fr. Etienne's expression. At 28 years old, Fr. Etienne, the Procurator, was the young hope of the house. There was also Fr. Aladel, aged 29,[8] recalled from the northern part of the country to be the confessor for the Sisters of Charity. The [spiritual] director was Fr. Richenet,[9] back from China.

The Superior General of the Sisters of Charity, whose office opened on to the broad flight of stairs, was Sr. Antoinette Beaucort,[10] born at Vic in the Meurthe *département*. She had been orphaned at an early age, brought up by a priest-uncle, and had joined the Company at the age of 14. Caught unawares by the Revolution and imprisoned in 1792,[11] she had to hide for a while before going back to community life at Royan, then at Mont-de-Marsan, and then in Paris. She had been bursar from 1824 to 1827,[12] and had a good head on her shoulders. Orderliness was close to her heart. She kept a close eye on birth and baptismal certificates in order to avoid any confusion between names given to the Church, to the civil registrar, and in religious houses (and the sisters were sometimes given a new name when they changed from one community to another).[13] Sr. Beaucourt left behind her the memory of an affable superior who knew how to "temper her refusals with so much kindness that you always came out of her room feeling comforted."

Above all, Catherine was in contact with Sr. Velay,[14] the first Directress, more usually known as "Mère Marthe." Born on October 21, 1770, she had been the last sister to take the habit at the age of 19 on May 30, 1790, hastily and without going on retreat beforehand. The Revolutionary Decree of May 25, 1792, compelled her to take it off again,[15] but she continued to minister to the poor, following the precept of Mother Deleau, the Superior General: "Give yourself in the service of the poor to anything that may be asked of you in all honesty."[16]

The superiors and formation personnel of that epoch had lived through a period of secret "goings-on," when Fr. Philippe,[17] Director of the Company, had come on visits while continually changing his clothes to ward off suspicion. Mother Marthe's instructions had a great influence on Catherine. The sisters of that time supported themselves with two guiding thoughts:

1) God alone, God in our superiors, in our companions [...]; in our hearts, to purify them; in our spirits, to enlighten them; and in our actions, to sanctify them.

2) Mary Immaculate.

Catherine pronounced that name with an infectious joy, with a faith that could move mountains, as she waited for all our Lady's power and goodness to be revealed to her.[18]

For Catherine, who had marked time for so long in a world not chosen by herself (the workers of the Faubourg St. Antoine, the stuck-up girls of the Châtillon boarding school...), the seminary was the gateway to life, heaven on earth, a world wisely established by St. Vincent in the way of God. Lit from within, Catherine lived a life that oriental liturgy manifests more explicitly: the anticipation of a life glorified by God. The communion of saints became a real experience, a world of encounters, of images, for earthly encounters are not all on one level. Moses knew it well: you do not see God without dying. To enter into communion with his invisible eternity, in the web of time that passes, is only done through the mediation of signs. Interior images are a gift from God in the very spirit of man. They are transparency itself when God and his elect give the sign. They allow the attainment of the communion of saints—a reality no less objective than the reality of the world itself, and one that is perceptible by our eyes through material signs. The sign does not prevent a coming together—quite the reverse: it realizes it. It is not so much a screen as a telescope that brings faraway stars nearer. God's gift can give perceptions that are more real than those of ordinary life.

This was the kind of thing that was happening to Catherine. As the "great festival day" approached when St. Vincent's body would be transferred, floating across the ocean of the Parisian populace, she wrote: "It seemed to me that I was no longer held by the confines of this earth."

Her spirit flew free, but her hands remained calm and steady at their work.

WORK AND DAILY ROUTINE[19]

Framework of the day

Catherine got used to the timetable and habits of the house. The rising bell rang at 4:00 A.M. (This was no different from her peasant habits, which had continued at Châtillon.) Straightaway a voice would be heard: "In God's holy name, please, Sisters, arise." And a whole chorus of voices, some still half asleep, others already clear and strong, would respond: "Blessed be God's holy name."

This first moment of the day was the time for the Sign of the Cross and the Act of Adoration prescribed by the Rule.[20] Catherine learned how to set out a *chemise* of a type unknown in Burgundy: its sleeves were enormous—much longer than one's arms. One had to learn how to fold it up differently each day so that wear and dirt on the easily soiled border did not show up in the same place every time.[21] At 4:30, it was time to go down to the chapel for prayer, which ended at 5:15 with the Daily Offering, the Angelus, litanies of Jesus, and a whole host of prayers for sinners, benefactors, travelers, the sick, the dying, and so on.[22]

Then came the "repetition": a customary time of sharing dating back to St. Vincent. The Directress would select two or three novices each day and address them with the following ritual formula: "Sister X, would you share with us the virtuous thoughts with which the Lord inspired you during your prayer?" The sister would go and kneel down before the Directress's table and submit to this, while everyone else stayed on their knees. She would begin with the ritual formula: "After having placed myself in the presence of God...." So, life had its forms and its formulas, which provided a framework, a filter, an enabler, even for confidential things.

Next, the novices passed on to housework. As a sturdy country woman, Catherine had been chosen for "courtyard work": sweeping outside and in corridors and cloisters; plus washing up saucepans and large cauldrons.[23]

From 6:00 until 7:00, time was set aside for those whose education had been lacking, in order to improve their reading and writing.[24] Catherine applied herself earnestly to this.

At 7:00, Mass in the chapel. The seminary sisters had no chair or bench, except on Sundays when benches without backs were put out for them.[25] There followed "breakfast" in silence: dry bread and milk soup.[26]

At 8:00 the Directress (equivalent to a novice mistress in religious orders) carried out the *Instruction on Christian Doctrine,* mostly based on the Gospel. There followed manual work: sewing, ironing, vegetable peeling, etc., during which the sisters were permitted to converse with each other piously, in a serious manner "and not in the form of recreation."

At 11:30 came the "particular exam," a directed examination of conscience, followed by what at that time was called "dinner" in good French, preceded by the *Benedicite* in Latin, whose formula is still used today in some monasteries: *Benedic, Domine, nos et haec tua dona....* Bless us, O Lord, and these thy gifts, which we are about to receive from thy bounty.

The meal was accompanied by reading, ending with the martyrology and grace, as in all monasteries at the time.

At midday, the Angelus was followed by a decade of the Rosary and then a time for relaxation when the sisters could talk to one another while sewing.

At 2:00 P.M., the Directress would give the second *instruction*, on the theme of St. Vincent's teachings, usually about love and service of the poor. The essential points in these instructions were recorded in a sort of catechism that emphasized three virtues: humility, charity, and simplicity, together with the utmost insistence on serving the poor:

> We should consider them as our lords and masters, recognizing how much we owe to them [...], we should be consistent in our devotion in order to acquit ourselves well of our duties toward our dear masters, the poor, neglecting nothing which could be necessary for the alleviation of their suffering [...] and above all we should take care to instruct them properly in the principal mysteries of our faith [...] so that they may live well and die well.[27]

St. Vincent had sketched out this ideal for the Sisters of Charity:

> Having as a rule nothing but a rented room for a cell, the streets of a town or the wards of a hospital for a cloister, obedience for an enclosure, fear of God for a grille, holy modesty for a veil–[the sisters] should, in any place in the world in which they find themselves, conduct themselves with as much purity of heart and body, as much detachment from created things, as much edification of their neighbor, as do religious sisters in their cloister.

At 3:00, the community would silently make the Act of Adoration of Jesus on the cross, which Catherine had done so fervently during her time at Châtillon. Then another period of work, more prayer in the chapel from 5:30 until 6:00, and then supper followed by "working recreation," as at midday.

At 8:00, the two points for meditation on the following day would be read aloud and, after another examination of conscience, the day would end with night prayers. At 9:00 the lights were put out.

Throughout the day, anyone encountering a gap in activity would be expected to profit from it by saying the Rosary.[28]

The week

Catherine got used to the habitual rhythm of each week: Wednesday was a day of abstinence, Friday a day of fasting[29] (Catherine had been doing that ever since her childhood[30]) with *coulpe* [public admission of faults] on Friday evening.[31]

On Sundays,[32] the offices were more solemn, and readings organized by the superiors replaced manual labor. On this day, too, the sisters taught each other the catechism "in order to make themselves capable of instructing children and the poor on the things necessary for salvation."

The months and the year

Each month, one day was set aside for silent spiritual retreat. Every year, the liturgical cycle brought order and variety into life: Advent; Christmas and the crib; dawn coming up in the long, candlelit winter nights; the harshness of Lent and the joy of Easter; Pentecost; then St. Vincent's feast on July 19.[33]

THE TRANSFERRAL OF THE RELICS OF ST. VINCENT[34]

But this year, St. Vincent's feastday was already here in mid-April: an exceptional festal day for the transferral of the relics and a new sign for Catherine!

It was not just an event for her and for the sisters, but for the capital: from the humblest person right up to the King, who perhaps saw the festivity as a possible way of shoring up his shaky throne.

Vincent de Paul had come through the Revolution without being eclipsed. His prestige as "Father of the poor" was so great that some patriotic sayings of the time linked his name with those of Rousseau and Voltaire.[35] It was better to take advantage of his widely felt humanitarianism and have people like that on your side rather than against you.

But this had not prevented the two communities founded by him from being dissolved and persecuted.[36] Nevertheless, Commissaire Delivry, whose job it was to clear out the Vincentians' church, had left them St. Vincent's body, preserved intact in its reliquary. They had hastily put it in an oak chest and transported it, thus concealed, to Monsieur François Daudet, nephew of the Procurator of the Congregation, and then to Maître Clairet, a notary. Fr. Daudet, the Vincentian Procurator, had taken it back to his quarters in 1795.[37] On July 18, 1806, he had returned it to the Sisters of Charity, at that time living in the Rue du Vieux Colombier. They had taken it with them on April 30, 1815, when moving to the Rue du Bac. On April 10, 1830, the body had been moved to the Archepiscopal Palace in Paris.[38]

The solemn transferral by which St. Vincent's body would return to its proper home began on April 24, three days after Catherine's arrival.[39] The Archbishop of Paris, Monsignor de Quélen, aged 52, one of the pillars of the Restoration, began the celebrations together with eight other Bishops at Notre Dame. Here, St. Vincent's body had been "carried by ten men, accompanied by twenty others, all vested in albs, who had begged the favor" of working in relays in order to "transport such a precious burden."[40] The relics were venerated by a "large crowd of people." After vespers and compline, the Archbishop took his seat with the Bishops, the Chapter, and the clergy. From the heights of the Notre Dame pulpit, Monsignor Mathieu, diocesan Promotor and Vicar General, gave the panegyric on St. Vincent. In his hands he held a little ivory crucifix that "the father of the poor had used to comfort King Louis XIII at the time of his death."

The next day, Sunday April 25, at 9:00, the Apostolic Nuncio, Monsignor Lambruschini, celebrated a Pontifical High Mass before the reliquary, which had been placed on a dais. It was a heavy silver shrine, seven feet long, made by Odiot for the sum of 40,000 gold francs. A huge crowd surrounded the Archbishop and twelve other Bishops.

At 2:00 P.M., while vespers were being chanted in Notre Dame, the procession started off toward the Vincentians' house, more than a mile away. The Chapter cross led the way, followed by numerous groups of people: "members of associations, inhabitants of Clichy, Christian Brothers," etc., each one with its own banner.[41] Then came infantrymen, drummers, and platoons of policemen. Four companies of grenadiers and four of riflemen surrounded the two rows of seminarians who themselves surrounded the clergy. A military band produced sparkling peals of sound from its brass instruments.

At the *Benedicamus Domino,* intoned by the Archbishop, the first of the three groups of ten men lifted the silver shrine off the dais. The shrine's focal point was St. Vincent's face, reproduced in wax beneath the black skullcap. Another group of ten men preceded the reliquary; the third group followed it. All thirty were laymen, "garbed in cassocks, albs, and silk belts of a different color for each group." Additionally, they bore St. Vincent's medal hanging around their necks on violet ribbons.[42] So dignified and devout did they look that the Nuncio took them to be "Parisian priests."

The reliquary was escorted on all sides by the Vincentians and the canons of the metropolitan Chapter. Then came the King's chaplains, the Bishops, and finally the Archbishop, preceded by his cross and his coat of arms, surrounded by assistants in copes, and followed by high-ranking functionaries. A platoon of police brought up the rear of the procession.[43]

However, there were also orphans and the poor: those who really counted for St. Vincent. They had not forgotten him. They were the crowd.

The reliquary made a halt in the square at l'Hôtel-Dieu, at the request of the nuns and the sick, while the long cortége spread itself out along the embankments and into the Rue des Saints Péres. Incensings, prayers, acclamations....

It was at this moment that 1,000 Sisters of Charity from Paris and the surrounding area (two-thirds of those in the whole region) joined the cortège: 800 in front of the reliquary, 200 behind. They were accompanied by fifty orphan girls.[44]

The seminary was there: a forest of 112 little bonnets. Beneath one of them was Catherine, happy to be escorting the man from her dream, the man responsible for her vocation. The crowd swelled, "avid to see the infinitely precious remains of the holy priest who had filled this great city with monuments and institutions created by his charity for the relief of the unfortunate," as the official report solemnly expresses it.[45]

The procession did not reach the Rue de Sèvres until 6:00. The houses were decorated. It was out of the question for everyone to go into the Vincentians' chapel. The crowd stayed outside the gateway, which displayed a painting of St. Vincent. Only a few privileged persons were allowed inside to hear what took place. The Archbishop, in the name of the Church, but also "in the name of the poor," gave back to the Superior General the body of him who was "the father" and the protector of those same poor.[46]

The Superior General of the Congregation of the Mission [the Vincentians], Fr. Salhorgne, replied. He celebrated the "public, solemn, and peaceful triumph of a holy priest...a sort of prodigy that our descendants would find it hard to reconcile with the indifference that is unfortunately so common today."[47]

And so, before Catherine's very eyes on that Sunday of April 25, an eight-day period began which witnessed a great crowd (and even King

Charles X, himself [48]) passing through the Vincentians' chapel. The sisters of the Rue du Bac, being such close neighbors (only 300 yards away), came every day. Among them was our young Burgundian sister, who would be celebrating her twenty-fourth birthday on Sunday, May 2. She felt as light as a captive balloon when its mooring ropes are cut.

It was not until twenty-six years afterward that Catherine drew up her experience at the request of her spiritual director. She did so in an objective, nonlyrical style, without writing it down, situating it precisely in time and in this new space where she was "no longer held by the confines of this earth."[49]

It was a semiconscious state, not a dream, and it was on the wings of a demanding desire that she came to the vision: "I asked St. Vincent for all the graces necessary for me and for [his] two [religious] families and for the whole of France. It seemed to me that they had the greatest need of them."

Catherine was thinking of the possibility of further revolution, but above all of the lack of renewal in prayer that characterized the early years of the century. Her own prayer was no longer solitary, as it had been on the cold flagstones of Fain les Moutiers. She was sharing in the preoccupations of the people and she was desperately filled with hope for St. Vincent's two families.

THE APPARITIONS (APRIL–DECEMBER 1830)

St. Vincent's heart (April 25–May 2, 1830)[50]

This was the longing that gave rise to the event:

Finally, I prayed to St. Vincent with a lively faith for him to teach me what I should ask for. And each time that I came back from St. Lazare [where I had paid a visit to the shrine], I experienced so much sorrow [that] I seemed to find St. Vincent in the community, or at least his heart.... [It] appeared to me every time when I came back from St. Lazare. I had the sweet consolation of seeing it [in the chapel at the Rue du Bac] above the shrine where the small relics of St. Vincent de Paul were exposed.[51]

The little reliquary was a small metal cabinet with glass windows placed to the left of the main altar. The vision of the heart took place above it.

It appeared to me, at three different times three days running:

White, color of flesh, announcing peace, calm, innocence, and unity.

Then I saw red like fire: which must light the flame of charity in people's hearts. It seemed to me that the whole community should renew itself and spread to the farthest points of the world.

And then I saw red-black, which brought sadness into my heart. Waves of sadness came over me and I suffered much in overcoming them. I did not know why, or how this suffering had to do with the change in government.

This is Catherine's own narrative. Twenty-six years after, her memory had preserved the fact of three visions whose colors signified for her *innocence, love,* and *ordeal.* Her confessor and Fr. Etienne were confused over the dating of these visions and placed them in *July,* at the time of St. Vincent's *feastday* (and not at the time of the *transferral* of the relics). They stylized the episode into two parts: the dark vision first, and then the bright red vision—the opposite way to Catherine.

According to their interpretation, which was in circulation from 1833 onward (i.e., twenty-three years before Catherine set down her version), she had not merely perceived the symbols but had also heard words inside herself.

For the dark vision: "St. Vincent's heart is deeply afflicted at the sight of the evils which will swoop down upon France."

For the bright red vision: "St. Vincent is consoled a little, for through the intercession of the Most Holy Virgin he has obtained the favor that his two families will not perish in the midst of those great evils."[52]

If we read Catherine's accounts carefully, we find that these *explicit* messages were not given to her until later on: at the time of the apparition of our Lady during the night of July 18/19, the feast of St. Vincent. This explains why Fr. Etienne and Fr. Aladel said nothing about the latter vision and placed the vision of their Founder's heart on this date. The official documents synthesized the predictions that Catherine progressively received. They were disseminated confidentially before being proclaimed publicly during the time that Fr. Etienne was Superior General, and they certainly stimulated the fresh growth of St. Vincent's two families. These promises were held in high regard since they were continually confirmed by extraordinary acts of protection recorded amidst the upsets of the century, from the July 1830 Revolution to the Commune of 1871.

For Catherine, the important thing was this new encounter with St. Vincent, whom she was "rediscovering" six years after her dream at Fain; but this time she was wide awake and it was hope which inspired this encounter under the sign of love.

But she did not make too much of it, relativizing the *sign* that it was given to her to see: "I seemed to find *St. Vincent,* or *at least his heart....*"

It was not a question of a heart of flesh—which was neither in the chapel nor in the shrine at St. Lazare, since it had been set apart as a relic and had followed an independent destiny. In 1790, Fr. Cayla, Superior General, had entrusted it to his Italian assistant, Fr. Siccardi, who had transported it to Turin, hidden inside a hollowed-out book. After various adventures, it had come back to Lyon on January 1, 1805, at the imperative behest of Cardinal Fesch.[53] Catherine knew nothing of this absent relic, but she was right to insist on the symbolic character of the apparition. It was not an anatomical object but an icon.

The three colors were not simply a picturesque color scheme. They carried a message, heavy with meaning. Catherine decoded that message with all the laconic strength of those under the influence of an intense perception.

The vision of the flesh color indicates not so much an actual color as the dimension of incarnation. This flesh color is white, the color of skin, not of blood, and it signifies "peace, calm, innocence and unity." Catherine had arrived in a convalescent community, glowing anew after the bloodletting of the Revolution. There she found things in a more tarnished and sometimes shocking state than the ideal she had created in herself. However, hope kept her from being negative. There was much at that time which needed reform: Catherine would soon be saying so, and the superiors were already aware that things needed to be done. But Catherine's vision went beyond the faults of the present and toward a better future.

The red-like fire of the second vision designates not so much a color as an interior ardor. What Catherine perceived was that radiance which, from the time of Abraham to the time of Moses (and even the time of Pascal...), provokes the use of the word "fire" when God is near.[54] This fire, irradiating St. Vincent's heart, "must light the flame of charity in people's hearts."

Catherine is not concerned with faults except as regards the going beyond them promised by the vision. The community should "renew" itself, she says (i.e., reform itself). This hope grows to encompass a universal dimension: "It seemed to me that the whole community should spread to the farthest points of the world."[55]

But the third vision turns to black and evokes "waves of sadness" in Catherine that can scarcely be overcome. Is this to be another revolution, with all its dead, like that of 1793? Here, Catherine's vision concentrated symbolically on the old monarch. Perhaps she had caught a glimpse of him paying a visit to St. Vincent's shrine. At least she knew that he had taken part in this celebration. In the context of her hierarchical world, where the sovereign (made holy by anointing) is a peak, like the father on a farm, the Pope in Rome, or the superior in the house, the King paying homage to St. Vincent takes on meaning. The Restoration, moving toward the last rays of a setting winter sun, had appeared to her only in a religious light before its fall back into a night of nothingness. Catherine Labouré was a peasant of old French stock, like Paul Claudel's Violaine, and she therefore attributed a certain holiness to this government. Despite the fact that her father had been a functionary in the earliest civil administration of the Revolution, she saw a sinister omen in the fall of this government: the corruption of the old religious world of which she was a part, and which, moreover, was knitted into the very depths of her being.

She now felt herself to be the carrier of a message greater than herself but which must remain a secret between her and heaven. She took advantage of her weekly confession—doubtless on Saturday May 1[56]— to confide it to Fr. Aladel.[57] But it was quite difficult for her to put into words what she had seen: this message of love, of promises, and of impending misfortune. Catherine found no sympathetic response on the other side of the grille. The black silhouette only rewarded her with fear and refusal.

"Another girl going off on a tangent and wandering in her mind," thought the confessor. He asked her to be calm and forget all about it. "Do not listen to these temptations" (did he add "from the devil"?). "A Sister of Charity's job is to minister to the poor, not to dream."[58]

Catherine was totally in agreement with a ministry of service, but this attempt at dissuasion astonished her, since the vision had multiplied tenfold her capacity for loving and serving. So why present these two things—service and "dreams"—as two opposing poles? At any rate, she accepted his advice without bitterness. "My confessor calmed me as much as possible, while turning my mind from these thoughts."[59]

As much as *possible!* Is it "possible" to calm ardors that come from God? Catherine fell back on wise, austere prayer and on the official formula and sacramental rites. She did not see St. Vincent's heart again. Above the reliquary, with its metal chasing, there was nothing but the religious painting of St. Anne sitting in a chair with the little Virgin Mary, hands on her mother's knees, learning to read.

Our Lord in the Eucharist [60]

Then something else altogether happened: at Mass, all of a sudden, the host became transparent like a veil. Beyond the appearance of bread, Catherine saw our Lord. It happened before she had time to resist as her spiritual director had counseled her. Could it be an illusion? Catherine concentrated her critical faculties...and no longer saw anything but the host and just the host. But when she let herself follow her internal motion—when she really started to pray again—then the host revealed what, ordinarily, it would conceal. It was neither a dream nor a state of overexcitement, but more like a mysterious doorway to Reality. Catherine summed it up like this:

> I saw [...] our Lord in the Most Holy Sacrament [...], all the time that I was in the seminary, except all the times when I doubted [i.e., resisted]; when that happened, the following time I would see nothing, since I wanted to get to the bottom of it [...], I doubted this mystery, [and] I believed myself to be mistaken.

She felt like Peter when he sank into the sea as he began to think of the improbability of it being possible to walk on the waters.

On June 6, 1830, Trinity Sunday, the vision turned black, just as St. Vincent's heart had done two months earlier. Catherine again used this word "black" to convey the impact of this depressing vision.

> Our Lord appeared to me like a King, with the cross on his breast [as always], in the Most Holy Sacrament. It [...] was during Holy Mass, at the time of the Gospel. It seemed to me that the cross sank [from his breast] on to the feet of our Lord. And it seemed to me that our Lord was stripped of all his vesture. Everything fell to the ground. It was then that I had the blackest and most somber thoughts.[61]

The vision of Christ's sufferings in his body, the Church, was formed on a model very close to the martyrs of the Revolution. Catherine's interpretation centered on the King of France. Theologians had at one time made his anointing an eighth sacrament, to enhance the title of God's representative that the Apostle Paul had already attributed to pagan sovereigns (Rom 13:14; 1 Tim 2:1-2; Tit 3:1). Catherine made a clear distinction between her *vision* and her *applying* it to the old King, whom she had glimpsed out of breath the previous April as he came to pay homage to St. Vincent.

"I do not know how to explain it," she admitted, "but I had the thought that the King of the earth would be lost [i.e., dethroned] and stripped of his royal garments."[61]

Catherine attempted to confide her "thought" to Fr. Aladel, but without success.[62] However, the things of heaven continued to give signs to her, resist as she might. The desire for God, which had inspired her vocation, blazed within its realization.

She was happy in the seminary: a lightweight inhabitant of the heavenly regions and yet tough when it came to sweeping courtyards or cleaning out cauldrons. It was certainly by accident that one day in the refectory she remained so absorbed in the aftermath of an apparition, so lost to the outside world, that she suddenly heard Sr. Cailhot, third Directress, calling to her: "Now then, Sr. Labouré, are you in a state of ecstacy?"[63]

Sr. Cailhot's tone was brisk, suspecting nothing. The form of words was usual when chiding people for absentmindedness—Catherine was not that kind of person. She started to eat guilelessly, as if nothing had taken place, and no more was said about the matter.

At the beginning of June, she received a letter from her elder sister, sent from the south of France on May 25, the month of Mary. Marie-Louise had only just learned that Catherine had gone into the seminary. She was a shade unhappy. "Your silence since March 4 has worried me a lot [...]. I was cross with you [...]." Having got that off her chest, joy overtook Catherine's big sister.

> I am no longer cross with you; I thank the good Lord [...]. If you have nothing special to say, you can delay writing to me for a little while [...]. Your happiness will be as perfect as one can hope for on this earth if you are amenable to all the good advice which will surely be offered you. You lost your own will on the road from Châtillon to Paris, I trust. Congratulations! Never try to get it back! The will of our superiors is certainly worth more than ours. Have you really realized that you are no longer in your own household, that you no longer know how to do anything? [...] My dear, in the seminary you must stock up with all the virtues [...], especially humility [...]. It is not hard to believe ourselves to be the least important of all when you think about it a little.

She asked Catherine to remember her especially to Mother Marthe, one of the bright lights of the novitiate: "Oh! How we love to discuss her wonderful instructions!"[a]

A mission for Catherine (July 18, 1830)[64]

It was indeed Sr. Marthe who gave the instruction in the seminary on the evening of July 18, 1830, vigil of St. Vincent's feastday. With warmth she recalled the Founder's piety toward the Virgin Mary. Catherine drank in her words. She had seen St. Vincent. She had seen our Lord.... She had not seen the Blessed Virgin, and so she was caught up in a new burst of feeling.

"I went to bed thinking [...] that, that very night, I would see my Blessed Mother. I had been wanting to see her for so long."

Sr. Marthe had given the novices a present: a tiny piece of the rochet (a kind of lace-trimmed surplice) that St. Vincent had formerly worn.[65] Before going to sleep, Catherine had a wild idea. She cut the piece of cloth in two and, as she herself says without beating about the bush, "I swallowed it and fell asleep thinking that St. Vincent would obtain for me the grace of seeing the Blessed Virgin."[b] She goes straight on with a "finally" which conveys the secret impatience of her time of waiting.

> Finally, at half past eleven in the evening, I heard someone calling my name. "Sister, sister!" Waking up, I looked in the direction that I had heard the voice coming from, which was toward the passage: I pulled back the curtain and saw a child dressed in white, about four or five years old, who said to me: "Get up promptly and come to the chapel. The Blessed Virgin is waiting for you." I immediately thought, "But someone will hear me." The child replied [to her thought[66]]: "Do not worry, it is half past eleven and everyone is sound asleep. Come, I shall wait for you."
>
> I hurried to get dressed[67] and went to the side of this child, who had stayed standing without going any farther than the head of my bed. He followed me—or rather, I followed him, all the time on my left, bringing rays of brightness wherever he passed. The lights were lit everywhere that we passed, which I found most astonishing. Much more surprising, when I entered the chapel[68] [...] the door opened on its own when the child had scarcely touched it with his fingertip.

In recounting her adventure in this ingenuous fashion, Catherine did not doubt that she was repeating St. Peter's adventure in the Acts of the Apostles (2:6–11) when he was set free from his prison: "During the night...the angel of the Lord made him get up.... The door opened in front of them by itself.... He had thought he was dreaming." Catherine goes on:

> My surprise was even greater when I saw that all the candles and candelabras were lit, which reminded me of Midnight Mass.[69] I still saw nothing of the Blessed Virgin. The child led me to the sanctuary, next to Fr. Director's chair.[70] There I went on my knees and the child stayed standing the whole time.
>
> As I found the time passing slowly,[71] I looked around to see if the sisters who kept watch in the house were passing through the gallery. At last the hour came; the child forewarned me. He said, "Here is the Blessed Virgin. Here she is."[72]
>
> I heard a sort of noise...like the rustle of a silk dress, coming from the direction of the gallery, near the picture of St. Joseph, which came and alighted on the altar steps, on the Gospel side,[73] in a chair like St. Anne's one. [However, it was not St. Anne in this chair but] the Blessed Virgin only[74].... It was not the same face as St. Anne.... I did not think it was the Blessed Virgin.[75] However, the child who was there said to me, "Here is the Blessed Virgin."[76] At that moment it would have been impossible to say what I had experienced, what was going on inside me. It seemed to me that I could not see the Blessed Virgin.

The whole of this first part has all the appearances of being a dream, like the Acts episode of the liberation of Peter who believed he was dreaming; but the narrative is studded with realistic details that do not fit well with the concept of a dream.[77] Catherine was afraid of the arrival of those on night duty who patrolled in the side gallery. She doubted the identity of the Virgin. Bernadette also shielded herself at the threshold of the first apparition when she saw that the trees were not moving in spite of the strange gust of wind.

Catherine was standing in the choir on the left, in front of the Communion table. She was carefully watching the chair in which the lady visitor was seated: it was on the altar steps and similar to the one in the picture hanging above St. Vincent's shrine—the one where St. Anne is teaching her daughter, the young Virgin Mary. If it was not St. Anne sitting there, could it be the Virgin? Could she have sat down in her mother's chair?

The child repeated: "Here is the Blessed Virgin!" But Catherine did not assimilate it. She stayed where she was, near Fr. Richenet's chair, which had been put there for use during the High Mass of St. Vincent.

It was then that the child spoke to me, no longer as a child but as if a man, the strongest man and with the strongest words.[78] Then, looking at the Blessed Virgin, I was at her side in a single bound,[79] on my knees on the altar steps, with my hands resting on the Blessed Virgin's knees.[80]

There, a period of time passed, the sweetest of my life. It would be impossible for me to say what I experienced.[81] She told me how I should behave toward my spiritual director and also several other things that I must not mention; the way in which to comport myself when suffering.

"With her left hand" the Virgin showed Catherine "the foot of the altar." It was there that she should come "and throw herself [...] to open her heart." Catherine continues: "I will receive all the comfort that I need [...]. She explained everything to me."[82]

What explanations did Catherine hear in the course of this close encounter with our Lady? She made two attempts to transcribe them at the end of her life on October 30, 1876, forty-six years after the apparition. We set out here the most complete account possible, collating the two versions.[c]

"My child, the good Lord wants to entrust you with a mission.[83]

"You will have plenty of suffering, but you will overcome it through the knowledge that what you do is for the glory of God. You will know what comes from the good Lord. You will be tormented by it until you have told it to him whose task it is to direct you. You will be contradicted.[84] But you will have grace. Do not fear. Tell everything with confidence and simplicity. Have confidence. Do not fear. You will see certain things. Give an account of them [i.e.]: what you will see and hear."[85]

What Catherine was being asked to tell with confidence was the visions and the words that would be given to her. This would be the medal whose production she would soon be asked to push for.[86] The apparition ended with: "You will be inspired in your prayers: give an account of them."[87] This promise of help was followed by a foretelling of misfortune.

"There will be bad times to come. Misfortunes will come crashing down on France. The throne will be toppled. The whole world will be turned upside down by misfortunes of all kinds" (the Blessed Virgin looked full of grief as she said this). "But come to the foot of this altar. There, graces will be poured out on all those, small or great, who ask for them with confidence and fervor. Graces will be poured out especially [on those] who ask him for them.

"My child, I love to pour out graces on the community especially. I love it very much, happily.

"[And yet] I am grieved. There are great abuses in regularity. The rules are not being observed. There is a great laxity in both the communities. Say this to him who is responsible for you, even though he is not the superior. He will be responsible for the community in a special way. He must do his utmost to reestablish the vigorous observance of the Rule. Tell him on my behalf to take care that there is no bad reading, no wasting of time, and no useless visits.

"When the Rule is [once again] vigorously observed, there will be a community which will come to join itself to yours. This is not normal. But I love it [this community].... Say that it should be accepted. God will bless [the communities] and they will enjoy great peace."[88]

This prediction became fact in 1850. Two communities entered St. Vincent's family: first that of the Sisters of Charity, founded by Elizabeth Ann Seton (who subsequently became the first canonized saint of the United States), then that of the Sisters of Charity of Austria, founded by Léopoldine de Brandis.[89]

"The community will enjoy great peace; it will become great," our Lady ended, but only to proceed to tell of imminent troubles.

"Great misfortunes will come. The danger will be great. However, fear nothing, tell others to fear nothing! God's protection is always there in a special way and St. Vincent will protect the community" (the Blessed Virgin was still sad). "But I will be with you myself. I have always watched over you. I will grant you many graces. The time will come when the danger will be great. People will think that all is lost. When that happens, I shall be with you! Have confidence; you will know my visitation and the protection of God and that of St. Vincent on the two communities. Be confident! Do not be discouraged. When all this happens, I will be with you all. But this will not be so for other communities. There will be victims." (The Blessed Virgin had tears in her eyes as she said this.) "There will be victims among the clergy of Paris; Monsignor the Archbishop" (fresh tears as this word was uttered) "will die."

This prediction did not come true in 1830; nor was it to do with Monsignor Affre's death when he was killed on the barricades in June 1848. Catherine's written account specifies the time: *forty years* after the 1830 vision.

Therefore, we are dealing with Monsignor Darboy's death in 1871.[90] Unfortunately Catherine did not set down this interpretation until 1876, after the event, but she remembered having said it to

Fr. Aladel many years before. As she put it, "At these words, I thought: 'When will [this] be?' I understood *forty years* very clearly." (The second version adds "and ten years after the peace.")[91] "On this point, Fr. Aladel answered me, 'Do we know if you will be there and I, too?' I replied to him, 'Others will be there if we are not.'"

The apparition emphasized misfortunes that would not be long in coming:

> "My child, the cross will be held in contempt. It will be thrown to the ground. Blood will flow. Our Savior's side will be opened anew. The streets will run with blood. Monsignor the Archbishop will be stripped of his vestments." (Here, the Blessed Virgin could not carry on speaking; grief was portrayed on her face.) "My child, the whole world will be plunged into gloom."

Finally, the vision began to tell Catherine about plans which would become more detailed later on: the new Association of Children of Mary that her confessor would found;[92] the celebration "with great pomp" of the Month of May[93] and the Month of St. Joseph;[94] "there will be great devotion to the Sacred Heart."[95]

Now let us return to the 1856 account in which Catherine relates the end of the apparition.[96]

> I stayed for I do not know how long. All I know [is that] when she departed I only perceived that something had been extinguished, then no more than a shadow that went alongside the [future] gallery [on the right],[97] by the same route that she had taken when arriving. I got up from above the altar steps and saw the child [there] where I had left him. He said to me, "She has gone."
>
> We went back the way we had come, everything still lit up and the child still on my left. I believe that child was my guardian angel, who had made himself visible to take me to see the Blessed Virgin, because I had prayed a lot for him to obtain this favor for me. He was dressed in white and a miraculous light went with him—that is to say, he was shining with light. He was about four or five years old.
>
> When I got back to my bed, it was two o'clock in the morning.... I heard the clock strike. I did not go back to sleep at all.

This long, very lucid period of sleeplessness lasting till the morning was what made Catherine sure that she had not been dreaming.

She wasted no time in passing on to Fr. Aladel the message destined for him,[98] particularly as she had a vivid memory of what the Virgin had allowed her to hear: "You will be tormented until you have told it to him whose task it is to direct you." Her petition was not well received.

Fr. Aladel could see nothing in it but "illusion" and "imagination." Doubtless the demands concerning reform of the two Vincentian families[99] found a strong echo in his own evangelical and radical thoughts and desires. He was one of the bright young hopes whom people were starting to put their reliance in for reorientation of the Company. Nevertheless, he said to himself, "What is this young sister poking her nose in for?" He found the thought of being elevated to being a founder [of the Children of Mary] shocking.[100] Could Catherine be trying to flatter him by pretending to give him a mission to fulfill? And as for the prophecy of misfortune in another revolution, he found it totally improbable. The transferral of St. Vincent's relics had produced much fervor among the people, and the rapid conquest of Algeria "promised great prosperity to France," or so it seemed to him.[101]

In the face of these optimistic prognostications, the Revolution indeed burst upon France before the end of the month, during July 27–29. The "Three Glorious Days" succeeded in bringing about simultaneously both the overthrow of the monarchy and the "bloody troubles" as paradoxically prophesied.[102] This is how Fr. Etienne felt about it:

> Churches are profaned, crosses overturned, religious communities invaded, devastated, and dispersed, priests hunted down and maltreated. The Archbishop of Paris is himself the object of the populace's fury and is obliged to put on false clothes and go into hiding ["stripped of his vestments," Catherine had said]. It really looks as if the bad days of 1793 have come to life again.[d]

What was more easily verifiable even than the predicted outbreak of violence was the protection of the Vincentians and Sisters of Charity. Menacing behavior seemed to stop at the very doors of their houses. One mob of young rioters, aged between 12 and 14, noisily began to attack the Vincentian house as 95 Rue du Séveres.[103] "We saw weapons being brought in here!" they said.

A good Father, still in his cassock, who had not even bothered to disguise himself like the others, came out to speak calmly to them.

"My child," he said to the ringleader, "do you want to see my weapons?"

"Yes, sir, show them to us."

The priest opened his breviary and showed him the holy pictures that, luckily, caught the interest of his young inquisitor.

"Would you like one?" Father asked. He handed over a picture and the boy went off triumphantly with it. The whole mob followed.

Another time, they came back again to take the cross off the façade of the house. But Fr. Etienne's courage and vigor saw them off quickly. After that, it was all over. Nothing further happened to disturb the peace.

So relates Sr. Pineau, seeing in this a realization of the promises given to Catherine.

Catherine had even gone as far as to provide details which appeared absurd: "A hunted Bishop will find shelter in a Vincentian house." This seemed like the last place in which anyone would choose to hide. But now along came an Archbishop, Monsignor Frayssinous, Minister of Worship under Charles X, to ask Fr. Salhorgne (the Superior General) for shelter. The latter thought it safer to send him on to St. Germain-en-Laye.[104]

Taken aback by these unexpected happenings, Aladel listened to Catherine with greater interest during the time of troubles,[105] but "without letting her see that he attached the slightest importance to her visions." After the upheaval, Catherine went back to a normal sort of confession: small, everyday sins, which seemed larger in her eyes because of her contrition and her humility. So her confessor started to hope that this young sister would return to being an ordinary penitent without fuss or visions.

The medal[106]

That was not the end of it. Four months later, Catherine came along again with definite instructions: to have a medal struck bearing an effigy of the Immaculate One whom she had seen radiating God's gifts.

That same day she had once again been seized with "a great desire to see the Blessed Virgin," a desire which came from outside herself.

> I thought that she would grant me this grace, but this desire was so strong that I was convinced that I would actually see her at her most beautiful.
>
> I perceived the Blessed Virgin at the same height as St. Joseph's picture [...], standing, dressed in white, medium height, her face so beautiful that it would be impossible for me to tell of her beauty. She had a silk dress, white like the dawn.

This time it was no nocturnal apparition but "half past five in the evening on November 27, during prayers, in the deep silence after the meditation topic had been given. Nor was it near the high altar, as the apparition in the chair had been, but on the right, on the same side as St. Joseph's picture." Catherine did not have to say more.[107]

She *saw* from her place (at the front on the right) where she was in the midst of a meditation, among the serried ranks of sisters, without anyone noticing. She confided her vision to Fr. Aladel under the seal of the confessional. This is what he recalled and distributed about the matter:

> The novice, while she was at prayer, saw a picture[108] representing the Blessed Virgin, in the way that she is customarily portrayed under the title of the Immaculate Conception, full-length and holding out her arms. [She was] dressed in a white dress[109] and a silvery-blue mantle,[110] with a veil the color of the dawn.[111] From her hands came rays of light, beautifully glittering and as if in bundles.[112] [The sister] at the same moment heard a voice saying: "These rays of light are a symbol of the graces that Mary obtains for all people."[113] Surrounding the picture she read the following invocation in golden letters: *O Mary, conceived without sin, pray for us who have recourse to thee.*[114]

Catherine's account tells us what her feelings were at that moment:

> Here, I do not know how to express myself concerning what I experienced and what I saw: the beauty and the glitter, the rays of light [...].
>
> "I pour out [these graces] on those who ask them of me" [Catherine heard. She made me] understand how pleasing it was to pray to the Blessed Virgin and how generous she was toward those who pray to her, what graces she granted to those who ask them of her, what joy she felt in granting those graces.
>
> At this moment, I scarcely knew where I was, I rejoiced, I did not know....

Aladel continued his narrative in terms coinciding laconically with those used by Catherine:

> A few moments later, this picture turned around and on the reverse side she could make out the letter M surmounted with a little cross and, at the foot of it, the Sacred Hearts of Jesus and Mary.[115] After the sister had had a good look at this, the voice said to her: "A medal must be struck on this model,[116] and those who carry one with an indulgence attached and who piously make this short prayer will enjoy the special protection of the Mother of God."[117]

This was how Aladel would describe the apparition later on.[118] But at the time he gave it a bad reception. This new manifestation of visions was a bad sign.

"Pure illusion!" he retorted. "If you want to honor our Lady, 'imitate her virtues' and beware of your imagination!"[119]

Catherine withdrew, apparently calm, "without becoming any more upset," according to her confessor.[e] But this was above all due to her own self-control and to the promised grace, for she had been badly shocked. Relieved by the act of having dared to speak, now she would try to obey.

Aladel took such little interest in the message that he did not record the date of this first apparition: November 27. Catherine recalled it much later on, in 1841.[120] Neither did Aladel count how many days after the event it was when Catherine came to tell him about it.[121] For him, the important thing was asking her firmly never to return to such topics.

Final apparition (December 1830)

But in December she saw the picture again. Later on she would set down her account of this "third apparition of our Lady"–the second and last concerning the medal. She "had not made a note of the time"–i.e., the date.[122]

Like November 27, it was at 5:30, after the giving of the meditation topic. It was signaled in the same way: the rustle of a silk dress. There were some differences: she came not from the gallery side but from behind the altar. And the "picture" of the medal appeared not "at the same height as the picture of St. Joseph," on the right,[123] but in the center, "near the tabernacle," a little behind.

The same "high-necked dress" on the Virgin: as Catherine put it, "the color of dawn"; the same "blue veil." The "hair parted down the middle, covered by a kind of headband decorated with a piece of lace two finger-widths long," she recorded in minute details, in similar terms to the ones she had used for the November 27 apparition. The rays of light which sprang from her hands "filled all the lower half in such a way that you could no longer see the Blessed Virgin's feet." As on the previous occasion, "a voice" made itself heard in the depths of "her heart": "These rays of light are the symbol of the graces that the Blessed Virgin obtains for those who ask them of her."

Catherine had the feeling that these words should appear "as a description at the foot," if an earthly picture were made of this heavenly vision.

This account of the third apparition does not speak of the reverse of the medal. Catherine merely ends with the Virgin disappearing "like something being extinguished" while she "remained filled with joy and consolation."

The apparition had the character of a farewell; and Catherine, whose days in the seminary were coming to a close, received this message: "You will not see me any more, but you will hear my voice during your prayers."[124]

This, then, was the end of the visions. They had all taken place in the chapel at the Rue du Bac.[125] Only the communications, or interior inspirations, would keep these visions alive.

Catherine was in a dilemma: on the one hand, the duty of making known the renewed request concerning the medal; on the other hand, obedience to her spiritual director, who wished to hear no more talk of these "imaginary things." She gave precedence to earthly obedience, since our Lady had not pressed her.

Receiving the Habit

End of seminary life

Seminary ended on January 30, 1831. Catherine received the habit. It was a day of silent retreat, and the ceremony was very simple. Twenty out of seventy-three of the sisters had reached the end of the seminary, whose full complement had been cut by a third because of the July Revolution. In the afternoon, Catherine and her companions cast aside their apparel (a kind of bodice, tied in at the waist, with a gathered skirt) and put on "the habit" (still black at this period). They put the cap *(toquois)* on their heads–a sort of bonnet on which was placed the starched *cornette* with its large wings, a well-known symbol of the Sisters of St. Vincent de Paul, from the eighteenth century until the time of the Second Vatican Council (September 20, 1964). Sr. Antoinette Beaucourt, the Superior General, greeted the twenty sisters. She fixed the *cornette* in place with a pin, called for that reason "the obedience pin" because of its close link in time with the submission or vow of obedience.

She exhorted the young sisters to the service of the poor[126]–and Catherine's desires and thanksgiving were already stronger than this exhortation. The next day, Catherine left the seminary.

First warning signal

"Before going on to her new destination, [she] spent several days in one of our sisters' houses"–so said Sr. Pineau in March 1877.[f] Sr. de

Geoffre adds a further detail: it was "a large establishment." Which one? Probably the "little houses" hospice nearby—an old leper house founded in 1494, in which St. Vincent's daughters installed themselves during his lifetime, in 1655. Then, as now, it occupied a site in the Bon Marché; its entrance opened on to the Rue de Babylone.

It seems that this short stopover may have been organized by Aladel so that he could inspect Catherine. He "found an excuse to call on the sisters of that house." Rumors of the visions of St. Vincent's heart had already been leaked abroad, rendered even more credible by the extraordinary protection that the sisters experienced during the July Revolution. "It was known that Fr. Aladel had certain confidences imparted to him. As soon as he appeared, the sisters surrounded him and plied him with questions, each of them trying to outdo the others." He kept his eyes open and was worried, since Catherine appeared more roused by these questions than he was himself. Would she betray herself?

No. "Unabashed," she was "the most eager of them all to take part in all the questionings, quietly and without unmasking herself in any way." Her confessor was impressed by this. Despite the severity of the reception he had previously given her, she had now managed to notch up quite a score—though he took care not to let this be seen. This same young sister who had come to him in shadow, full to the brim with inopportune visions and messages, was, then, not a prey to ostentatious behavior, but totally mistress of herself and capable of keeping the secret! This was a kind of charism. At that time, Aladel did not know of the second (and final) apparition of the medal. Catherine, obedient as always, had not dared to speak of it to him. His vivid impression of that day was that "the Blessed Virgin was helping the sister to keep her secret and that this secret was agreeable to her."[127]

*Assumed to be a portrait of Catherine's mother, Madeleine (left);
Pierre, Catherine's father (right).*

The entrance of the farmhouse where Catherine was born.

Catherine's cradle in her parents' bedroom.

Catherine's dovecote. The interior framework contains 1,121 pigeon-holes, each capable of housing two pigeons.

Catherine's kitchen nook, located on the left as you enter the principal room with its two fireplaces.

The principal room of the farmhouse where Catherine ruled for twelve laborious years.

Saint Vincent de Paul, painted by François de Tours.

The Hotel of Châtillon, where Catherine attended seminary. The balcony opens onto the Superior General's office. The seminary was located underneath, the dormitory above. The third attic window from the left is the spot from which Catherine set out for the chapel on that famous night of July 18–19, 1830.

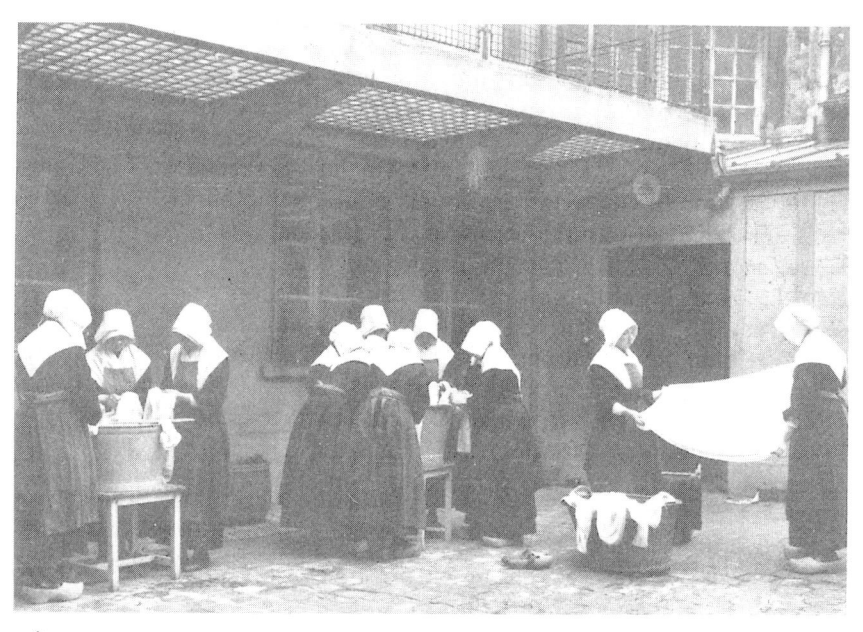

The seminary photographed at a time when the habit was still that of Catherine's day (1830).

Painting by Lecerf (1835). The two last visions of the heart—red-like fire and red-black—are combined in a single artistic composition. It is an exact rendition of the chapel and clothes worn by Catherine, which the painter had never seen.

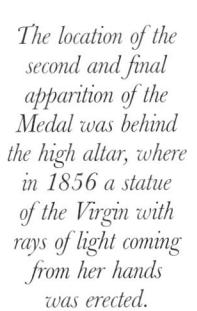

The location of the second and final apparition of the Medal was behind the high altar, where in 1856 a statue of the Virgin with rays of light coming from her hands was erected.

J. M. Aladel, Catherine's confessor (1800–1865).

Apparition of the Virgin with rays of light coming from her hands, as interpreted by Brother Carbonnier. The picture is preserved at St. Lazare. Fr. Aladel often celebrated Mass at the altar above which this painting hangs.

One of the first Miraculous Medals struck by Vachette at the Quai des Orfèvres in 1832. The rays of light are tiny and symbolic. The trefoils are Vachette's trademark, and they are found on both sides of the coin. The two lines above the two hearts on the reverse side are purely ornamental. Catherine did not ask for them, neither did she find fault with them; they appeared on the medals that she wore and distributed. This is the very first representation of the apparition as appeared on the frontispiece of a book published in 1833, a year before those of Le Guillou and Aladel.

CHAPTER IV

First Steps at the Enghien Hospice

From reception of habit to vows (February 5, 1831–May 3, 1835)

ON FEBRUARY 5, 1831, CATHERINE rang the doorbell at 12 Rue de Picpus: the Enghien Hospice to which she had been assigned.[1] Four Sisters of Charity made her welcome[2]; young and old were on the lookout for the new arrival.

She was 24 years old and had nearly twice that number of years remaining to her, all of them to be spent at this very place. It was in the Commune of Reuilly, a desolate suburb to the southeast of Paris, three miles from the Rue du Bac—and only two and a half miles from Charles Labouré's restaurant, also on the east side of Paris but further north.

The Enghien Hospice had only been in existence for twelve years. The Duchess of Bourbon had founded it in 1819 in memory of her son, the Duc d'Enghien, who had been shot in 1804 in the Vincennes trenches on Napoléon I's orders. She had set up the Hospice in the Rue de Varenne for the purpose of caring for convalescents after treatment in the Paris hospitals, as well as for twelve aged and poor women. Her heiress, Madame Adélaïde d'Orléans, sister of Louis-Philippe [King at the time of Catherine's arrival], had transferred the foundation to Reuilly in 1829,[3] supplementing the responsibilities of the house with the care of fifty elderly servants of the d'Orléans family, in order that they might find a decent existence there after having cast off their glittering livery.

Fr. Aladel had Catherine assigned to such a nearby suburb to be able to more easily keep an eye on this young sister, so normal in her everyday work, but so disturbing because of her visions.

Kitchen, Garden, and Henhouse

The house with its vaulted corridors opened on to a garden which stretched for 2.5 acres as far as the Rue de Reuilly. Here was the ground where Catherine would soon find as much work as she was capable of.[4]

Too young to work at caring for the elderly men, some of whom were sometimes a little forward in their manner,[5] Catherine was allocated to the kitchen. It was very soon apparent that she knew what she was doing. Farmhouse practices rapidly came back to her—those little tricks of the trade that had been perfected by her experience in the Labouré restaurant, whose clientele had demanded more in the way of refinement and novelty. Catherine treated the elderly folk like customers worthy of respect.

The only blot on the horizon was the head cook, Sr. Vincent, aged 35.[6] This sister, one of the founding sisters of the house, had a good reputation for great self-denial and sensitivity—but she was parsimonious. Catherine liked to give generously and found these restrictions intolerable. "You must put up with this workmate with patience"—so Aladel replied imperturbably in the course of a visit to Enghien to hear confessions.

This was the pathway of virtue. How could this be at cross-purposes with serving—and even loving—the poor? Troubled in her heart, Catherine did her best without managing to achieve true submission. Was she really so little cut out for virtue? Humble, she tried to persuade herself that this was so.

She had been entrusted with the henhouse, and here everything went well.[7] In this realm her competence was unrivalled, as it was in the vast garden where the townswomen worked to no purpose whatsoever. This became her domain. She administered, organized, and defended this territory against the sparrows and other predators, animal and human.[8] Gradually she changed the working methods and made of the land a small farm in the Burgundian fashion. Here she found her roots, although in less fertile soil.

In this way, as she had learned at Fain, she realized one of the dreams of St. Vincent, whose "non-productive" work tormented him so much that he wrote on July 24, 1655:

> We live off the patrimony of Jesus Christ, off the sweat of the poor.... I often have this thought, which throws me into confusion: "You wretch! Have you earned the bread that you're going to eat—this bread which comes to you through the work of the poor?"

St. Vincent's analysis in the spirit of the Gospel was nothing less than radical. For Karl Marx, the work of the poor merely gave a thing added worth. St. Vincent, however, felt that the poor were purely and simply the only legitimate producers of the bread that he ate....

As a farm woman, Catherine was way above such problems. She ministered to the poor by producing their food, a little more of it each year. To the thousands of chickens and pigeons would soon be added milk from the cows that she would be introducing into the cattle shed at Reuilly. The tiredness engendered by this sort of work was a tonic for her conscience.

THE MEDAL AT LAST

Catherine rejected

The return to exacting physical work had dried up Catherine's visionary qualities. She had only spoken once about the medal to Fr. Aladel after the November 27 apparition; and he had brought so much authority to bear in forbidding her even to think about it that she had kept the second apparition (in December) strictly to herself. But if she now "no longer saw" (as our Lady had told her), a voice inside urged her to pass on her message. So in the spring she gave in to this inner prompting which tormented her so much. It was a waste of time; Aladel saw her coming and forestalled any outburst. His orders were unchanged: you must ward off illusion.[9]

Catherine felt relief at having spoken, and Aladel congratulated himself at seeing her leave him so quietly. But the inner voice continued pushing at her. What should she do when faced with these contradictory instructions from our Lady on the one hand and God's representative on the other? In the autumn, she summoned up the courage to reply to our Lady: "He does not want to listen to me." ("He" was Fr. Aladel.) "He is my servant," answered the voice inside her, "and he should be frightened of displeasing me."[10] So in the autumn Catherine tried again to get through a third time[11] to him on our Lady's account. "The Virgin is angry," she brought herself to say.

Aladel remained like marble; but these words affected him and tormented him in his turn. Could he be a "bad servant" of "her whom he loved to call 'Refuge of Sinners' "? Perplexed, he allowed Catherine to talk for longer than the first two times, but without revealing what was troubling him. In the same way, he sent her off without giving her anything to hope for.[12]

This time, however, he discussed the matter seriously with Fr. Etienne, Procurator General of the Vincentians. Etienne was a friend whom he had already talked to in vague terms about the impression he had been left with by the predictions of the Revolution in July 1830. These two bright young hopes of the Company, already burdened with many responsibilities though they were barely 30, often shared their anxieties and their plans with each other. They knew very well how much caution the Church demands when it comes to apparitions.[13] Nevertheless, they put the case before Fr. Salhorgne, the Superior General, who was not at all opposed to it.[a]

"I shall soon be having a meeting with Monsignor Quélen, the Archbishop of Paris, on congregation matters. Why don't you come with me?" Fr. Etienne had said to his confrère. "We'll take the opportunity to submit this request...along with others."

What would the prelate think? They asked themselves as they went in to see him.

They were very surprised! The apparition of Mary in the mystery of her "original grace" was deeply attractive to him.[14] The rays of the Sun of Justice–Christ–what a beautiful illustration of this mystery! Yes, Mary, the woman clothed with the sun as depicted in the apocalypse, wished to put forth the radiance of him whom she had brought into the world.

"I see no drawback to striking the medal," concluded the Archbishop.

Indeed, it conformed very well with faith and piety. It could make a contribution to the giving of honor to God.

So the way was now open, with all the prudence demanded by the Church in such a case. "There is no question here of prejudging the nature of the vision nor its circumstances. We are simply going to distribute a medal. The tree will be judged by its fruits."[15]

So the scheme got under way, but not hastily. Aladel established a design, reduced to the essential characteristics. For the obverse side of the medal, the invocation to be inscribed–*O Mary, conceived without sin...*–seemed to invite the engraving of a "classical" rendering of the Immaculate Conception, in accordance with the Archbishop's wishes. The model would therefore be Bouchardon's statue in St. Sulpice, but with the rays coming from the hands–that new characteristic as seen in the vision. For the reverse side, Aladel was somewhat at a loss.

Contrary to his usual custom, he consulted Catherine in the confessional at Reuilly.

"Wasn't there another inscription, as there was on the front?" She could no longer recall, but she would pray about it. At her next confession she gave the reply she had received in prayer: "The 'M' and the two hearts will be sufficient."[16]

Cholera

Everything was due to start at the beginning of March 1832.[17] But cholera suddenly launched itself on Paris on March 26, right in the middle of festivities. The epidemic came from Russia via Poland. It provoked attacks of torrential diarrhea that necessitated hospitals making holes in their sickbeds so that the excremental flood could flow directly into buckets deployed to cope with the disaster. In the space of four or five hours, the body of a healthy man would be reduced to a skeleton. The death toll mounted in an appalling upward curve:

DATE	NUMBER OF DEATHS
April 1	79
April 2	168
April 3	216
April 4	542
April 8	769
April 9	861, and so on.

Altogether, there were more than 18,400 deaths officially recorded—in fact, over 20,000, since official statistics and the press artificially depressed the figures to avoid undue panic.

Doctors who came rushing to Paris to get information on the epidemic only succeeded in spreading it around the provinces. Prominent physicians treated not so much the sickness itself as its symptoms: diarrhea, attacks of cramps or vomiting. Hot water bottles and hot baths were set against the chill which encased the sick in an ice-like cocoon. Bloodletting, calomel [mercury chloride], and opium were used to try and stifle the spasms whose strength seemed to concentrate in the inexhaustible excretions. Dupuytren, basing himself on the dodge used by Hamburg prostitutes "to conceal their periods," applied lead acetate in order to obstruct the feces. Others prescribed the emetic ipecac "with the aim of substituting regular, artificial bouts of vomiting for natural ones," following the principle of *vomitus vomitu curatur* (cure sickness with sickness). Chafing and frictions were practiced by Récamier and Chaumel, while chamomile, valerian, mint, ether, and laudanum were Velpeau's remedies at the Hospital de la Charité. At the Hôtel-Dieu, Magendie saved eight out of twenty patients through alternating potions of punch and chamomile, together with acetate of ammonia. Broussais published the triumphant successes of his method: internal consumption of marshmallow and ice, external heat treatment with steambaths, poultices, and leeches behind the ears and on the back of the neck. These rather strange prescriptions acquire a kind of logic when one learns that he thought cholera to be a form of "gastroencephalitis." Leeches placed in the anus were designed "to draw motions in the center toward the periphery." He claimed to have cured thirty-nine out of forty patients. The *Gazette Médicale* disputed this figure and said it should be twenty-four cures out of 129. Broussais sent his witnesses to Jules Guérin, the editor. It was at this point that the death occurred of one of his patients: Casimir-Perier, President of the Council of Ministers, "despite having been treated by him." It was now every man for himself.[18]

In the hiding-place where he had taken refuge, Monsignor Quélen learned of the plague. A riot among the populace had hounded him out of his palace on January 15, 1831; he had been forced to take refuge in the monastery of St. Michel and subsequently in the Caffarellis' home.[19] Immediately, he returned to his people in distress, celebrated Mass in the house of the Sisters of Charity (in the chapel where the apparitions had taken place), and then went straight to the Hôtel-Dieu. Fr. Etienne was worried that the prelate was running the risk of violent attacks and insisted on accompanying him to the hospitals; but the Archbishop's gesture had overcome any hatred that there might have been. His prayers and his blessings mingled with hope.[20] At his request, Fr. Etienne opened St. Lazare to the sick and was caught up in the bustle of this ministering work where drama and the unforeseen cropped up daily in an increasing spiral. The same went for Aladel, whose health was seriously affected by fatigue.[21]

Vachette strikes the medal

The epidemic seemed to die down at the end of May. Newspapers announced its demise. At last Aladel was able to contact Vachette the jeweler at 54 Quai des Orfèvres: he ordered the medal from him. Unfortunately the epidemic struck up again in the second half of June. Panic was redoubled,[22] but the manufacture of the medal was already under way. Vachette delivered the first 1,500 on June 30.[23] The first was given to the Archbishop, who wasted no time in having a statue made for his bedroom—a statue "on the model shown to the sister."[24]

Catherine received her medal at the beginning of July, within her community, though nothing was done to single her out or reveal her secret. She looked at the effigy. No document suggests that she had already seen a sketch of it, so what did she feel at that moment? Above all, joy that our Lady's request should have been fulfilled after such an apparently hopeless impasse. There was the Virgin on one side, with the rays coming from her hands and the words of the invocation; there was the cross and the two hearts on the other side.

Catherine was concerned about liberties taken with interpretation: by Aladel, who had stylized the design on the model of Bouchardon's Virgin; by the metalsmith, who had put on the reverse side the stars left out on the obverse (around our Lady's head) and had added two little horizontal lines and a trefoil (his trademark?).

Aladel had allowed him complete freedom as regards detail, knowing that the manifestation of an ineffable and luminous vision in the tiny bas-relief of a medal can only be an interpretation. At Lourdes, the Abbé Peyramale would soon be facing the same problem with Bernadette and the sculptor Fabisch, commissioned to make a statue that accorded with the vision. Peyramale would have to muffle the visionary Bernadette's disappointment in deference to a renowned artist who had interpreted the vision "according to the rules of art." At any rate, it was impossible to produce a totally faithful impression reproduction.[25] Catherine did not dwell on the details—she was too happy now that she could see that the basic essentials had been brought about: the invocation, the rays coming from the Immaculate One, the signs of the cross and of love. At the time of the medal's first distribution, Catherine showed nothing but approval. "Now it must be propagated,"[26] she said, confident that God would do the rest.

If she had felt any disappointment in the physical realization of the project, the first cures and conversions would soon reassure her beyond all expectation.

First rays of light

At first the medal was distributed by the Sisters of Charity in the Paris region at the time of the renewed outbreaks of cholera.[27]

In Paris, at the school in the Place de Louvre, little Caroline Nenain (8 years old), from the parish of St. Germain-l'Auxerrois, was the only one in her class not to wear the medal and the only one to catch cholera. The sisters gave her a medal and she recovered straightaway. By the next day she was back in the classroom.[28]

In the diocese of Meaux there was a woman in Mitry who seemed a hopeless case; furthermore, she was pregnant. She was given a medal and gave birth most successfully. Everyone was astonished at the good state of health of both mother and child. In the same village a crippled child, on whose behalf "famous doctors" had been consulted in vain, began to walk on the first day of a novena during which the medal was laid on him.[29]

Another very popular cure was that of a young man of 16 who had epilepsy (according to some) or rabies (according to others) after having been bitten by a dog (November 21, 1832).[30]

There were also conversions: on June 13, 1833, the sister applied a medal to a soldier from Alençon who was "mad with rage and blaspheming." He began to pray, contrary to all expectations, and composed himself for death with serenity, even going as far as to say, "What grieves me is that I have come to love so late and that I do not love more than I do."[31]

The medal was distributed without any explicit reference to the apparition. To do that would have meant setting up a canonical enquiry and referring it to Rome, where such dossiers were not welcomed. The Curia knew only too well the risks of illusion and exaggeration, the problems of finding out the truth, and the shadow that such celestial messages cast upon the earthly authority of the Magisterium. The Archbishop had authorized the striking of the medal with a concern for avoiding such difficulties.[32]

Tidal wave

But success burst the banks of discretion. All the talk about the miracles provoked questions on the origins of the medal and impromptu answers. Rumors grew to the proportions of a tidal wave. Letters of gratitude arrived spontaneously at St. Lazare,[33] together with requests both for more medals and for explanations.

On August 5, 1833, Fr. Lamboley, a Vincentian and refugee in Spain during the Revolution, sent an account of the apparitions. Not only did he narrate the apparition of the medal, but also those of St. Vincent's heart–those apparitions beloved of the "two families" founded by him.[34]

By February 1834, before any account had been published, the medal was already being generally described as *miraculous*.[35] The problem was, how to channel this movement without getting into an awkward position with the Holy See, by whom the premature propagation of revelations and miracles was forbidden?

First publication

Abbé Le Guillou found the answer. A Breton priest, an artist and musician, he had been summoned by the Archbishop to Paris to become one of his advisers. His proposal was that an informatory piece should be published in the modest surroundings of a *Mois de Marie* [Mary's Month].[36] It was an accepted fact that these pious books included "miracles" and "lessons," freely narrated, as illustrative pieces in order to stimulate religious fervor. The medal would be presented thus. Le Guillou therefore asked Aladel for a letter in which he would recount the apparition (anonymously). The letter, drafted on March 17, 1834, was short and to the point: barely a page long and as cautious as one could wish.

> Toward the end of 1830, *someone* told me about a vision which, *so she said,* she had had while at prayer. She had seen, *as if in a picture,* the Blessed Virgin....

Some "acts of cures, conversions, and protection" were cautiously qualified. Le Guillou made it clear that the medical men were still nonplussed. In different ways they were saying, "It's a marvel!" Some of them were ironically pronouncing, "It's magnetism!"[37]

The *Mois de Marie* was published on April 10, 1834, with the personal approval of the Archbishop. It was very quickly (and cautiously) recorded by a young man of 21 named Frédérick Ozanam. Now, anyone who wanted information could be told: "Read Le Guillou, page 317."

This first exposure provoked a desire for a separate pamphlet on the medal. This was what the public wanted.

Aladel made up his mind to write it himself, still anonymously.[38] He expanded a little on the condensed account that he had produced on March 17 and revised his draft twice, not without some corrections–all of which demonstrates his uncertainty. He clarified the visionary's identity a little: it was no longer "someone" but a certain "Sister M..., a novice in Paris in one of the communities devoted to the service of the poor."[39]

In his manuscript, Aladel cautiously wrote that "she believed she saw."[40] In the published version, he brought himself to say, "she saw, while at prayer, *a picture*."[41] But this last word relativized the apparition, and what followed emphasized that "the Blessed Virgin" appeared in it "as we are used to seeing her represented under the title of the Immaculate Conception."[42] These precautions would be a protection in case Rome began to get anxious.

When he received the proofs of the pamphlet in July, Aladel asked Catherine for authorization to divulge (while of course respecting her anonymity) what she had said in the confessional and to acknowledge that permission. He added a note to this effect: "The person to whom this revelation was made has given permission to make it known to pious souls."[b]

On the same occasion, Aladel rectified (by means of another note which was not in the manuscript at all) an omission that Catherine had indicated with considerable passion:

> A little while back, Sister M...told us of something that we had omitted in describing the three visions. It is this: the graces, portrayed by the rays of light, fell upon a certain part of the globe that was at Mary's feet; and this privileged part of the globe was France.[43]

The *Notice* appeared on August 20. The account of the apparition was still brief and reduced to its essentials: neither a description of the apparition, nor colors, nor details. Aladel spoke as if the "three visions" mentioned by him were exactly identical and well separated in time, by intervals which he modified in successive versions. This was followed by a collection of reports of physical and spiritual miracles, including the cure of a dumb woman, that had taken place in Constantinople as early as June 10, 1834.[44] Ten thousand copies of the *Notice* were printed. It was sold out in less than two months[45] and remained out of print for the next two months.

The second edition, which finally appeared on October 20, disappeared even more rapidly: all gone in less than a month, despite a printing of 15,000. The actual print-run for the third edition was 37,664.[46]

Ten million medals

Accounts of the cures reached other parts of the world: the United States (1836), Poland (1837), China and Russia (1838) and Abyssinia (1839). By the latter date, there were already more than ten million medals around the world. Numerous metalsmiths were producing them. Monsignor Vachette was totally overwhelmed and had no time to take action against the many rivals and counterfeiters.

How can one explain this circulation? Was the cholera epidemic responsible for "launching" the medal? The theory seems obvious but does not stand up to scrutiny. The doctors at the Pasteur Institute, noted for its work in the human sciences, have found a clear distinction between large-scale psychosociological reactions in the case of the plague and that of cholera. *Plague* provokes a feeling of divine punishment and stimulates religious sentiments. *Cholera,* with its grotesque attacks of diarrhea, tends rather to provoke derision and anger against civil authorities. The blame is laid at their door, rather than at God's.

Above all, the great increase in the medal's diffusion had not begun when the epidemic ceased in the autumn of 1832.[47] At the beginning of 1834, when cholera had already been forgotten for over a year, scarcely 10,000 medals had been distributed. The 50,000 mark was not reached until the beginning of March,[48] 150,000 during the summer and a half million in the autumn (at the end of November).[49] From that point on, the movement acquired a worldwide dimension, independent of any particular events.

Thanksgiving

Catherine was in a state of thanksgiving, for this lightning-like expansion was accompanied by conversions, cures, and acts of protection, which formed the substance of everyday conversion. Faith, which had seemed impotent, was now curing, converting, protecting. The Good News proclaimed by Isaiah was becoming a fact: "The blind see, the lame walk, the poor have the Good News brought to them."[50] For the people whose religious tradition had not been uprooted by the Revolution, it was a reawakening. The medal was a bible for the poor, an icon, sign of a kindly and powerful presence: that of Mary in the communion of saints,[51] the light of Christ, the shadow of the cross under the sign of the only Love, represented in the form of a heart on the reverse side of the medal. Catherine was happy. What had been asked of her in the night was now bursting into reality.

CATHERINE'S EXPOSURE

But simultaneously the secret was being threatened. Questions were being asked, guesses being made about "which 1830 novice" had

had the vision.[52] And the most perceptive among those trying to guess actually put Catherine in some difficulty.[53]

Alarm of 1835

The year 1835 was when the number of medals already struck exceeded a million.[54] The superiors were astonished by the renewal in religious fervor and vocations, and commissioned the painter Lecerf to produce two pictures commemorating the visions of 1830: the heart of St. Vincent and the Miraculous Medal. It was for the second of these that the greatest trouble was taken to ensure exactitude of detail. Aladel gave his attention to the question of the colors—particularly the silver-blue mantle. The painter reproduced the interior of the chapel at the Rue du Bac with great accuracy as it was before enlargements. His interpretation was not scrupulous—the obverse and reverse of the medal were represented in a single painting. It is not impossible that Aladel had been able to question Catherine briefly on one point or another; and he certainly arranged for her to see the two pictures after they had been hung in the seminary. The visit was discreet and low-key, doubtless on an occasion when Catherine was making a retreat at the motherhouse, but the door was left open, as was usual and proper. While the confessor and his penitent were in silent contemplation, a sister came in and, pointing to Catherine, said naïvely, "It is surely this sister who had the vision!" Fr. Aladel was embarrassed. He turned toward Catherine, who had begun to smile. She replied, "People are good at guessing, aren't they!" At which the sister, who thought she had gotten it right, exclaimed, "Oh well, in that case I don't believe it anymore. If it had been her, you'd never have asked her to tell me!"[55]

Risks

The discreet method of distribution authorized by the Archbishop had now been overtaken by events. The medal was now known all over the world as "miraculous." And everyone knew that it had come from a vision. Legally speaking, the Roman offices had been set up precisely to denounce abuses of this sort. But there was doubtless no harm in waiting since in Rome itself Cardinals Lambruschini and Rivarola had taken up the cudgels on behalf of the medal. In this very year, 1835, they had the medal struck at their own expense and sponsored the Italian edition of Le Guillou's book.[56] But if the Holy Office decided to involve itself under the seal of its formidable secrecy, these influential people would not be enough. Something had to be done.

PROCEEDINGS IN ABSTENIA[57]

Monsignor Quélen accordingly began proceedings with the object of guaranteeing the grace-filled activity at its source. Apparitions, medal, and miracles—all would be scrutinized according to the methods established in the eighteenth century by Pope Benedict XIV.[58]

Refusal

One obstacle was immediately apparent. The essential testimony would be that of the visionary herself—but up to now Catherine had only spoken under the seal of the confessional.[59] Even Etienne himself had no idea of her name.[60]

The Archbishop asked to see her, even if it had to be with her face covered and no attempt to detect her identity. But he met with a refusal and gave in.[61] Canon Quentin, entrusted with the proceedings by the Archbishop, came up against the same obstacle.[62] Near the beginning of his report (1836) he states:

> For the enquiry to proceed in a regular fashion, it is certain that ecclesiastical authority should have received details of the vision from the lips of the sister herself. *She it was who should have given notice to the authority* of all the circumstances surrounding the apparition of the picture. In the end, it was her solemn oath that ensured and guaranteed the fidelity and the truth of her account.[c]

Since he so clearly defines what his duty was, why then did he agree to do without this evidence? The answer is that Catherine's confessor, who had "invited" her "to appear before the ecclesiastical authorities [...] encountered such an aversion to this that he was not able to overcome it."[63] This was in 1835.

Around December of that same year he reiterated his requests, asking her this time "to be kind enough to make her own declaration to the promotor," but she formally refused to do so.[c]

To get himself out of this dilemma, Canon Quentin made a last effort, probably in January 1836, before the initial interrogations took place. However, concerning this final request, Aladel notes: *"An astonishing thing*. Now this sister recalls scarcely any of the circumstances of the vision, and therefore, any attempt to obtain details from her would be completely useless."[c]

This last argument certainly was astonishing, for the strange amnesia[64] was not a sufficient reason for excusing Catherine from appearing at the proceedings. On the contrary, it demanded a close look at the nature and cause of the amnesia. When, how, and why did this "forgetfulness" come about? How long did it last? Was it providential, pathological, or diplomatic? Any argument based on amnesia is even more disconcerting for us today, given that Catherine's memory returned on each occasion when she had to explain herself. Furthermore, she was able to write down detailed accounts of the apparitions a long time afterward: in 1841, 1856, and 1876.[65]

Aladel's motives

We can catch a glimpse of the conversation between the spiritual director, a little stiff-necked, and the peasant girl, anxious to protect her secret.

"But I don't remember anything more!"

Without a doubt there was some truth in those words. The memory of a trance-like state is fragile and fleeting, more so than a dream, for it arises from the grace of a single moment. But we can also surmise that there was also a hefty dose of peasant caution.

"I don't know.... I can't remember...."

This ancient reply, deeply rooted in the subconscious memory from generations back, arose spontaneously within her in difficult situations.

Misermont, vice-postulator of the canonization process, put forward a third theory: that the Blessed Virgin stipulated that Catherine should keep the secret. But neither Aladel, nor Quentin, nor even Catherine ever said that. This was a belated mystical or apologetic inference. If it really was the reason, why did Aladel not say so during the proceedings?

He could have used his authority to summon her, in the public interest—even using the mission she had taken on as a justification. Why did he not do so? Was it from a sense of delicacy regarding the promised secret? Surely it was. The secret had appeared to him as "agreeable to the Virgin herself and protected by her," according to his biographer, Boré.[d]

But it seems likely that Aladel was also influenced by a concern to avoid confrontations regarding a mission that he had interpreted in his own way and with simplifications. The enquiry would produce an awkwardly ill-timed and useless stirring up of differences of details, it would provoke discussions on the production of the medal, and it would create an embarrassment scarcely propitious for a grace-filled religious movement in full flight.

Aladel did not decide to protect the secret from any possessive motive. He had preserved his anonymity and had no ambition to be steward of the movement. In 1835, he even asked to be sent off on the missions,[66] just at the time when the circulation of the medal and his own *Notice* were reaching victorious proportions.[67] Only his promotion to Third Assistant at the August Council meeting put an end to this plan. He could, however, have been apprehensive about the possible confrontation between his outline account and Catherine's more complicated details, not to mention the change in an unobtrusive relationship of conscience existing between confessor and penitent—and all this to satisfy the needs of the enquiry. Secrecy would protect the conduct of a large undertaking. But, even if Aladel could, the historian cannot avoid raising the question of what tensions and differences might have arisen between him and Catherine regarding the apparition itself. There, then, is a riddle that virtuous and apologetic arguments have never managed to conceal.

The Promoter's point of view

If Catherine and Aladel's motives for keeping silence remain rather blurred, they are totally clear when it comes to the Promoter. Well aware of the necessity for evidence from the visionary herself if the enquiry was to come to a normal conclusion, he finally bowed before the secrecy of a conscience and "the king's secret." "God has his own ways in all things," he said formally.[e]

His decision is very understandable, taken in the context of his life. As a young priest of 26 during the 1793 Terror, he found himself under the unqualified and schismatic Bishop of Loir-et-Cher; he therefore went back to living as a layman. He went to Paris and earned a living by going into public administration. His career reached a high level and he used his position to save persecuted priests. At the end of the Revolution, Abbé Desjardins, who had been sending these priests to him, suggested that he should take up his priestly ministry again. The experience acquired by Fr. (once more) Quentin brought him "supervision of the temporal affairs" of the diocese of Paris. In this way he became a Canon, Vicar-General (1833), and finally Promotor responsible for canonical questions. He liked to repeat the words that his Archbishop had used when entrusting him with his juridical functions: "Remember that, in the Church, there is no such thing as a King's Procurator; but, following the example of Jesus Christ, in your tasks be always a man of mercy. Justice of this kind does not lose its way."[68]

His decision, however much law and history may regret it, sprang therefore from a higher priority—that of the Gospel.

What Catherine avoided

Catherine's life and holiness turned it to good account. She thus escaped from a formidable ordeal—formidable both from a psychological and physical point of view. Delivered up to the judges and then to both adversaries and admirers, she would have gotten into inextricable difficulties. No doubt she would have shown evidence of hidden resources that we can know nothing of, but what price would she have paid? In all probablility her life would have been shortened like Bernadette's was.[69] But none of this was her fate, nor her choice. She remained incognito for God alone and for the service of the poor in which she involved herself with all her heart.

So the cause of the Miraculous Medal was for Catherine only "contumacious proceedings" [proceedings *in absentia*] in the sense of "refusal to appear before a tribunal," not in the etymological derivation where *contumacia* means "pride." Quite the opposite. Aladel and Etienne were correct, then, in attesting that "the sister's aversion to appearing is simply the result of her humility."[70]

Here, humility blended with a fair sprinkling of caution and realism. Catherine would have guessed what kind of affronts she might have had to endure after choosing differently, given the condition of women at the time and her own subordination in particular.

Although it is not possible to elucidate further the divergences between Catherine and Aladel around 1835–1836, the facts witness to a basic agreement between them.[71] If she had really felt herself betrayed, she would surely have seized the opportunity to extricate herself from contradictions. We cannot blame her reserve or timidity, for we will later discover how bold she could be when (peacefully) confronting armed and formidable opponents.

Faced with this deadlock, why did Canon Quentin persist with the proceedings right up to the production of a final report in 1836? He hoped to find a way out by another route. The impressive harvest of miracles gave him hope that the medal could be established in good standing. As far as the apparition itself was concerned, he counted on resorting to a juridical process, used in belatedly opened canonization proceedings where eyewitnesses are not available. He would have Aladel and his confidant Etienne recognized as "qualified witnesses," speaking with authority.[72]

Let us not dwell on the proceedings, which terminated abruptly, as they are only indirectly relevant to Catherine's life. However, instead of an appendix on the enquiry, we should at least have a look at a dual portrait of Catherine.

First, Fr. Aladel's description in his deposition of February 16, 1836:

> A country girl [...], she only had a very ordinary and basic education [...]. Nothing out of the ordinary [...]. Piety: [...] simple and straightforward [...]. Her devotion to the Blessed Virgin had never been manifested exteriorly in any noticeable way, but [...] it is known that she has great confidence in the Blessed Virgin [...]. She is very simple [...]. Nothing [...] excitable [...]. On the contrary, she is of very cold and even apathetic appearance.[73]

Fr. Etienne, who was questioned on February 19, confirmed that Fr. Aladel had spoken to him of Catherine in the following terms:

> Very pious girl, very simple in all her ways as in her devotion. Pure life [...] and marked by an especial devotion to the Blessed Virgin [...] very calm imagination [...] and in no way susceptible to excitement.[74]

Vows and Hurt

While all this was going on, Catherine imperturbably continued her ministry to the poor.

The end of an ordeal

In the kitchen, the elderly appreciated this young sister who served them generously when Sr. Vincent Bergerault was not nagging behind her. Catherine hid her impatience at the parsimonious cook, confessed it, but never managed to resign herself to the situation. Sr. Savart took pity on her. After two or three years at Enghien, she summoned

Catherine and said to her with a broad smile: "From now on your work will not be in the kitchen, but in the laundry."

So Catherine took up washing, ironing, and mending. It was something that she could do well, one of the skills of a peasant woman. Linen is the honor of a house. Catherine took special care over the clothes of the poor, making sure they were clean and properly patched.

Catherine and the old men

Soon she was being tried out in the old men's room. These old men were not always easy to deal with, and their language and lustful behavior disturbed the younger sisters. Solid and firm, Catherine soon commanded their respect and this was her work from then on.

Vows (May 3, 1835)[75]

No doubt she was confirmed in this work on the occasion of making her vows, which she did (as the custom was) at the end of five years, on May 3, 1835, Good Shepherd Sunday. In Enghien's modest chapel, after the elevation of the chalice, her voice sounded out in the little community, still only five strong: "I, Catherine Labouré, in the presence of God and all the heavenly court, renew the promises of my Baptism; and to God I make my vows of poverty, chastity, and obedience...."

To the three vows, the Sisters of St. Vincent de Paul add a fourth, dear to Catherine and already deeply rooted in her life: "...and [I vow] to work in the corporal and spiritual service of the sick poor, our true masters, in the Company of the Sisters of Charity. I ask all this through the merits of Jesus Christ crucified and the intercession of the Most Blessed Virgin."

Thus Catherine put the seal on her first five years of sterling service, prepared for by her peasant upbringing.

A replacement

But this beautiful day was not free from shadow. The previous year, on April 26, 1834, Catherine's elder sister Marie-Louise, who had been twelve years ahead of Catherine, had left the Sisters of Charity in accordance with the freedom that St. Vincent had given his daughters: to choose each year whether or not to renew their decision.[76]

It was an incomprehensible shock for Catherine. Boosted in her vocation as a Sister of Charity by Marie-Louise's enthusiasm, she nevertheless did not feel betrayed by her sister's departure. Yet it was all the more disturbing in that her elder sister's vocation had, to begin with, been a success from every point of view. A Sister Servant at 33, Marie-Louise had told Catherine (who was then still searching for her own pathway) of her irreversible happiness. She would never have left her place, she wrote, not even to be queen!

Her letter of August 1831, which arrived about the time Catherine was "making her début" at Reuilly, showed the same enthusiasm. Her only concern was that Catherine should apply herself to all her "duties with simplicity, guilelessness, gaiety, diligence, and openness of heart," and that she should remain at this level.

> A Sister of Charity who has charity [...] gives satisfaction to all who surround her. Seeing her, they say, "There is the image of God! What humility! What compassion! What leniency! What goodness!" Someone who admires a Sister of Charity says to himself, "If God is so good in his feeble creatures, what will it be like when we see his infinite perfection?" How happy are those Sisters of Charity who have some resemblance to God! He could never disown them! [...] My dear Zoe [...], let us admit that we are bad painters, aren't we? We only know how to mess everything up. What are we to do? Not be discouraged! [...]
>
> Your sister who is for life in the love of Jesus and Mary,[77] Marie-Louise.

And yet, at this period Marie-Louise had been smitten by and was under the influence of a calumny so serious that she had been "deposed" in 1829; she was no longer a superior. She was reduced to the ranks of a simple "companion"–first of all for two years in the same house where she had been superior, a traumatic situation in which she remained in contact with her adversaries. Two belated transfers–to the hospital at St. Cloud in 1832, then to the hospital at Tarbes–came too late. Something had been broken.

On April 2, 1834, at the very moment when the first brochure on the medal was due to appear, Marie-Louise was recalled to the motherhouse, where the confrontation was not a happy one. The Labourés had their pride. They had a lively sensitivity and a way of speaking as impetuous as it was laconic when they were in difficulties. Smarting under the injustice, Marie-Louise stiffened up. She had lost that energy which gives meaning to life and makes possible an austere and sometimes heroic everyday existence.

The vows that Catherine pronounced a year later took on the character of a "replacement"...as she awaited her sister's return. Yes, Catherine was praying with obstinate hope. If so many miracles had taken place in the Company over three years, why not this one? She had not been bowled over by the shock. Strong enough for two, in this as in everything else, she waited for the dawn.

Chapter V
Time of Fruition

THE PERIOD FROM CATHERINE'S VOWS and the proceedings in absentia (1836) up to the War and the Commune (1870–1871) has up to now scarcely had any attention from historians. It could just as well have been one long layer of fog. And yet it was a season of fullness in her life: the time of fruition.

"At the hub of medical science"

It would be illusory to think of this period of time as the sort of blandly happy existence of people with nothing of interest in their lives, no history worth knowing about. Catherine gave the appearance of being a solidly built girl in whom everything is well adjusted. This impression is belied by the following extract from a letter, written on June 11, 1841, in which Sr. Cany expressed her sympathy: "You will find yourself at the hub of medical science without being able to obtain any relief from it."[1]

Catherine had been taken to the hospital with "sciatic pains" for which no cure could be found. This was extraordinary. How could this handicap be reconciled with her efficiency in so many different directions? Her niece, Léonie Labouré, who visited her often from 1850 onward, confirmed the existence of this physical handicap and explained how Catherine had resolved the problem beyond the stage of complaining.

"She had pains in her knees: it is a family illness and I suffer from it myself. If we tried to express pity for her, she would reply that it was nothing and that as long as she could carry on working she would be quite happy."[2]

Sr. d'Aragon also noticed it. "Despite her appearance of excellent health, she suffered all the time and no one showed pity for her."[a]

Those who sow in tears will reap in joy (Ps 126). The psalmist's maxim does not exclude the possibility of reaping in pain and putting on a brave face. This is the secret of courage, one of Catherine's secrets. We should not forget it as we admire the vista of useful and fertile years– such a vista as Bernadette must have dreamed of when she was reduced to working as a sick person. In these mature years, Catherine's happiness was realized in the Lord's path: "If anyone wants to come after me, let him renounce himself and take up his cross and follow me" (Mt 16:24).

So let us now visit Catherine's gardens, astonishingly varied as they are, from the most commonplace to the most secret.

THE EARTHLY GARDEN AT REUILLY

A new farm

First of all, there was the garden that Catherine tended between the Rue de Picpus and the Rue de Reuilly. The earth, on the edge of an expanding Paris, was not like the rich soil of Burgundy. But here Catherine rediscovered her demanding and austere peasant habits. Sheepfolds tend to be viewed through rose-tinted spectacles in illuminated manuscripts on the saints, but you need to be queen and have a whole army of servants to turn the countryside into a pastoral paradise. This was not the case with Catherine.

Contrary to town girls, Catherine knew that a henhouse does not make money on its own.... It is not enough just to give out grain, collect eggs, sell or kill livestock at random. Before selling, you have to fatten them up, look out for vitamin deficiency, sickness, incursions by rats and other predators–including humans. And anyone trying to come in scrounging would soon find out who was boss in this garden....[3] Little by little, Catherine transformed the garden into a kind of little farm where animals could prosper. It was probably she who introduced pigeon-keeping, little known in the area.[4]

Cows and accounts

Catherine had established the cowshed, where there were always at least two cows and sometimes three. She bought the first on March 19, 1846, for 480 francs,[5] but she had to have it treated when it fell ill. She got it back on April 18, and sold it for 260 francs, a loss of 220 francs. All this was recorded and lessons learned, but she was not discouraged. On May 10, she bought a second cow for 310 francs and sold it in October, this time with 10 francs' profit. In the meantime this second cow had produced 1,272 pints of milk. This was encouraging. But problems started again with the third cow. Catherine bought it for 400 francs the same day and had to sell it the following October for 240 francs: nearly 50 percent less, a loss compensated for by a milk yield of 2,436 pints. In this way she lost on average a good hundred francs on each of her cows.

The fourteenth cow rectified the situation. Catherine bought it for 420 francs on August 19, 1851, and sold it at a 30-franc profit (450 francs) six years later on March 31, 1857. From 1852 to 1861 the profits and losses more or less cancelled each other out. When Catherine sold at a loss, the deficit was minimal—and there were the exceptional cases of the eighteenth cow, sold at a 40-franc profit on June 1, 1855, and the twenty-fourth cow, sold at the buying price. But after that the disappointments came on apace. Prices rose from 300 francs to 400, then to 500 and even 600 francs—and gold francs at that. The twenty-seventh cow, bought at 500 francs on January 21, 1860, was sold for less than half that price on November 26 of the same year: "Because of sickness." The thirtieth and last cow, for which 580 francs was paid on November 1, was sold at a loss of 120 francs on October 13, 1862.

The new superior at that time, Sr. Dufès, had arrived on October 18, 1860. She was worried. The operations with the cows were hampering a rather tight budget. There was no room for pastoral paradises with the Sisters of Charity! Sr. Dufès was unhappy and asked to see the accounts. Catherine totaled up her figures: they were in perfect order, but the totals showed the size of the deficit: in seventeen years, Catherine had lost 3,655 gold francs in buying and selling cattle. She may have been a good farm woman, but she was not a good livestock dealer. At Fain, this had been her father's private province and he had never initiated her into it. Catherine was too straight to play this game—thus she sold for less than she paid. If there was an exception for the eighteenth cow, this was due to an accident. Catherine was so proud of it that she had been unable to hide the fact in her accounts book. Indeed, she ended the *curriculum vitae* of this worthy animal on an unusually lyrical note: "This cow produced 16,302 pints of milk in five years and eight months."

She was so loath to part with the animal, which was starting to go downhill, that she gave the other cattle dealer the impression that the cow was a real treasure. In this way she managed for once to sell above her buying price, and this with a cow at the end of its useful life.

Number thirty-one

Catherine did not resign when Sr. Dufès asked her for accumulated accounts (1862). Still one step ahead of what she was doing, she had already written in her book "Thirty-first cow, bought on...." Those words were destined to remain suspended on the whiteness of the page. Sr. Dufès was immovable and Catherine obeyed. She was sorry that there would be no more fresh milk, so much appreciated by the elderly and not accounted for in the books.[6]

Rabbits and pigs

All the same, Catherine was by no means unemployed. Pigs[7] and rabbits[8] now appeared in her accounts book up until 1875.

"Bibi"

From 1861, we also find entries for one horse, then for several. We know that the name of one of them was "Bibi" and that he was fairly temperamental. Sr. Levacher tells us:

> One day, we had to go in the cart to the motherhouse at the Rue du Bac. Sr. Vincent wanted to go via the main roads because it was easier for the horse, who was, moreover, well known for not being exactly docile. Sr. Catherine, however, would have preferred to go another way. For what reason? I really can't say. All I remember is that she had a teasing dig at Sr. Vincent and said, "Get on with you! You want to show off your horse, your Bibi! What's more, he's handsome, your Bibi!"[b]

Poultry

Poultry was the consistent basis of Catherine's work. As at Moutiers, she sold chickens in order to buy other things for the farm.[9] Most of the eggs, it seems, went straight into the house and were eaten there. But it was a significant amount. In 1861, the thirty-nine hens laid 2,626 eggs.[10]

The dovecote was better stocked. In 1864 alone, Catherine sold 313 pigeons. Sales dropped to 194 in 1867 and 1868, but rose again to 257 in 1870.[11]

Final reckoning

Did Catherine earn the community's livelihood with her farm? Overall, the answer is yes. If she lost out in selling cows, those same cows produced 97,258 pints of milk at 50 centimeters a time: 48,629 francs, which exceeds the total losses (purchases of foodstuffs for the cattle came to 33,859 francs).

The pigeon breeding was equally on the plus side for the fourteen years (1861–1874) during which records were kept: 3,656.85 francs spent on maize grains; 4,852.70 francs realized through sales; a profit, therefore, of 1,195.85 francs.

In the same way, the poultry accounts for the four years recorded (1861–1864) seem positive. Feeding and upkeep accounted for an expenditure of 900 francs. The value of eggs sold came to 775 francs, let alone sales of chickens which amounted to 203.50 francs—not counting the ones that were eaten in the house.

These columns of figures sum up in a page or two a whole year of activity—farm woman, hen-breeder, pigeon-breeder—and Sr. Dufès found them amusing. But Catherine had learned her figures very late in life and she felt accountable for the well-being of the poor. She knew that, according to St. Vincent, a Sister of Charity "should be able to give a good account of herself."

The principal expenditure was on horses (30,627.05 francs, just for feeding them during the fifteen years from 1861–1875). But this was expenditure on "energy," which today would be spent on cars, pure spendthrifts without alimentary value for capital or for revenue. A means of transport was necessary for the community—people and goods.[12] And then again, the horse turned the pump that brought up water for the tank in the attic of the house.[c]

This farming work was more important for Catherine than it might seem, from the point of view of her human as well as her spiritual roots. Catherine had reared thousands of chickens, had hand-milked more than 100,000 liters, and so on. The job of providing nourishment was no one else's task; it was her own. She liked to be able to get enough for everybody—fruit and vegetables, eggs and fresh milk, all welcomed in the daily fare.

A reminiscence supplied by Sr. Olalde gives a taste of what this brought into everyday life.

> One evening, the sister cook had forgotten to make any soup. When the time came for the meal, this sister exclaimed: "Oh, good Lord, I haven't made any soup!"

Sr. Catherine, without scolding her, said calmly, "Don't upset yourself, sister. I have just milked the cows. Everyone will be happy to have fresh milk this evening!"

The sister in question was indeed Sr. Vincent, the parsimonious cook—the one who was making her suffer.

SERVICE OF ALL KINDS[13]

The elderly

As well as "yielding fruit" in a peasant-woman fashion, Catherine worked in all other areas, too. She had of course started off in the kitchen and then moved to the laundry (where she still kept an eye on things). She helped out with the really big jobs and always had some smaller task at hand during recreation time. But her main function was looking after the elderly.

Catherine was firm, impartial, and ruled with an orderliness that always caused things to run smoothly. She was able to forestall any kind of disorder by putting everyone on the right course in time. Above all, she loved the elderly and was loved by them in return. Her work was generally considered to be difficult; one had to be able to hold one's own with old gamekeepers, manservants, butlers, gatekeepers, and so on—all of them preoccupied with the good old days, their splendid liveries, etc. If Catherine had a "fault," it was that she did not scold very often or for very long, according to Sr. Dufès.[d] On the occasions when she did, it was all over quickly and she immediately went back to her normal state of silence and kindness. Often she would put off giving a correction. On one occasion, she put an incorrigible drunkard to bed (he had come home quite incoherent), but waited for the next day to have it out with him. And when he begged her pardon, she told him, "It's not me you should be asking for pardon, it's the good Lord."

Catherine was good even with the most disagreeable, just as if the "wicked ones" (as people used to call them) had the right to special attention and indeed even slight preferential treatment. She saw them as they were: wounded creatures crying for help and knocking themselves against walls and against people—like children who need courage and self-esteem restored to them.[e]

However, she did not let herself be taken for a ride—far from it. She had a sense of justice and reacted quickly if anyone overstepped the mark.[f]

Her best weapon was her fairness and consistency—and of course her goodness itself, which disarmed any bitterness or hostility on the part of these old servants who were marked for life by the elevated ranks they had once held. She helped some of them to discover prayer and the Mass, like a light at the end of a previously blocked tunnel. For the hospice was indeed the end of the road for them—a waiting room for death—and the architect had even provided a mortuary, on the right of the entrance to the chapel.

Catherine served the elderly generously and never tired of asking them, "Do you have enough?"

How soothing for these older folk, haunted by a fear of "missing out." Was Catherine a psychologist? At any rate, she was certainly good for them and acted instinctively rather than in a calculating way. When someone did not like one kind of food or another, she made sure the person got something else instead.[g]

Looking after the elderly also entailed organizing the "reception area," which Catherine did. This task was known as "being at the door," and it had to be manned continuously from 7:00 in the morning to 7:00 at night. Catherine filled in whenever she had a free moment, or at times when it was otherwise difficult to ensure continuity. She kept the place clean and quiet, with no bits and pieces left lying around—almost like a monastic cell.[h] She would take some small piece of needlework with her and would greet visitors pleasantly, whoever they might be (benefactors or poor people), listen politely, and, without superfluous chatter, take them wherever they needed to go.

The poor

According to her companions, Catherine loved "the poor especially"; for her, they were the suffering members of Jesus Christ.[i]

As with the elderly, Catherine's attitude to the poor was instinctively shot through with St. Vincent's recommendation:

> Truly, it was never God's intention in setting up this Company that you should be looking after bodily welfare *only...,* rather, our Lord's intention is that you should help the souls of the sick poor.[j]

Almsgiving was a joy for Catherine, Sr. Maurel tells us,[k] but no less so was the giving of God's consolation—the wellspring, the best she could give, into which she plunged so deeply.

"Disappointed" at not being able to do more on the material side of things, Catherine did not confine herself to comforting words while washing her hands like Pontius Pilate. No, she would keep on looking for some way of remedying the impossible: rent payments to avoid eviction, medicine, finding a tool so that a workman could earn his daily bread....

"No one ever complained about the welcome they got from her."[l] "I never heard tell that she had dissatisfied anyone."[m]

The Blot

"Always pleasant," "even tempered,"[n] "straightforward and very kind," Catherine did not like wasting time and put a sober and rapid stamp on this "reception" service of whose roster she was in charge. But there was a blot on the landscape here—and it was her fault!

One day, around 1860, a tearful woman rang the bell. She must have been about the fiftieth caller that day. "Blaisine!" exclaimed Catherine, embracing her. It was an old seminary companion: Sr. Lafosse. Her mysticism had fueled belief in her vocation, but she soon showed herself irretrievably hampered by a disastrous psychological state. Her bursts of goodwill always seemed to run off into forgetfulness, tactlessness, blunderings, and hurtful words, which Catherine herself did not escape. Moreover, she alternated between states of excitement and depression, between gross overeating and exaggerated fasting. During the time when Catherine was settling into a stable life at Enghien, Blaisine had "gone through" fourteen houses in twenty-five years—a record. Twice she had left the Sisters of Charity, only to return in a calamitous state. The third time she left, on April 14, 1855, it was with no hope of returning. Now she was well on the way to becoming a tramp.

Catherine did not beat about the bush. She managed to persuade the superior and took the woman in—not that anyone thanked her for it: she got nothing but complaints. "That girl has lost her head," or "Her brain is addled," the sisters would say when Blaisine produced one of her outbursts. Catherine was under no illusions. She absorbed the recriminations and kept Blaisine at arm's length. Only she had any influence over "the Blot," as Blaisine was known, and this was only through Catherine's temper and the fruits of her work. Only Catherine could persuade her to eat when she was in the midst of one of her depressive phases and refusing all food—and this was because Blaisine knew that it was Catherine who had had the vision of the medal. What is more, she said so (in confidence!) when Catherine's back was turned, and this did not make it any easier for Catherine to preserve her anonymity.[15]

THE FAMILY GARDEN

Catherine had not lost contact with her own people. The family was large and there were both great joys and great anxieties, all of which she shared in effectively.

Jacques goes to Paris

Her brother Jacques, the third child, got married on July 18, 1835, and went to Paris. Henceforward he would be visiting Catherine two or three times a year.[16] He brought along the babies—first Louise, then Léonie (born in 1842). Much later on Léonie would be a witness in the canonization process.[17]

Tonine's marriage

On September 11, 1838, it was the turn of Tonine—Catherine's sterling companion at Fain—to get married: rather late in life, as she was almost 30. Looking after their father had kept her on the farm in a village where people only rarely left to go elsewhere. She had also inherited the job of caring for Auguste, the baby of the family, now aged 29 and still crippled and rather odd. Tonine finally married Claude Meugniot, a timber merchant at Viserny. Catherine was pleased for her sister, but sad for her father and "little" brother. She helped to fix Auguste up with their brother Antoine, who was buying the family house and took him on as he was.[18] Nine months later, on June 14, 1839, Catherine received the news of the birth of Marie-Antoinette, Tonine's eldest daughter, with whom she would soon have a special relationship.[19]

Father's death

Pierre Labouré did not live more than six years after Tonine's departure. He died on March 19, 1844, in a house that had become sad and deserted. Another Parisian brother, Joseph, was notified by Antoine and wrote to Catherine three days later.

> He had been very ill [...]. He was buried yesterday, Thursday the 21st instead. As we were not able to be present for his last hours, we want to organize a Mass and family reunion. I will let you know the date....[20]

Catherine had not realized how much her father had been deserted—and now that he had died of loneliness, her heart felt bruised because of it. Everything rushed to the surface on September 15 of the same year, 1844, when her elder sister, Marie-Louise (the one who had left the Sisters of Charity), proposed to go back to Fain "to look after Auguste." Go back to Fain now that Papa was dead? No, no! Catherine's heatedness shows how deeply she had been wounded:

> Going to look after a brother is a very good thing, which everyone will approve of. But they would also have approved of it if, ten years ago when you left the community, you had *gone to render the final services that one does for old people, for a father as afflicted as ours was in his old age [...], dying in estrangement, even though within his family; deserted even within his family.* Everyone would have commended it had you gone to render him those last services that a child renders to his [or her] parents at the time of death [...]; especially when one is free to do so, as you were.[21]

It was the only time in her life that Catherine, who had felt sick at heart when she left her father's service, now regretted not having this "freedom." "Don't be surprised, then," she finishes up, "if you aren't viewed in a very good light in the family, and don't expect to be well received."[22]

Here Catherine was combining her dual suffering—the abandonment of her father and the broken vocation of her elder sister—two tragedies that could never hope to be absorbed into a single grief.

Would Marie-Louise come back?

The upshot of the letter was strained, as Marie-Louise told Catherine that she wanted to come and see her at Enghien. This, however, would cut across the rules of the community concerning those who had "left." What could Catherine do? Having dissuaded Marie-Louise from going back to Fain, she was now dissuading her from coming to the hospice at Enghien.

> My dear friend, as for your proposal about coming to see me, it would be most inconvenient because you are known to most of the sisters in the House. I do not advise you to come. You tell me that it will be a sacrifice to leave me. I thought your sacrifice had been made ten years ago and I thought you had made it cheerfully. I did not think that it was still to be made. I have made my own sacrifice, *which has cost me so dearly, and the good Lord knows the suffering I have had.* Yes, only God and Mary, our kind Mother, know it! And once again this suffering is recurring!

Here, Catherine is still talking while under the influence of personal injury: indeed, it's the same wound. The death *of* her father, far away and cut off, awoke in her the memory of that death *to* her father through which she had had to reach her vocation. And the same memory drew up from the depths of her soul that sense of the duration of time, which is at the root of all philosophical peasants: "Up until now, I have had the feeling that you would go back into a community. But *I see the time passing and it has already gone*. Yes, time flows on every day...."

Catherine had watched ten years go by since her sister had left in 1834. Catherine did not go into the question of how her sister had been wounded by the calumnies, or the fact that she had been able to find a new, respectable, and useful life as a teacher in Paris. Catherine could not resign herself to the present.

> The past is no longer in our power; the present is in our power, but the future is not. Let us take the opportunity of giving ourselves utterly and completely to God, holding nothing back. Think of the letter I wrote to you six years ago [this letter is not extant]: I made you the most beautiful proposals and you refused them all. Now I am placing everything in the hands of the good Lord and the Blessed Virgin—your patron saint. I commend you to the Blessed Virgin as to a tender Mother [...]. May she take you under her protection! I beg you to pray for me. Farewell for the time being and perhaps forever.

Was this a parting of ways? What was Catherine driving at? She did not know. She had been led to this point rather than coming to it herself, torn between persistent setbacks and the ineradicable, between the rules of the community and her hope. No! She would not submit to a breakup. Suddenly she bounced back: "It is TO BE HOPED that we will see each other again, but when?" The problem was a disciplinary one and Catherine came back to it:

> You know that when people have left our community we may have no further communication with those who have left. You know our holy Rules. And, more than ever, at the moment fervor is being renewed in the community as if it were the period of St. Vincent himself....

Without exerting any pressure, Catherine set forth the solution that she had finally (and painfully) come up with:

> Our good Mother is entrusting me with the task of telling you a thousand and one things on her behalf. She is always ready to render you every possible good service and you can count on her goodness on

every occasion. She still loves you and would be pleased to render you service. If, however, you have something to communicate to us, you can come on any day of the week except next Thursday. You know at what times we are free. Write to let us know the day and the time that you can come to the *Dames blanches* community on our street [Rue de Picpus], number 15 [...]. There is a chapel at the far end of the courtyard where you can wait for me. Kindly *say to the Brother that you are waiting for my superior and me.*

Farewell, my good sister. I embrace you with all my heart and am, for life, your most devoted sister.

Marie-Louise's pride reacted badly to this letter. The negative side of it hardened her severity; yes, indeed! She went back to Fain to take care of her brother. It was there that God and charity would best be served!

How could Catherine be so sure of her sister's vocation? She persisted, writing again on September 29.[23] She had just reread the letter that Marie-Louise, ablaze with passion, had sent her at the dawning of her own vocation in 1829: an enthusiastic hymn to the life of the Sisters of Charity.°

Catherine copied out the letter and sent the original back to Marie-Louise in order to confront her with herself at the time when God was speaking to her in this way. The emotional tension was so high that Catherine alternated between the second person singular *(tu)* and the second person plural *(vous)* in addressing her sister—doubly a sister, in fact, since she was not only Pierre Labouré's daughter, but also St. Vincent's; and this was indeed only a month after the election of Fr. Etienne, which rekindled such a flame in the two spiritual families.

> I am sending you [sing.] back a letter which will doubtless give you [pl.] pleasure. You [pl.] written [*sic*] [it to] me at the time when I wanted to enter our community [...].
>
> You [pl.] should now apply to yourself [pl.] the good advice you [pl.] gave me and ponder well on these words [...]:
>
> *If at this moment there were someone powerful enough to offer me not just a kingdom but the whole universe as my possession, I would consider it as no more than the dust on my shoes; as I am quite convinced that in possessing the universe I would not find the happiness and contentment that I experience in my beloved vocation.*

Caught up in the ardor of her plea, Catherine added the penultimate word *beloved*, which was not in the original. She continued, on the second page: "You [pl.] preferred this happiness—to what? I hardly say it!—to a temptation."

Catherine made herself seem stubborn and severe because it seemed so clear to her that God's light and the future were there, beyond all Marie-Louise's unyielding. Did she think she was God to preach like this? No, she was preaching to herself, too; after *tu* and *vous*, she begins to use "us" *(nous)* and to speak with humility.

> It must be admitted that we are weak when *we* do not put all our trust in God, who knows the very depths of our hearts....

Next, Catherine attacked Marie-Louise's final stand, the last defense that her head erected in contradiction of her heart: making God into the backer for her runaway projects.

> In nearly all your [pl.] letters you [pl.] talk to me about a *miracle,* as if the good Lord produced them without rhyme or reason. We must really be poor creatures if we think that the good Lord will work any miracles for us!

Catherine, who knew what she was talking about, did not believe in random miracles regulated by personal whims. She went on:

> [It was certainly a miracle] when you [pl.] left the community! Alas! God knows if it was one! Did our Lord and the Blessed Virgin preach about their miracles? Where is our humility? It's a long way from theirs! To be more accurate, we have no humility at all.

Catherine's conclusion was an ironic urging for her to run away.

> Farewell. I advise you [sing.] to go to the family home. You [pl.] will find solitude, and there the good Lord will speak to your [pl.] heart.

What emerges here from this Jacob-like struggle is that it is this double death that marked Catherine's heart and sent her flying back on a sort of rebound toward our Lord and our Lady. It also extended the letter that, having reached its limit at the foot of the second page, now continued sideways up the edge of the first page:

> Ponder well on the death of our mother—which you witnessed—and that of our father, which is still very recent [...]. This is the best way to find grace before God.[p]

And this is just what happened.

Marie-Louise soon hastened to a meeting in the Rue de Picpus. Doubtless everything was sorted out gently with Sr. Montcellet, the efficient superior who was the first to give full scope to this house in the slum quarters of the suburb.

On June 25, 1845, the Council agreed to reinstate Marie-Louise in the Sisters of Charity, "in view of the circumstances obtaining at the time of her leaving and her edifying conduct since then." She was to receive the habit again at Enghien, at the age of 50. Thus it was in Catherine's community that Marie-Louise cast off her lay clothes to put on once again the winged coif, probably on July 2, the feast of the Visitation. How Catherine had prayed for this! There could be no greater joy than this "visitation" for the two sisters, reunited in the wake of our Lady and St. Vincent! This was a joy hidden in the depths of the heart, for which no words could ever be found.[24]

However, it was but the doorway to a fresh separation, for on July 2 itself, Marie-Louise received her posting to Turin with three other sisters, resulting from a decision of Fr. Etienne. She arrived there on July 19, in the community of San Salvator. She served as a stretcher bearer in the Italian war and did not see Catherine again until 1858, when she was recalled to the motherhouse in the Rue du Bac.

Jacques' death

In 1855, Jacques fell ill. Catherine visited him at 18 Rue des Postes (now Rue Lhomond). He himself asked for the last rites. She gave him the Miraculous Medal, putting it around his neck.[25] After his death on April 17, Catherine's contact with the family became more regular. She became a pillar of strength for Adélaïde, the widow, and their daughter Léonie, aged 13.

Problems with an artist

Around 1855 there was a new arrival in Paris—Antoine-Ernest, the son of her brother Charles, the wine merchant-cum-restaurateur whose establishment had been the scene of the testing of Catherine's vocation. Antoine-Ernest had come from Semur-en-Auxois to continue his studies. Catherine looked at this unsettled young man, aged about 20, with the "air of an artist" about him. He was a violinist in his spare time, but a very talented one. Lo and behold, he managed to get into the orchestra at the Opéra! Paris was a dangerous capital city for someone of his sort! This time, Catherine panicked. By sending her his only son, wasn't her brother entrusting her with responsibility for him? The scruples cultivated by the Church at that period suddenly swept over her. Her nephew had lodgings nearby—lodgings found thanks to her, no doubt. She would go and see him, like a mother hen....

Antoine-Ernest did not much like being inspected by a *cornette!* One morning—late for Catherine, who got up at 4:00, but early for him, a real nightowl—she found him *still* in bed, the table piled high with empty bottles and dirty glasses. She could not control her anxiety: "So, you live it up here! You bring women in here!"

"No, just friends!" And he added coldly, "This is my place here. Don't come back again."

Born in 1834, Antoine-Ernest had now reached the age of maturity and Catherine knew what that meant. She realized her mistake and never set foot inside the place again.[26]

He came to Enghien at the beginning of 1861 to introduce his wife, Claire Letort, to Catherine. The marriage had been celebrated at Puligny in Burgundy on January 14, 1861. On the pretext of a honeymoon journey, he went to Paris and took up his work again at the Opéra so that he could offer his spouse a pleasant winter—a guileless stratagem. He went back again in succeeding years, but he never saw his aunt again. He even forgot to bring along his first child to show her (Charles-Antoine, born June 8, 1863). Catherine was now monopolized by Tonine and her children. Antoine-Ernest and Claire took umbrage and preferred the company of Marie-Louise, now back at the Rue du Bac.

Tonine in Paris

Catherine's concern for Tonine's family is a story in itself. It could well have been a fourth-rate novel, so improbable did it seem. Tonine arrived in Paris[27] in 1857, two or three years after Catherine's violinist nephew. The capital had always attracted the Labourés. Her husband was a capable and generous man who had sold his business in timber and high-class vineyards. His weakness was that he could not take the smallest amount of alcohol—rather a handicap in his profession. The slightest slip in this respect turned him into a madman—and Tonine suffered because of it. To get himself out of this vicious circle, he had wound up his business affairs and found a post on the railways.

Catherine was full of joy at being once again with her childhood intimate friend and at meeting the latter's three children: Marie-Antoinette (18), Charles-Albert (17), and Philippe (13). In 1858, she had the eldest child received into the Children of Mary at Reuilly by Fr. Aladel himself. She was there, tears in her eyes.[28]

Philippe's vocation

In March 1858, at the time of the Lourdes apparitions, Catherine learned through Tonine and Marie-Antoinette that Philippe had stayed with the priest of his village.

"Do you want to be a priest?" she asked him when she saw him again.

"I think this is the path for me," replied Philippe, who was nearly 14, "but I can't promise anything."

Something was drawing him to the priesthood. But he grumbled about the Latin that the "good Father" of the village wanted to teach him. This unpleasant imposition made him doubt his vocation. Be a priest? Yes! Be initiated into these mysteries? Certainly not! However, he would get around this obstacle.

Catherine got the Vincentians to take him on as a student at the college at Montdidier (Somme), thanks to some financial help from one of her companions. She felt very accountable for this and so one day said to Philippe, "If you don't wish to become a clergyman, you must tell me."[29]

At 17, he would not forget the unusual provocation that she cast at him toward the end of his studies: "If you want to join these men, you will be accepted. It's possible to become a superior quite soon, then go to China, like Fr. Perboyre. You can travel and see sights and also come back again."

> She said this with a cunning expression, as if she had read it in the future. I took it as a joke, but everything took place to the letter and in the very order she had stated. While she was talking to me, she held in her hand a little wooden reliquary containing a small piece of fabric used by the future Blessed Perboyre.[30]
>
> On August 9, 1863, she accompanied me when I entered St. Lazare. And in the meantime she had taken me to visit Fr. Etienne, the Superior General. In all this, she acted with the most delicate charity and with the consent of her superiors [...] but *never exerting the slightest pressure on me*.[31]

She had understood. A person's freedom must be respected, even if that entailed moderating her own zeal.

Claude and conversion

Meanwhile Philippe's father, Claude Meugniot, had been struck by a locomotive in January 1861. Thirty-three months of tribulation began. Like many middle-class people of the time, Claude was something of an unbeliever. Religion was a woman's affair. Catherine was concerned. She visited her brother-in-law, but his ideas were simple and well-defined: "It's not worth it! We've got one saint in the family already. We won't be damned."

Nevertheless, Catherine (the saint...) urged him: "I'm praying for you, but you must pray too!"

Claude was still skeptical: "She [Tonine] wants to convert me, Zoe, but she won't manage it!" Without acrimony, he added: "All the same, she's a good girl."

In his letters, Philippe kept harking back to his father's state of health. He wanted news, but his family made a point of concealing the news from him for it was not good. By the autumn of 1862, the doctor saw no further cause for hope. However, to their astonishment, Claude's health improved slightly. Marie-Antoinette went to tell Catherine. "You see," she replied, "you must never give up hope!"

It was at this time that Claude became a convert, affected by this medical remission. From that time on he became a "model of patience," according to his daughter, Marie-Antoinette. He lived for another year, often able to stand up. It was the last respite, for he died on October 26 in the Rue de Châlon.

"We always thought among the family that his conversion had been due to the prayers of my aunt," Marie-Antoinette later said.[32]

Deaths

The same time of trial occurred the following year. Antoine Labouré, the fourth child, came to Paris for an operation. He went to see the Meugniots,[33] whose resources were running low. Catherine visited him. The operation was not a success and he died at Fain on August 26, 1864.

Hubert, the eldest, died at Nuits-St. Georges the following year, July 17, 1865; he had been owner of a fine vineyard enterprise that continued after his death.[34]

Catherine also prayed for her brother Pierre-Charles, who no longer practiced his religion. He would die a long time after her at age 84, on January 1, 1889.[35]

America and widowhood

Marie-Antoinette Meugnoit got married on October 15, 1864.[36] She was 25. Her husband was the brilliant Eugène Duhamel, aged 32, with all the charm of an adventurer. Like his late father-in-law, he was making his career on the railways where he had a good position.

A year later Marthe was born, on August 4, 1865,[37] the first child of the new family. Catherine did not delay in going to see her, for the Duhamels also lived in the twelvth *arrondissement* (the Empire had incorporated the former village of Reuilly into it).

In December 1866, Marie-Antoinette was on the point of giving birth to a second child when Eugène suddenly disappeared.[38] Had he been killed? The police investigated the matter, but did not succeed in finding a body. Marie-Antoinette went into mourning.

On January 22, 1867, Jeanne-Caroline was born. The baby's crying replaced the mother's—and she bravely took her new charge into hand.[39]

The two surrogate mothers of Fain, Tonine and Catherine, were there to help: resolute Catherine, with her undaunted faith in God who would look after everything, even the impossible; and Tonine, with her good sense and her portmanteau of bitter experiences. One day she said to Catherine, "If I had known what would happen to me, I would have become a nun like you."

Catherine replied, "Each to his or her own vocation! You would not have the consolation of having given a son to God."[40]

Catherine did not content herself with merely giving spiritual advice. She looked after her little nieces, whose upbringing without a father posed so many problems, not least of which were financial. No help was forthcoming from the Meugniot side of the family. Catherine brought them some sustained assistance[41] and was able to interest her superior in this dramatic situation.[q]

Two years after Eugène's disappearance, Marie-Antoinette was summoned to the Ministry of Foreign Affairs.

"Madame, it's about your husband."

"Yes, sir, he's dead...."

"No, Madame, he is alive!"

Marie-Antoinette fell down in a faint. She learned the rest of the story when they got her back home. While in America a friend had been surprised to meet Eugène, whom he thought had been murdered. Eugène had opened up a successful laundromat. The friend had not dared to mention it to the family, but had informed the Foreign Ministry.

How had Eugène ended up in America? One fine day, it seems he had taken a train to Le Havre, where he had been tempted with the offer of a good job in America. A ship was just leaving. Idiotically, he embarked on it. It was only as the European coast disappeared over the horizon that he realized his stupidity. Once he had arrived, a month later, he could see no other way out than to build a new life on the new continent in the hope of returning one day to his loved ones, bringing with him success and financial fortune. He found an America in a state of reconstruction after the Civil War, Lincoln's assassination, and the abolition of slavery (1869). The North was at that time attracting immigrants to help it to establish its dominance and exploit its victory.

But why had Eugène gone? Was it due to some misunderstanding? Not at all. He was a sensitive and attentive husband. Was there perhaps another woman? No! It had to do with his mother, who was very possessive. He was the youngest in his family; she was a widow who had fastened on him as her last bastion against solitude–someone to keep her company in her declining years. To keep a better hold on him, she had gotten him to take over all her financial affairs (as her husband had done), complete with "her taste for spending money without proper regard for the actual situation." Despite his excellent job, Eugène was hard put to provide for the needs of *two* households, especially his mother's extravagant one. Marie-Antoinette loved her husband. Naïvely, she had thought that she would win her mother-in-law over by kindness. Each month (without even telling her own mother, Tonine) she handed over "an envelope containing a portion of her housekeeping allowance." But that was not the problem. The mother-in-law harassed her son, trying to lure him with the wonders of America and the prodigious possibilities there. Oddly, she would prefer to lose this son than share him with her daughter-in-law.

Eugène tried to keep everyone happy. He could emigrate there *with* Marie-Antoinette. The young wife did not know where the pressures were coming from and tried to reason with her husband: "Take the boat with me pregnant and little Marthe only 17 months old? It would be sheer madness!"

Weak and torn between two women–his mother and his wife– Eugène had left in order to escape from the intensity of this tearing apart; he had also been intoxicated with the thought of the journey. Remorse and shame gnawed at him. He tried to ignore these by throwing himself into his work. He cherished the idea of coming back home having made his fortune–this would bring his family happiness.[42]

Let us now jump to the final episode, which takes us beyond Catherine's death. Eleven years after his departure, Eugène came back for the 1878 Exhibition. He had a stand which "attracted considerable business through two Negresses." He had made his fortune. He joined up again with his friends, but did not dare to go and see his wife. This was understandable. But he had a burning desire to see his children again. The school was warned and held him at bay. He kept watch at the exit and first went up to his younger daughter, Jeanne.

"It's Adrienne, isn't it?"

He had decided on this name with his wife before the birth, but things had turned out differently.

"No! It's Jeanne!"

"My child, would you please permit me to kiss you?"

A whole other world assailed and agitated him. He was seized by an immense desire to do something for his wife, who had lost all confidence in him, and for his children whom he had abandoned with insufficient financial resources. He left for New York, full of schemes for transferring money and so on.

But fortunes come and go overnight on the other side of the Atlantic. A fire ravaged the entire area where he had put up wooden houses. He was not insured and his health could not stand the shock. He came back to France, ill and looking like an 80-year-old though he was only 57. Marie-Antoinette had refused either money or to take up life with him again after what seemed to her an inexplicable desertion. She felt strong. By this time, Catherine was no longer there; she had gone from henhouse to heaven. Marie-Antoinette refused to see her contrite husband. It was her two daughters who dragged her into the bedroom at the clinic where he lay ill. Ruined, Eugène fell out of his bed and threw himself on his knees, sobbing at the feet of his wife. He died shortly afterward on September 14, 1889.[43]

Now let us go back again to Catherine's lifetime.

Philippe's ordination

Philippe Meugniot was ordained a priest on May 22, 1869, at St. Lazare. This was a great joy for Catherine.

An abundance of fruit

The family gardens bore much fruit. There was material aid for Marie-Antoinette. Catherine had saved her from misery and despair.

She helped her to become a staunch woman, at once mother and father of her two fatherless children and she later became a pleasant and matriarchal grandmother for the third generation.

Two vocations came about through Catherine: Marie-Louise's, rebuilt; Philippe's, awoken and sustained right to the end.

There were reconciliations with God for her brothers and her brother-in-law, unbelievers or half-believers, convinced as they were that "one saint in the family" was quite enough.

There were so many small things—mostly long forgotten—that it is amazing that Catherine did so much for her family. And yet none of it detracted from her normal duties.

One time when Marie-Antoinette Duhamel went to see her, Catherine was in the middle of milking the cows. She carried on squirting the warm milk into a foaming bucket and gave her niece a beseeching look from underneath the cow, saying, "Give me a chance: I'll be as quick as I can." But once the milking was over, she gave her her full attention.

Catherine's devotion to her duties sometimes irritated her relatives. For her, duty was everything. Léonie Labouré was familiar with this aspect of Catherine and so she would arrange to come "at recreation time." Yet she would still sometimes have to go and look for Catherine.

"I'm almost sure she's in the chapel," Léonie would say. "I'll go and see." And sure enough, she nearly always found her there.[r] She would move about to attract attention, but in vain. Catherine's eyes would be fixed on the tabernacle and she would seem to have turned into a statue. She was completely with God. On one occasion when she had finished, Léonie made a face and said, "I've been waiting for you for ages."

Catherine replied, "You were not in the street, you were close to the good Lord. You can never have too much of that."[44]

Léonie also tells us that Catherine was extremely punctual and used to send them off as soon as the bell rang.[s]

St. Vincent's Gardens

To Catherine's joy, the "gardens" which flourished the best during this period were St. Vincent's: his two "families," the Vincentians and the Sisters of Charity.

Catherine's vocation had been awoken in her by a wonderful dream and she had been aware of the decadent practices following the

Revolution.⁴⁵ Our Lady had sent her to bring pressure to bear on her confessor so that things might improve.

> The Rule is not being observed. Regularity leaves much to be desired. There is a great laxity in both the Communities.ᵗ

Setting things right initially

Cures, conversions, acts of protection—all produced a new sort of climate. Every day the impossible would happen and what took place would provide food for conversations and for prayer. "Haven't you heard what happened?..."

The reforms made headway and there was no more compromising or cheating. Boots and silk fabrics disappeared, as did painstaking preparations for self-beautification. In 1834, Mother Boulet re-established uniformity: gray habit, standard *cornette,* and regularity in all things.⁴⁷

New light in retreats

On May 25, 1838, after a lecture given at the Rue du Bac on the Holy Name of Mary, Catherine made a note of her resolution to "take her as my model at the beginning of all my actions [...] think whether Mary did this action, how and why she did it, and with what intention. Oh! How beautiful and consoling the name of Mary is!"⁴⁸

During a retreat in May 1839, Catherine also resolved to "offer myself to God without reserve [...] accept every little irritation in a spirit of humility and a spirit of penitence [...]. In humbling myself, may his Holy Name be blessed!"

Well before the vision which would appear again in the days immediately preceding the 1848 Revolution, Catherine had turned toward the crucified Lord: *We believe in thee, O holy cross; thou makest reparation for us. Our hope is in thee. We pray to thee to sanctify the just and convert sinners.*

In 1841–1842, the spiritual exercises were given by Fr. Etienne, now Procurator of the Congregation of the Mission. Catherine found here the inspiration to "truly observe our Rules—and not simply stick to the letter of the law—above all in little things. If we truly observe the little things, we will do the same for the big things, in order to imitate our Lord. We must take him as our example."

The same retreat confirmed in Catherine the possibility of combining action and contemplation: "[I resolve to] bring together the roles of

Martha and Mary. O Mary, make me understand what it is to be a good Sister of Charity."[49]

Following our Lady's example

Fr. Aladel's retreat, given at the end of the month of Mary in 1843, "broadened Catherine's horizons," and we can see there a tremendous inspiration. Two insights, to begin with: Mary standing at the foot of the cross; Mary in the upper room with the apostles. Catherine noted:

> [We should] wait in silence for the gifts of the Spirit. Mary was in the upper room with the apostles. She kept silence while awaiting the descent of the Spirit. What a lesson for us! Mary is our example [...] O Mary, make me love thee and it will not be difficult to imitate thee.[u]

From then on Catherine made prayers of entreaty for the renewal of St. Vincent's two families, following the promises received in 1830. She contemplated the *biblical source of her vision:* the woman clothed with the sun in Revelation, chapter twelve. From this text she drew some very concrete resolutions:

> It is necessary to *persevere* [...] following Mary's example. When she reached the throne of the adorable Trinity, the eternal Father clothed her with the sun, put the moon under her feet, and then placed on her a diadem of twelve stars.[50]

Through Mary, she perceived that serving the poor led to a "sweet death":

> Mary loved the poor and a Sister of Charity who loves the poor will have no fear of death. She will feel a great consolation because she has truly served the poor. No one has ever heard that Sisters of Charity who loved the poor had terrifying fears of death. Quite the opposite—we have seen them filled with the sweetest consolations, dying the gentlest of deaths.[v]

In 1843 Catherine brought the month of Mary to a close by offering our Lady "a bouquet of resolutions":

> Imitate Mary.
> Place everything in her Immaculate Heart, in this sanctuary in which our Lord deigned to live.[w] The three virtues of our holy state: humility, simplicity and charity [...] are the basis of our vocation [...].
> We must enter this sanctuary, never to leave it again. [...] Yes, it is into this sanctuary that we must cast ourselves, with the confidence that Mary will grant us all the means necessary for our salvation. It is in this

sanctuary that we will find humility, gentleness, patience, kindness, and charity, as well as the other virtues. Yes, we will derive all the virtues from there, yes, all the graces and all the fruits that we have received during this month, during this retreat, we must gather them all together and offer them to Mary, our good Mother.

Resolution: to let no day pass without practicing some virtue of the Blessed Virgin [...]. We will not find it difficult since everything that she did and everything that she practiced is already done by us in our work: our very vocation makes us do it.

O Immaculate Heart of Mary, obtain for us this great grace for the two families of St. Vincent.[51]

Resurrection

The following August 4, Fr. Etienne was elected superior of the two Congregations.[52] He was 42. On August 15, feast of the Assumption, he closed the assembly by renewing the Act of Confidence in Mary, which had been made for the first time on August 15, 1662, two years after the Founder's death. This Act was derived from one made by the Sisters of Charity in 1658, while St. Vincent was still alive, on the feast of the Immaculate Conception.

> We have recourse to thee [...]. May it please thee to receive us all in general and each one in particular, under thy holy protection [...] and to plead our cause with infinite bounty; may the little Company of Sisters of Charity, of which we are members, also hold thee as its true and only Mother.[53]

Right from his first circular letter, dated September 8, 1843, the new Superior General openly mentioned the apparitions as the source of the grace that was now buoying up St. Vincent's two families. Catherine's heart must have leapt with joy when she read these lines of his:

> I cannot fail to recognize such an obvious intervention on the part of Mary, August and Immaculate, who has given us such extraordinary tokens [...] of her tenderness [...]. It is her powerful mediation which obtained from God the grace that our two families should not perish in the midst of the misfortunes that overwhelmed us and that he should use this as a way of reviving faith. Can we find another reason for such *incomprehensible numbers* of vocations that are showing themselves everywhere [...] or for such prodigious developments [...] in our Company in the very midst of the tempest?[54]

The following year, on the anniversary of his election, Fr. Etienne clarified his thoughts in a forty-page letter, in the course of which the influence of Catherine's visions was even more evident.[55]

Catherine's thanksgiving burst forth in a letter to her sister written on September 15, 1844:

> At this moment, more than ever, there is a renewal of fervor in the community, as in the time of St. Vincent. If there have been abuses, now *everything* is being renewed![56]

Catherine was not afraid of emphasizing *renewed,* nor of saying *everything*. It was a renewal starting at the roots and working from the inside. It pervaded the entire lifestyle more and more: prayer, human relationships, initiative, generosity, efficiency.

The nomination in May 1845 of Mother Mazin as head of the Sisters of Charity accentuated this movement. According to the evidence of one sister:

> She was a straightforward and simple person, capable of understanding St. Vincent's successor and of pursuing the work of reform with him. We almost believed ourselves to be back in those happy times when our Venerable Louise de Marillac, under the guidance of the holy Founder, was laying the first foundations of the growing community [...]. The superiors' wishes were everywhere welcomed with obedience and accomplished without resistance as soon as they were voiced—sometimes even before that! What a beautiful sight the motherhouse was then! Piety, recollection, unity produced a delightful place and the serenity visible on every face bore witness to the common happiness.[57]

The two families were immersed in thanksgiving carried along by a renewal in quality as well as in quantity. The power of Fr. Etienne's régime lay in the fact that he gave pride of place to charismatic impulse, given by grace, but at the same time linked this to observance of the Rule, in such a way that ardor and order reigned together in fruitful harmony—such a harmony as inspired Catherine's own life.

On January 1, 1855, Fr. Etienne was able to sum up the general feeling thus:[58]

> The Company, having climbed painfully out of its own ruins, had not more than a very feeble and sterile existence—it had very little hope of taking up once again the happy position it had held in the Church—when suddenly *a mysterious voice announced to the Company that God would make use of St. Vincent's two families to revive faith.*

"The voice" that Fr. Etienne was referring to was the one that Catherine had heard. He went on:

> Not long afterward, in the motherhouse chapel of the Sisters of Charity, *the apparition of Mary Immaculate* took place *which gave birth to the Miraculous Medal*. This was in 1830, and it was then that a new era began for the Company.

Up 'til then, in spite of the efforts that Fr. Etienne outlines here:

> [The Company] had appeared quite incapable not only of getting back on its feet again but of preserving, through its former life, anything more than a final flicker of light which looked as if it must soon go out. At that time, vocations were rare and erratic. The Company had only a few listless houses in France; overseas, only a few abandoned houses where old missionaries sadly came to the end of an apostolic career which had been filled only with tears and suffering and no possibility of assuaging this grief with the consolation of something to hope for. But after this apparition of Mary Immaculate, everything changed its face. Life seemed to be rekindled within her breast. Already in 1831, colonies of missionaries inspired with the purest and most ardent zeal crossed the seas and went into the Levant and into China to forge with our overseas missions new links for the chain of generations that the Revolution had broken.

A hymn of acknowledgment and thanksgiving if ever there was one! Fr. Etienne painted a picture of the worldwide expansion that followed on the heels of this qualitative change.[59] The seminary's establishment grew in number, from less than 100 to more than 500. A huge building had to be built to house them all. Even this was not enough, and the process of formation had to be split up among different countries and provinces.

With the Vincentians, the same movement took place. Houses in their death throes received fresh blood in the form of an influx of the young. Houses had to be founded at top speed, with young superiors whose own formation had barely finished. In 1839, the fathers made foundations in China, the sisters in Smyrna. In 1842, it was Algeria and so on.[60]

Fr. Etienne put it this way:

> All this took place in the course of the twenty-four years that have now passed since the apparition of Mary Immaculate. Who could not see in this a wonderful intervention from heaven? Who would not feel the

same sentiments of admiration as St. Vincent and say with him, "The finger of God is there"?

His conclusion avoids triumphalism by following the same path as the Founder:

> All this has as its base something which is essential for St. Vincent's children: *the virtue of humility.*

The two Vincentian families were merely instruments, but the light of the medal was worldwide. Its expansion could not be calculated, but was of the order of one billion. Conversions were recorded in ever increasing numbers.

Catherine saw all of this.

In 1837, there was a letter from Fr. Perboyre, a missionary in China and highly respected by Catherine, telling how the medal had freed a madwoman who had perhaps been possessed.

By the beginning of 1842, Catherine had heard a piece of news which was spreading like wildfire: all the presses were talking about it. A young Jewish banker from Alsace, recently engaged to be married, had gone to Rome. Alphonse Ratisbonne was rather critical of Catholicism, but a French friend, Théodore de Bussières, challenged him to accept the medal and he was converted suddenly in the church of St. Andrea delle Fratte. The Virgin appeared to him, just as on the medal. "She said nothing to me," he said, "but I understood everything." This happened on January 20, and the new convert had already been received by Pope Gregory XV by the end of the month. The Cardinal Vicar made official proceedings on the basis of conversion, in canonical form as the Romans know how. All the witnesses spoke about it, from his friend to priest-confidants and even to the sacristan.[61]

Ratisbonne, who entered Holy Orders, asked to see the sister who had been the first to see this same vision. He wanted to share it and confirm its grace. But Catherine had made her choice—discretion and work—and she refused to see him.[62]

Advances and problems at Reuilly

At Reuilly, Catherine's community, the general renewal manifested itself in the laboriousness of day-to-day life. The house had been planted in a peculiar location, totally lost on its noble foundress. "A real sore thumb," Sr. Dufès would soon be saying.

Founded and subsidized by King Louis-Philippe's immediate family, the vast new building reared up in the midst of a seething, poor area. St. Vincent's daughters worked there, trying to be all things to all people, with no political motivations but simply impelled by the demands of the Gospel. Here was the hub of the house at Reuilly, soon to take on a dramatic form.[63]

Sr. Savart, Catherine's first superior (1819–1844),[64] had not shut herself up inside the property as if it were an island. Catherine retained a glowing memory of her. "She was a fine old lady," said Catherine. "Every year she had the first fruits of the garden taken to families living in the area or to her beloved old men; until they had had their turn, the sisters could touch nothing." This opinion did not change, right up to Sr. Savart's death thirteen years later on December 29, 1844.[x]

Sr. Montcellet, who followed her in 1845, opened the era when new foundations were made for serving the locality. In 1849, the year cholera struck, she set up the "Providence St. Marie" at the other end of the garden. This consisted of classes and a refuge, built but not paid for, to take in anyone in physical or mental misery, including young children sent out to work and outrageously exploited. In 1850, she founded a small boarding school for those orphaned in the cholera outbreak. The following year, she was elected Superior General (June 9, 1851).[65]

Sr. Mazin, former Superior General, replaced her for a few months only (1851–1852).[66]

Sr. Randier was next, from 1852 to 1855: an authoritative woman who more than anyone else combined a good brain with a fertile generosity. Catherine liked her fourth superior very much, but she was soon moved elsewhere.[67]

Then came Sr. Guez (1855–1860), an intelligent woman who was very appreciative of Catherine and who established excellent relationships at all levels. But she too was moved on.[68]

The development established by Sr. Guez had been rapid. The house was torn between the elderly's residential hospice and the all-consuming needs of the locality, between the task that had been entrusted by the d'Orléans family and the demands made by human misery. The royal family's administrator protested at Sr. Guez's departure, as did the sisters themselves.

Then came Sr. Dufès,[69] Catherine's last superior. She arrived on October 18, 1860. Thirty-seven years old, she had great plans and an iron will, both of which she put unstintingly into the work of relieving the huge amount of human misery in the area. Her youth and initiative took the community's breath away and the sisters tried to defend the customs established by two Superior Generals. They wanted to use Catherine, a solid "elder stateswoman" who had already passed her silver jubilee, as a focus for resisting the new régime, which the elderly did not like. They even went so far as complaining to the exiled Queen Amélie, and this produced a lot of uneasiness. Catherine never joined in with this sort of argument. She defended authority, going so far as to bring all the young sisters together to tell them, "Don't you get mixed up in anything."[70] In the heat of debate, she would even add, "The superior is the same as the good Lord!"[y]

Sr. Dufès indeed owed Catherine more than she could ever repay, narrowly escaping being relieved of her duties (like Marie-Louise had been).

Difficulties tended to surface again and again. Sr. Combes (aged 28) came in 1861 and found herself involved in them. "Several times I was urged by Catherine to submit myself to the superior," she recalled.[z]

The same was true of Sr. Maurel d'Aragon (aged 21) who came in 1862. Catherine got her to come to her office one day and said to her, "Our life is faith–faith to see God in everything, in our superiors, in things which happen." For the rest of her life, Sr. Maurel understood that only God's work matters, not disputes. [aa]

The disputes were the elderly's. They felt put to one side in this busy beehive which stirred up their nostalgia for life in the château. Catherine understood the importance of the poor people of the area, but had to soak up all the old men's grumblings and try to get them to think and feel more positively.

Sr. Dufès gained the upper hand in masterly fashion, but it was certainly difficult to obtain a peaceful co-existence between the two houses at opposite ends of the garden: the hospice founded by the d'Orléans and the desperately pressing work among the local people. In 1865, doubtless after fresh complaints to Queen Amélie, Catherine said to Sr. Cosnard (24 years old), "Enghien will move to a château...." She thought she saw this "Loire château" with "Hospice d'Enghien" inscribed on it. She did not live to see the fulfillment of this premonition, which only came about in 1901.[71] It was exceptional for Catherine to impart a confidence in this way, but she certainly developed a real trust in Sr. Cosnard, a 24-year-old Normandy girl capable of appreciating Catherine's example. All her life Sr. Cosnard was able to remember the little "practical secrets of poverty" that Catherine brought her from the time of her arrival in 1864.[bb]

⚜

What a hidden treasure Catherine's welcome to those young beginners must have been! "When I arrived (1858), it was Sr. Catherine who welcomed me and was the first to embrace me with much kindness," Sr. Clavel affirmed.[cc]

The unity of the house owed a lot to the heartfelt welcomings and to the advice, based on a deep and practical experience, that Catherine gave to the new arrivals: Sisters Millon (1859), Combes and Thomas (1861), Maurel d'Aragon and the Breton girl, Tranchemer (1862). In Catherine, nobility and the common folk were intermingled in the service of the poor within a community without distinction of rank. First impressions of Catherine would be prayer, smiles, and darning! The most perceptive could tell how astonishingly saintly Catherine was.

Sr. Cosnard would record later on:[dd]

> Others were perhaps as perfect on the outside, but none of them gave the same impression of a soul blotted out by the love of God and of the Blessed Virgin and completely divorced from itself.

⚜

In 1856 or 1857 Catherine noticed a 27-year-old sister who had been sent to Enghien for a few days to change her ideas. Did Catherine guess what was wrong? She approached the sister in the garden as she was walking through from Enghien to Reuilly.

"My little one, you've got a bad thought turning over inside your head!" She had scored a bull's-eye. The "little one" replied: "I came into religious life to care for the sick and I shall never be able to speak in front of everybody!"

Sr. Fouquet had been allocated to the refuge at Boulogne in August. What made her ill was not looking after children but being exposed to the public, since at that time anybody (adults included) "could come in and take part in the lessons given by the sister to the children." Sister concluded forlornly, "I'd rather go back to my family."

"Cheer up," said Catherine, with her solid Burgundy accent. "I will pray to the Blessed Virgin for you. Promise me that for a year you will do the same. You will pass your exams and you'll persevere in your vocation!"

In fact, Sr. Fouquet overcame her repulsion during a period of two years, after which (in 1858) she was sent to the house she had always wanted to go to, at Nesle (Somme), to look after the elderly there–like Catherine at Enghien![ee]

In 1860, when she arrived, Sr. Josephine Combes, who was 29, unwisely let out a secret to one of her companions. How did Catherine know of this? "She reproached me for it," Sr. Combes recalled and added, "later you'll see!" A little while after, the companion renounced her vocation and returned to the world.[ff]

Having by now gained the support of her community, Sr. Dufès pressed on, despite financial difficulties that were impossible to get out of. *The Providence St. Marie,* built in the Rue de Reuilly a long time previously, had still not paid for. The superior was beset by bills to pay. One day she did not even have enough to pay the baker, so she went into the chapel to place her problem in the hands of our Lady. Shortly after that a lady visitor in the entrance, having asked where the box for offerings was, put something in it and went on her way. Sr. Dufès found that she had left exactly the amount required to pay the bill.

On her arrival in the house, she had felt sick at the sight of children of First Communion age rolling around in the streets, dead drunk. These were "winders" as they were called–children exploited by the wallpaper factories that became prosperous through Reuilly's misery. Those factories treated the children like "absolute drudges," Sr. Dufès observed. Most of the children never made their First Communion– and those that did were not properly prepared, so the celebration unfolded almost as if this frustrated area, cast down by misery, was in some way taking its revenge.

The government at last began to take some notice of Reuilly's "Chinese Quarter," and at its request the responsibility for the sisters' school, set up for these very children, was soon taken on by the local Commune itself.

The little boarding school had been started in 1850 by the Archbishopric for children orphaned in the cholera outbreaks;[72] it saw a flowering of vocations. Sundays were devoted to the laborious toil of teaching the children (including the "winders" from the wallpaper factories) reading, writing, and catechism. A seemingly endless expansion of work necessitated a corresponding expansion of premises and personnel and gave rise to a glut of novices. Following the cholera outbreak in 1866, the attics had to be fitted out to take in fresh orphans. When Catherine arrived at Enghien, there had been five sisters; by 1860, when Sr. Dufès arrived, there were twenty-nine; by 1870, forty.

The expansion of the community was a stimulus to acts of generosity, but at the same time there were incidents to keep people on the alert. At 4:00 A.M. on Shrove Tuesday, February 17, 1863, a serious fire broke out in the wallpaper factory adjoining the Reuilly chapel. Flames licked the sisters' roof, threatening to engulf the whole house.

"We were aghast," wrote Sr. Philomène Millon. "But Catherine quite calmly prayed in front of the statue of our Lady in the garden. She reassured Sr. Dufès and the rest of the community: 'Don't be afraid! It will stop and no harm will come to you!'"[73] Against all odds, this is precisely what happened.

⚜

The children who were taught catechism in the parlors of the house were the offspring of the 1848 insurgents. They were a noisy lot, and one day built a barricade in the Rue de Picpus, which was normally very quiet. The result was that the older people, former servants of the aristocracy, were absolutely terrified. They had always said that the sisters were making a great mistake in attracting vermin like this! They took their complaint to the highest level. In the depths of her exile, the Queen abandoned her customary benevolence to ask Sr. Dufès not to take on any more of these turbulent young people.[gg]

Sr. Dufès would not give way at all. The future of these youngsters was God's future in this forsaken locality. At 79 Rue de Reuilly (next to 77, where the sisters had first begun) the community owned a huge plot of land, leased to a rope manufacturer. He was laying down very expensive terms for the termination of the lease. Sr. Dufès mobilized her resources of prayer. The sisters immediately organized perpetual adoration for a whole night. Next morning, the leaseholder came around with a reasonable set of proposals that Sr. Dufès was able to accept. She built classrooms and a playground and founded a boys' club. There the young people were formed, educated, and catechized from 1864 onward. When given permission to join a new Children of Mary Association, organized by Fr. Etienne, they did so enthusiastically.[hh]

In 1868, the royal foundress became anxious as she saw "her good work pushed to one side" by such a great increase in activity. This was not the object of the foundation that she still subsidized to the tune of 500 francs per bed, 600 francs per sister, and twice that for the chaplain. She brought all her weight to bear, but Sr. Dufès would not budge. After all, the royal family had only founded the Enghien house. Now there were two houses. The twenty-five sisters involved in the work of the surrounding locality—and those twenty-five were not subsidized—would live at the other end of the garden, in the Rue de Reilly: they would include Sr. Dufès herself, who was thus able to distance herself from the problem. The community exercises and prayers had been transferred to the Rue de Reuilly since the previous year, 1867.[74] Only those sisters working with the elderly would be left at the hospice in the Rue de Picpus. Catherine was put in charge of them, and Sr. Dufès entrusted her with the keys.[75]

This solution necessitated fresh building once again. Financial burdens grew as big as the houses themselves. One day, Sr. Dufès was out begging for money—not for her own needs but for Notre Dame des Victoires. One woman asked her a great many questions. There was already too much to do that day and this just seemed like more time being lost, but the lady made a note of the address. A few days later she called in at Reuilly and gave Sr. Dufès 30,000 gold francs for the house, in memory of her deceased daughter.[76]

Good for anything

What was Catherine's place in this community? Although in charge of the hospice, she was not a part of the deliberations and decisions. People did not set much store by her. She was merely "the dependable sister," a milkmaid and peasant who was good for anything. This seemed natural for her; and as she seemed happy, things were not taken any further. She especially liked to see the young people of the house and posed no problem for anyone. No one had any cause for complaint because of her, whether at the "reception desk" or anywhere else. She was a good worker, sorting out a thousand-and-one problems, whether material or personal. She carried out her work quite normally and no one thanked her for it.

Sr. Dufès, however, had been confidentially informed that Catherine was the visionary and she treated her with severity. Sr. Cosnard tells us:

> Five or six times I saw Catherine on her knees before Sr. Dufès, who was telling her off for things she had not done and for which she was not responsible. It was really quite savagely done. Although innocent, Sr. Catherine did not make excuses. Nevertheless, it seemed to me that some kind of struggle was going on inside her. Her lips moved as if she were about to say something [...]. The struggle always ended in the triumph of humility.
>
> I was so moved [...] that I [...] asked Sr. Dufès how she could treat [her] in this way. [...She] answered in a very firm tone of voice, "Sister, leave me to do it; I feel myself impelled to do so!"[77][ii]

The superior's severe attitude was a bad example that spread. This unpolished Sr. Catherine, whose accent and apron smelled of the cowshed, was considered as negligible by some of the educated sisters in the community. Sr. Clavel tells us emphatically that one of them "humiliated" and "ridiculed" Catherine, even going so far as to treat her as an "idiot" and a "simpleton."[78][jj]

But Catherine's welcoming personality was a haven for newcomers, often ill at ease or embarrassed when faced with new jobs to do in this accursed area. She gave them advice about entering into the life of the community, about obedience, but above all about poverty and the service of the poor. She initiated them into the constant mending and darning that made such a contribution in economical terms and allowed the community to *give* more than would otherwise have been possible.

If the domestic staff loved her, this was because she gave them her attention.

Cécile Delaporte, the 20-year-old laundress, fell ill when she arrived in 1868. It was Catherine who went to visit her (as Bernadette would visit Jeanne Jardet, the sick servant at Nevers, forgotten under all her burdens). In the great freeze of the tragic 1870–1871 winter, Catherine took Cécile "an eiderdown and some cordial." Cécile also recalled:

> One day I was giving out irons to the sisters who were doing the ironing. She saw that I was hot and she gave me a glass of milk.[kk]

Some sort of electric current ran between Catherine and humble people, between her and children. Those who were puzzled or embarrassed went to her as if she were a beloved grandmother, a staunch member of the household...but would later leave the "old lady" when they had learned to fly with their own wings....

The elderly were grateful to her for keeping the hospice in good order at a time when it was becoming a side issue in the ever increasing work of the community. And this orderliness was to Sr. Dufès' advantage, for the founders might have withdrawn without it. Catherine did not spare her resources. Astonishingly, she seemed to be everywhere at once: garden, poultry yard, front door, and especially with the poor. She kept the rough and menial tasks for herself. It was always Catherine who waxed the floors of the old men's rooms with the heavy "galley-slaver" polisher. Everyone thought, "She's strong, Catherine is." But this sort of work was really not right for someone of her age, now approaching 60. She was surprised sometimes to feel her heart weakening. She would take a breather and start again. What you want to do, you can do....

⚜

Catherine also acquired a discreet but solid reputation as someone to keep watch with the dying. She went without sleep whenever the frequent death throes of the elderly residents required it. Three or four died each year among the men alone. Catherine skillfully combined physical care and prayer. All those with whom she kept watch found peace. Unbelievers were reconciled and sometimes died "holy deaths," or so those in the house would say. At the end of her life, Sr. Dufès could say that there was not a single one who was not reconciled to God.

Sr. Elisabeth de Brioys, who came from a high-ranking family but was herself "of fine judgment and great virtue," also received this final act of service from Catherine. Elisabeth had been a Sister of Charity since 1820. Despite tuberculosis with complications due to meningitis, she had been accepted for her qualities of soul. On August 24, during the summer of 1863, she came out of a coma. Very lucidly she suddenly said to Sr. d'Aragon, who was keeping watch with her, "I am going to die. Fetch Sr. Catherine. Tell her not to leave me."

It was late. Sr. d'Aragon put off doing anything about this seemingly premature request. Anyway, wasn't she there herself? At 11:00, the sick woman asked the same again. Catherine had been in bed since

9:00 and was fast asleep. Sr. Claire shook her. Catherine woke up with good grace and pulled on her *cornette*. She took up her position near the dying woman, looking at her kindly with her blue eyes, praying calmly. At 4:00 in the morning, the rising bell sounded. Catherine continued to pray. The sick woman's death rattle became more pronounced but more peaceful. She died at 6:00 as the first rays of the sun appeared on August 25. Catherine left her and went back to work.[79]

The "garden" of the Children of Mary

One point in this area of development was particularly dear to Catherine's heart–the one she had been entrusted with passing on to Fr. Aladel:

> The Blessed Virgin requires a mission of you.... You will be its founder and director. It is an *Association of Children of Mary* to which the Blessed Virgin will grant many graces. Indulgences will be granted to you.... Many feasts will occur. The month of Mary will be celebrated with much pomp and be observed by all.[80]

The realization of this sprang up of its own accord in 1838, at a time when Fr. Aladel was Third Assistant and helper of Fr. Etienne, who was then Procurator. Bénigne Hairon, born at Beaune in 1822, began a group of *Children of Mary* in the same town on December 8, 1838, when she was only 16. As she said herself, she was "the first one of all" as far as the Sisters of Charity were concerned. The Association was constituted on February 2, 1840. From then on it spread rapidly almost all over the provinces: St. Eulalie de Bordeaux on March 19, 1840, St. Flour in 1841.... The first Parisian Association was started at St. Louis-en-l'Isle on December 16, 1845. Fr. Etienne then named Aladel director of the new movement. On June 20, 1847, he went to Rome and obtained an audience with Pius IX during which the Pope agreed and signed a faculty "to establish in the schools run by the Sisters of Charity" an *Association* under the patronage of the Immaculate Virgin, with all the privileges enjoyed by the Association established in Rome long before by the Jesuits.[81]

In 1848, Aladel published a *Manual of the Children of Mary* which was reprinted regularly: 25,000 copies in less than ten years.[82]

In 1851, the movement reached Reuilly,[83] where there were thirteen candidates. On November 21, Aladel went in person to found the Association there with the assistance of the chaplain, Abbé (later Cardinal) Pierre Coullié. He gave the medal to the first three candidates: the orphans Esther, Antoinette, and Zoe. The following December 8, others followed. The group elected a president–Caroline Huot, aged 12, a lively and ardent child.

One might ask if all this was done under the influence of some kind of millenarist illusion. The answer is no, for the Reuilly records show that the movement went steadily downhill. The register for February 20, 1853, informs us that instead of a "solemn meeting of the Children of Mary" there was:

> no council, no new admissions. Little by little fervor is diminishing [...] Our meetings during the week are being worse attended each time. The Children of Mary seem not to understand anymore the ineffable happiness of belonging to their [...] loving Mother. This title, so sweet, now appears to be just a vain name and this blue ribbon [...] a frivolous ornament.[84]

But the charisma, despite being drained from within, found its second, deeper, wind. Thus, in 1858, the group welcomed Marie-Antoinette Meugniot, Catherine's niece.[85]

In 1860, Caroline, the first president, fell ill. She was 21 and had held office for nine years. Her physical decline seemed to intensify her fervor and the quality of her "testimony." Emaciated and transparent, but always joyful, she presided over the meetings with words so full of light that divine inspiration could be seen in them. "What she said was so 'right' and so exact that it showed that the good Lord was dictating her words"–so said the register the day after her death, December 17, 1859.[86]

Catherine remained watchful. Her advice and example were a support for fervor.[87]

THE SECRET GARDEN

In the depths of her heart Catherine kept her garden closed, defending its privacy with a rare efficiency. Her big clogs, her dirty peasant's apron, and her discretion–these were the ramparts behind which her secret was sheltered, a secret more threatened than it might have seemed.

Anonymity at risk

It was getting more and more difficult to conceal the identity of "the novice of 1830." It was in the 1850s that rumors began to spread...when superiors and others either actually knew or could guess who the visionary was.

In 1855, during her seminary, Sr. Charvier heard tell that *the sister who saw the Blessed Virgin now works at looking after the cows in one of the Paris houses.* "Now in fact," she relates:

> I was sent to the house at Enghien [...], working morning and evening at the same job as Sr. Catherine. The idea came to me that it was perhaps this Sister Labouré who had seen the Blessed Virgin. I observed her from up close, too, I found her very pious and very humble, and yet I said to myself, "No, this cannot be she who saw the Blessed Virgin." I did not find her to be enough of a mystic.

Nevertheless, the idea kept going around in her head. On an unspecified date,

> seeing on the mantelpiece a little statue of the Blessed Virgin which had on the forehead and under the veil a little scalloped headband, I asked Sr. Catherine point-blank: "Sister, was the Blessed Virgin like that when you saw her?"
>
> She answered: "Be off with you, mind your own business."
>
> Her tone was severe but not anxious, rather as if I had made a stupid mistake.

Sr. Charvier kept an eye on Catherine. In chapel, she often "gazed at the statue of the Blessed Virgin."

"Sister," she asked one day, "instead of looking at the tabernacle, why do you always look in the direction of the Blessed Virgin?"

She repeated the question but "never had an answer." Catherine "turned her back on me and went off."[88]

Also in 1855, the Abbé Coullié, future Cardinal Archbishop of Lyon, who was then a young chaplain at Reuilly, was "warned" of the visionary's identity but respected her "absolute discretion."[ll]

Cécile Delaporte, who had come to Reuilly as an orphan in 1856, gave evidence that it had not been long before she had heard it said that Catherine had seen the Most Holy Virgin, and after that she had kept her eyes on "Catherine's attitude," so "calm" in her spiritual exercises and her occupations. Despite Catherine's lusterless exterior, she was for Cécile both an example and an image.

> "The Blessed Virgin made a good choice," I said to myself. My companions had the same impression as I.[mm]

Between 1856 and 1857, Sr. Kieffer, "Sister of Office" [i.e., Assistant to the Directress] at the seminary, heard a "whispered" rumor there that "the sister privileged to see the apparition of the Miraculous Medal was at the Enghien Hospice and that her name was Catherine."[nn]

In 1858, Marie-Louise Labouré, back from Turin at the motherhouse, was visited by her niece Léonie and said to her *sotto voce* as she showed her the Director's chair in the chapel: "Embrace this chair, for the Blessed Virgin sat in it when she appeared to Sr. Catherine."

Léonie later admitted, "I did not understand, for in the family we only called her 'Aunt Zoe.' I was intrigued, but did not dare to ask questions. It was after her death that Aunt Louise herself told me whom she had meant."[oo]

Sr. Clavel was allocated to the house at Enghien in 1858. She did not succeed in penetrating the mystery, in spite of the fact that she had been told, "You are very privileged to be sent to the house where the sister is who saw the Blessed Virgin." She did not go out of her way to find out, but soon discovered what people thought, through veiled references and whispered allusions. "Several of my companions knew, as I did, it seemed to me, but by the grace of Providence we never talked about it among ourselves, much less with Sr. Catherine."[pp]

When Sr. Dufès was elected superior in 1860, Fr. Etienne told her in the strictest confidence.[qq] How long had he himself known the identity of the visionary? He did not know in 1836. Doubtless it was from the time of his election.

Sr. Henriot came to Reuilly in 1861, where she was assigned to lacework. She "sometimes heard her companions saying, as they pointed out Catherine, 'there is the sister who saw the Blessed Virgin.' However," she added, "we did not attach much importance to this sort of talk."[rr]

Sr. Combes, who came in the same year, tells us who was the main source of this secret information—the one who helped to man the door: Blaisine "The Blot." "It was Sr. Catherine who saw the Most Holy Virgin," she said to Sr. Combes.[ss]

Sr. Tanguy's story was this: "I was sent to the house at Enghien in 1863 [at the age of 25] and I was told, 'You are going to the house where the sister is who had the revelation of the medal,' and the speaker added that it was Sr. Catherine Labouré."[tt]

Sr. Caseneuve, who came to Paris from Moutiers in 1866 with her superior, Sr. Séjole (the one who had received Catherine as a postulant at Châtillon), assures us that she "had guessed a long time previously." [uu] From the time of the first news about an apparition of the Blessed Virgin, she had said, "That can only be Sr. Labouré!"[vv]

About the same time it appears that Sr. Dufès allowed herself to be pressured by persuasive relations or benefactors who wanted to "see the sister who saw the Blessed Virgin." At first she had refused as always, but in the end had given in.

"All right, then! I'll take you to the elderly people's refectory where the sister in question is serving."

"They had scarcely come in" when Catherine "slipped away to the great astonishment of her superior, who had never seen her behave like that." How had she managed to sniff out this trap? After the visitors had gone, she went to Sr. Dufès and asked her "not to subject her to any more visits like that."[ww]

Sr. d'Aragon, the source for the preceding incident, places the following one in the year 1867. It was at the motherhouse, where she had attended a retreat given by Fr. Chevalier. He had spoken of the Blessed Virgin and the "Miraculous Medal" in his final sermon and had told Sr. d'Aragon that he was coming to Enghien the next day. Sr. d'Aragon told Catherine about this and–what a surprise!–Catherine, who was usually content to stay at home and "normally very happy to see Fr. Chevalier," went "looking for" Sr. Dufès and asked her permission to spend the whole day with the sisters at Drancy. Sr. d'Aragon reported Catherine's reaction to Fr. Chevalier, who replied, "I'm not surprised, for I did speak about the Miraculous Medal and Sr. Catherine, having attended the retreat, must be embarrassed at the thought of seeing me again."[xx]

If we are to believe Fr. Pouget, from 1879 the seminarians at St. Lazare went to the Enghien chicken run to hide themselves and try to get a look at the one who had seen the Blessed Virgin.[yy]

These dated incidents, together with others less exactly dated, show that the news was gradually getting out. Catherine kept the rumors under control by her discretion and perhaps even by sowing seeds of doubt. Whenever her intuition caused her to suspect something, she made herself scarce or laid a false trail, using her flexibility and vigor as well as her peasant cunning. All this became increasingly difficult as the years passed,[89] but fortunately the discreet nature of her environment helped tremendously.

The gardener

Catherine knew full well that she was in no way the gardener of this secret garden. The gardener was Aladel,[90] who wielded the authority of God and the Church. He it was who possessed knowledge and power in a world which she thought complicated. Her peasant sense told her that unreal impulses ended up in failure. She could see how incapable some sisters were of raising pigeons or chickens in spite of any amount of good will. She knew that she herself was on a losing ticket when it came to wheeling and dealing. In fact, she felt herself to be quite incompetent in any area that she had no knowledge of.[91]

The successes of which she was the instrument did not go to her head. Like childbirth, everything went along swimmingly under a strong impetus, but not without frequent painful thrusts.

Her relationship with Aladel remained difficult and tense. Her confessor was always on the lookout for exaggeration or sheer illusion. The matter of the medal had been sorted out–now leave it alone! But Catherine came back to it–not because of any new apparition, however. It was the voice of our Lady inside her that reminded her of the mission that our Lady had given her and its consequences. How was it that the chapel which her heavenly visitant had made a source of grace was still closed to the public? Why wasn't the anniversary of the event commemorated by a pilgrimage or a special, solemn Communion?

Fr. Aladel's opinion was that all of Catherine's requests came out of her own head. He asked her to accept this. He received her with severity, humbled her, and showed her the door. He found the whole thing a chore, more especially as the medal's success tended to give rise to other apparitions. Beware of the extraordinary mental gifts of the illuminati sect and its like![92] Moreover, he was only a simple confessor and had no power over the chapel. In 1837, Fr. Grappin had replaced Fr. Richenet (who died on July 19, 1836) as Director of the Sisters of Charity. Aladel did not succeed him until 1846. Nevertheless, our Lady had made Catherine understand that it was to him that she must confide everything she had been entrusted with.

Requests turned down

What tormented Catherine from 1839 was the setting up of an altar and a commemorative statue on the spot where the first apparition had taken place, to the right and looking toward the altar. This statue should have a globe in its hands–a detail forgotten so far. Catherine made up her mind to speak. She even dared to persist within the darkness of the confessional. Fr. Aladel got hot under the collar and his displeasure overcame his usual discretion: "You're worse than a blasted wasp!"[93]

His outburst reached some acute ears on the other side of the black curtain. "The very confessional trembled" was the impression of one witness to this incident.

The request was turned down. However, in 1841–1842, Aladel, who was actually very much at one with Catherine despite surface tensions, seemed to succumb to persuasion. The success of the Miraculous Medal, the one hundred thousand copies of his pamphlet which had now run out of stock again,[94] compelled him to publish a new edition. He revised it. The Rue du Bac chapel was too small now and needed enlarging;[95] a new seminary for 500 young sisters needed building.[96] All this required thought and planning. In the end, Catherine's persistence paid off. Did Aladel actually ask her on August 15, 1841, to provide a written account of the apparition of the medal? Or did she do it of her own accord in order that he should read it but not have to be bothered by listening to her? This written account emphasizes descriptive details:

> Above the veil I saw her hair parted in the middle. Below, lacework three centimeters across without gatherings—in other words, lying lightly against the hair. Her face was quite exposed.

But what really mattered to Catherine were the wishes that she had already submitted orally. At a time when daily Communion was not given, she asked for

> a [supplementary] Communion for every community on the day when [the Virgin] appeared (November 27), and also for the apparition of St. Vincent's heart. All indulgences will be granted to you. Everything you want will be granted to you [...]! The good Lord will thereby be given glory. This will put fresh fervor into every heart.[97]

Catherine exhorted her confessor:

> I believe that you will leave no stone unturned to get this done as quickly as possible, so that it can happen on the Saturday before the First Sunday of Advent [anniversary of the first apparition of the medal]. I beg you to ask this of our Most Honorable Father.

She did not dare to add that she was asking for it in the name of God, let alone the name of our Lady. She simply transmitted the "interior request," just as it was given to her, principally concerning the altar:

> It is now two years that I have been feeling urged to tell you to have an altar to the Blessed Virgin erected or placed on the very spot where she appeared to me.[98]

But above all, this altar had to include a statue of the Blessed Virgin, just as Catherine had seen her, on this spot. She stressed a new detail. Our Lady held "a large ball in her hands, which represented a globe.[99] She held her hands at the height of her stomach, in a very relaxed way, with her eyes raised toward heaven."[zz]

It was an imploring look and a gesture of offering on behalf of this world—her children whom she loved to protect.

> Here, her face was totally beautiful. I could not describe it; and then suddenly I noticed rings on her fingers, rings with precious stones. Some were more beautiful than others, some larger and some smaller, which gave out rays of light, some more beautiful than others. These rays came out [...] always spreading out [like a fan] so as to fill all the lower part. I could no longer see her feet.[aaa.]

The voice made her understand that there was not enough hope.

> The precious stones which give out no rays of light are the graces that people forget to ask me for.[bbb]

Jesus said, "Ask and you shall receive." Catherine knew well that God's love is powerless over us if we do not ask for it.

In this year, 1841, Catherine's pressing demands gave rise to a supplementary inquiry. For the first time, the details she gave were written down on a sheet of paper in the form of a specification which would be given to the artist Letaille in order to realize the image she was asking for. The "essential" consisted of the following:

> The Blessed Virgin lightly holds the globe in her hands, she illuminates us with a bright light. It is important really to feel this light, which brightly lights up the earth, particularly against the hands from where the source of light comes. The Blessed Virgin looks at this earth with motherly tenderness. Around, there would be: *O Mary, conceived without sin, pray for us.*[100]

This note is not in Aladel's handwriting, nor Chevalier's, but perhaps was done by Fr. Jacques Perboyre, brother of Fr. Jean-Gabriel.[101]

Letaille, following these details, drew a sketch of the proposed picture: a Virgin standing crowned with stars, the moon under her feet, according to the book of Revelation, chapter twelve, and the specification sheet. She held an enormous globe in her hands—a surprising way of making sure that the rays of light coming from the hands did not hide the globe.

Catherine was hopeful, but the project was dropped. Thus, her "torment" was prolonged. Her notes had obviously been the inspiration for

Letaille's sketch, but it was not possible to say the same for the painting done in 1842–1843 by François Carbonnier, a former pupil of David, who had joined the Vincentians as a brother. Many claims have been made for him because of his talent as a painter. He certainly knew the secrets of color and composition. But his academic style was not Catherine's and she seems to have remained remote from it. It is said that Aladel often used to celebrate Mass at the altar beneath this picture, and the complacent testimony given by Fr. Chinchon regarding the exactitude of this work has been given more importance than it merits.[102] A proper examination of the facts themselves is less favorable. Brother Carbonnier doubtless conscientiously got his details from Aladel; but in the picture there is no crescent moon under the feet, nor the twelve stars around the head, nor the "light cloud under the crescent moon" that is to be found on the specification sheet given to Letaille. The pennon with *O Mary, conceived without sin*...does not form a semicircle with the ends at the same height as the hands—a detail that Aladel was well aware of—but is in a flattened arc for ease of reading. The position of the hands, turned toward the ground (which great play had been made of) seems to be simply a result of Carbonnier's own personal interpretation. The underlying problem was still the same; artists should not be departing from the official model as "laid down" by the medal itself, by Lecerf's picture (1835), and by the engravings in the later editions of the pamphlet (1836, 1842). The "essential unique details" given on the sheet for Letaille[ccc] were therefore not taken into consideration. Aladel was against this globe, which introduced a different vision and ran the risk of bewildering the fervent. The globe in the hands, together with the one under the feet, would have introduced *two* representations of the world on one and the same picture; and then, the hands were closed, not open. Was the new image to become the proper representation of the apparition? If so, how was it to be explained? A rectification? A complementary image? Another phase? Another apparition? Aladel was in favor of keeping things as simple as possible and did not want to get involved in a morass of this kind. To hell with details! In order not to change the stylization that had already proved its worth with the people of God according to traditional canons, Aladel burnt his bridges behind him.

The Virgin with the globe had not been realized, but the 1841 inquiry was not without its results: it had produced Catherine's first autograph writings on the apparitions and then the 1842 definitive edition in which Aladel specified the colors of the apparition, following the manuscript sheet given to Letaille. Nevertheless, he changed *heavenly* blue to *silvery* blue.[103]

The 1848 cross[104]

Catherine did not resign herself to this setback, nor was her desire extinguished by it. Her meditations were still as it were studded with twinkling lights for St. Vincent's families, for the world, and for France—especially the France that she felt so vividly in Paris. The vibrations of this populous part of the world had lived within her since the time when she had first come into contact with these "glowing" people at her brother's workmen's restaurant in 1828 and 1829.

On the threshold of the Revolution in 1848, as previously in 1830, a symbolic and prophetic rush of wind caught Catherine up in itself: she accepted it as a grace, as a request, and all this was in the context of a new climate: latterly the "religious radiation" of Chateaubriand was coming about. Hostility toward medieval obscurantism had given place to a nostalgia for the Gothic Middle Ages and for the Church herself: a charismatic and poetic movement centered on the medal had started to swirl around. Ozanam carried it with him when he founded the St. Vincent de Paul Conferences in 1833;[105] Newman hung it round his neck on August 22, 1845, two months before his conversion on October 9.[106]

Catherine did not go into these things. She scarcely had time to read. But a vision suddenly and freely took place within her, as previously: what was given to her was the triumph of the cross, a triumph that had to be BROUGHT TO LIFE. A monumental crucifix must be erected in Paris. It would strengthen the bonds between Christians and Christ crucified. Catherine could give no more meaning to King Louis Philippe's downfall than to Charles X's in 1830. She had completely turned toward the future with God.

> This cross will be called the cross of victory. It will be the object of much veneration. From all over France and from countries further away, even from overseas, some will come because of devotion, others on pilgrimage, and still others through simple curiosity. And of course special protections will occur that will be thought miraculous. Not a single person will come to Paris and not come to see and visit this cross as if it were a work of art.[ddd]

Catherine did herself a disservice by writing *lard* (bacon) instead of *l'art* (art)—from the sublime to the ridiculous, which caused Aladel to smile. But Catherine went on unperturbed, leaping now from the future to the past:

> At the foot of the cross will be represented the whole of this revolution, just as it took place. The foot of the cross seemed to me to be 10 to 12 feet square and the cross itself from 15 to 20 feet high. Once erected, it appeared to me to be about 30 feet high.

The dimensions were more modest than Claudel's when he was planning an underground cathedral at Chicago with a spire 700 meters (2,300 feet) in height.

> Under this cross will rest some of the dead and wounded from during such painful events [...].

Among these dead, Catherine picked out one (as in the 1830 vision) with especial intensity.

> Here, an arm appeared and a voice was heard, saying
> *Blood is flowing!*
> Pointing out the blood:
> The innocent dies, the pastor gives up his life.

Could this be Monsignor Affre, who on June 25, 1848, died on the barricades where he had come to bring peace? Or perhaps Monsignor Darboy, shot as a hostage during the Commune, on May 24, 1871? Catherine's words seem to apply to the latter,[eee] even though her phraseology fits better with Monsignor Affre.

> The cross appeared to me to be utterly beautiful. Our Lord was there as if he had just died—the crown of thorns on his head, hair disheveled at the back, head bowed toward his heart. The wound on the right side [...] appeared to me to be three finger-thicknesses long, and drops of blood fell. This cross seemed to me to be made of a strange and precious wood, with gold or gilded decorations.

This lifelike vision was full of hope. Catherine felt impelled to present it to Fr. Aladel.

"Here we go again!" he thought and reiterated his stereotype advice against illusions. Catherine tried again—in vain. She therefore decided to take up her pen on July 30, 1848.

> Father, this is [...] the third time that I have spoken to you about this cross, having consulted the good Lord, the Blessed Virgin, and our blessed Father St. Vincent on his feast and right through the octave, during which I abandoned myself totally to him and begged him to

remove all extraordinary thoughts from me on this subject and on plenty of others. Instead of finding relief, I feel myself more and more impelled to give you everything in writing. So, obediently, I am doing so. I think that I will no longer be troubled by it. I remain, with the deepest respect, your daughter most devoted to the Sacred Heart of Jesus and Mary.

She cast this final plea onto paper, like casting a bottle into the sea. She left page three blank and used part of page four for the address (often done, in fact, to economize on envelopes). The mode of address was according to the traditional formula, ceremonially repeating the title of the recipient:

Father
Father Aladel*le*
Director of the Sisters of Charity

Another mistake? Catherine had misspelled the Director's name, putting it in a feminine form. Before sending it, she added a sketch to the first page to show the placing of the cross and, underneath it, a description in tiny handwriting, all squeezed together, to fit on an already rather full page. The overloading was a symbol of the torment she was undergoing.

At the moment when the cross rose up, passing through a part of Paris to bring terror into the heart, coming to a halt in front of Notre Dame, it was being carried by several men who appeared to me to have angry faces. Finally, they abandoned the cross. It fell into the mud and they ran off. It seemed to me that a sudden chill inside them had made them run off, abandoning everything. This cross was covered with a crêpe veil.

This vision, full of colors, was interpreted by Catherine similarly to the vision of St. Vincent's heart:

The white touching the head of our Lord is innocence.
The red [is] the blood that flows [...].
The blue is deliverance by the Blessed Virgin.

It does not seem to have crossed Catherine's mind that these were the colors of the French flag–but in reverse order.

She gave an actual account of her visions without trying to give them a meaning. What was the link between the image of profanation and the triumphal cross to be erected? Was it an act of reparation? She gave no indication. All this seems rather peculiar today, but the vision was strongly rooted in the consciousness of the people in the middle of that century. At that time, the cross had prestige and popularity. The apparition of a luminous cross at Migné (in the Vienne *département*) in 1826 had left a lasting memory in people's minds. Other apparitions likewise. The cross appeared more often than the Virgin at this epoch.[107] It was during this period that *calvaires,* or wayside crosses, were erected by the thousands all over France, as if in riposte to the iconoclasm and blasphemies of the beginning of the century. In the middle of the 1848 Revolution, on February 24 (doubtless shortly after Catherine's premonition), a cross seized during the invasion of the Palais Royal had actually been carried in triumph by the rebels—one point in common with Catherine's vision. The riot that resulted from the pillaging of the Palais Royal had transformed itself into a procession to take this crucifix to the church, according to contemporary reports.

> Last Thursday [February 24], just when the crowd had invaded the Tuileries and thrown furniture and tapestries out of the windows, a young man who belonged to the *Conférence de St. Vincent de Paul* ran as fast as he could to the chapel, fearing [...] that sacrilege would take place [...]. The pious young man begged some national guardsmen to help him to take away the sacred vessels and the crucifix [...]. In the courtyard, voices were raised against the men carrying their precious burden. So the one carrying the crucifix lifted it high in the air, crying, "You want new life? Well, don't forget that you can only have it through Christ!"
>
> "Yes, yes," replied a great number of voices, "he is the Master of all of us." Hats were thrown in the air at the shout of "Long live Christ!" [*Vive le Christ!*]
>
> The crucifix and a chalice without a paten were carried in a kind of procession to St. Roch, where the curé took them in.[fff]

That was the difference between 1848 and 1830. In 1848 the revolutionary Parisian crowd spontaneously acclaimed the cross of Christ. Catherine perceived this; and if the cross she had asked for had been erected, there could have been a rapid expansion like that of the Miraculous Medal. This movement would have been the logical crowning point of her visions—it would have re-centered them on Christ. Catherine was deeply impregnated by this logic. She expressed it in one of her last utterances when, on her deathbed, she gave witness to her joy at being able to go to "OUR LORD, THE BLESSED VIRGIN AND ST. VINCENT." These words sum up the theme of her visions, but in reverse order. Catherine had begun with St. Vincent in April 1830; she had continued with the Blessed Virgin from the summer of 1830 onward; and everything came to a climax with this triumph of our Lord's cross in 1848, in the same line as the eucharistic visions of 1830. Not without difficulty, St. Vincent and the Virgin had provoked a response in Fr. Aladel. The grandiose plan for the cross did not. The idea was buried and Catherine suffered because of it. The very desire of the Lord and her mission both seemed to her to have been cut off. Torn between the vision and obedience, she had freed her conscience by writing. Now she took refuge in the Lord and never talked about the matter again.

An altar and a statue

But she was still tormented by wanting an altar, with the Virgin holding the globe, which would commemorate the apparition and open up the chapel to its destiny as a place of pilgrimage.

Fr. Aladel, increasingly involved with the development of the Children of Mary, therefore kept himself aloof from Sr. Catherine. In 1851, Fr. Chinchon (aged 35) became her regular confessor at Reuilly; he remained so until 1875. He listened, but was no more cooperative than Aladel had been. Was it at his suggestion or Aladel's that in 1856 Catherine produce a handwritten account of the first apparitions: St. Vincent's heart and the one (totally unknown hitherto) in which the Virgin had given her a mission, on July 18, 1830?[108] These writings would remain most secret.

However, something was done as a gesture toward her wishes. The enlarging of the chapel, begun in 1849, included a new high altar behind which a statue of the Virgin with rays of light would be placed, following the model of the Miraculous Medal.

The government presented two blocks of white marble in thanks for the nursing and care given by the sisters to the cholera victims. The first was carved for the altar. It was placed 1.5 yards behind the old one, thus coinciding with the last vision mentioned by Catherine (December 1830).

The other block was destined for the statue, but as a result of a financial disagreement with the sculptor, the statue was not finished until 1856. It was preceded by a plaster one.

These things were done more within the context of enlarging the chapel than in order to comply with Catherine's wishes. "It was not quite what she was asking for," as Sr. Hannezo knew well. ggg Neither the place nor the form were exact. "She was not completely satisfied with the statue of the Blessed Virgin because she was not portrayed as Catherine had seen her [...], holding the ball of the world in her hands."hhh

Fr. Chinchon realized that Catherine was complaining to him about the "attitude" that Fr. Aladel had given to the Virgin. The same went for Fr. Chevalier. And it was on the site of the *first* apparition of the medal, *on the right* and not in the center, that she wanted the altar to be. At least the statue would commemorate the apparition and would respond to the wish to make the Rue du Bac a place of pilgrimage.[109]

But the community was increasingly numerous, with over 500 novices at this period, and this prevented the chapel from being opened to the public. Catherine derived great benefits from the chapel every time she went and would have liked to share them extensively.

Lourdes and the Rue du Bac

When Catherine heard people talking about the Lourdes apparition (1858), she said, "It's the same one!"[110]

"What is most extraordinary," wrote Sr. Dufès, her superior, "is that, without having read any of the published works, Sr. Catherine was more conversant with what had taken place there than those who had actually made this pilgrimage."[111]

According to Sr. Tranchemer, her companion, Catherine said, "You know, these miracles could have happened in our chapel."[112]

Apparently she said the same to Sr. Millon: "If the superiors had wanted it, the Blessed Virgin would have chosen our chapel!"[113]

According to Sr. Pineau, Sr. Dufès found "in Catherine's belongings a piece of paper; on it were written these words in the sister's own hand: 'My kind Mother, here no one wants to do what you want: manifest yourself somewhere else!'"[114]

"On different occasions," Sr. Cosnard tells us, "Sr. Catherine went to great lengths to persuade me that the pilgrimage of Notre Dame des Victoires [whose Association wore the Miraculous Medal] and the Lourdes pilgrimage had been granted by the Blessed Virgin in order to compensate for those that the superiors had not seen it necessary to authorize via our chapel. 'However,' she said to me several times and with a remarkable tone to her voice, 'pilgrimages will come there just the same.'"[115]

The torture of not being listened to made Catherine a little stiff and tense at certain times. She would have lost sleep over it and stretched things out of proportion if she had not found a source of peace at the foot of the altar as our Lady had promised her.

FR. ALADEL'S DEATH (1865)[116]

On Sunday, April 23, 1865, Fr. Aladel gave an inspired lecture. He recalled the apparitions of St. Vincent's heart. Since 1856, he had certainly known the manuscript in which Catherine told the story; but if he was inspired by it, it was in a very free manner. According to Catherine, in fact, the heart had appeared:

> Three days running
>   White, color of flesh [...]
>   Red like fire [symbol of] charity [...]
>   And then [...] red black.[iii]

Aladel reversed the order, from dark to light:

> St. Vincent's heart appeared darkly, vested with a color in no way like real life. But at the end of the novena, when it was revealed again, it had refound its red coloring; a reflection of the heavenly blessedness surrounded it.[jjj]

It is a pity that the confessor did not tell us the authority for his interpretations and their reasons. At least he paid tribute to the anonymous visionary:

> It was to one of you that [Mary] first revealed the dogmatic truth of her Immaculate Conception [...]. It was on the eve of the sad events of July 1830....[kkk]

After this inspired piece of instruction, Aladel returned to St. Lazare. The following evening, bad news from Dax: Fr. Etienne, Superior General, had fallen ill–the irreplaceable guide of this whole grace-filled movement and such a friend! Aladel was overwhelmed. He set the two communities to praying and threw himself into it as well.

Next day, April 25 and feast of St. Mark, the brethren were amazed to find that he was not there. Normally they could set their clocks by him, his habits were so regular. However, they did nothing about this for the moment. The sister in charge of the community sacristy was worried because he was late for Mass for the first time ever. She ran to St. Lazare to tell them there. Someone went up to Aladel's bedroom and found him there, unconscious, sprawled face down on the floor. He had had a stroke, and he died the same day at about 3:00 P.M.

Thus, the final words of his sermon can be seen as a kind of premonition:

> When, in our final hours, after the *Consummatum est* of our last sufferings, our soul leaves the body which holds it captive, if our Blessed Father St. Vincent finds in us a strong spirit of faith, great charity, and the love of predilection for the Immaculate Virgin, it is to her that he will present us and Mary Immaculate will lead us to Jesus.

His brethren thought that he had offered his life in exchange for the threatened life of Fr. Etienne.

On Thursday, April 27, the funeral rites were celebrated by Fr. Eugène Vicart, who would succeed Aladel as the sisters' spiritual director and as the Superior General's advisor. The altar servers at this liturgy were Vincentian students for the priesthood. One of them was Catherine's nephew, Philippe Meugniot (20 years old at the time). He retained an "astonishingly striking" memory of the ceremony:

> I was the thurifer. When turning around to perform some ceremonial function or other, my eyes alighted on Sr. Catherine, who was in the front row with her superior [Sr. Dufès]. I was startled by her radiant physical appearance. I could not explain it [...]; was it a memory [...] and a heavenly reflection of the relationship that she had with the venerable deceased man?

This serenity was soon to be troubled by fresh disturbing torments.

CHAPTER VI

The War and the Commune
(July 1870–June 1871)

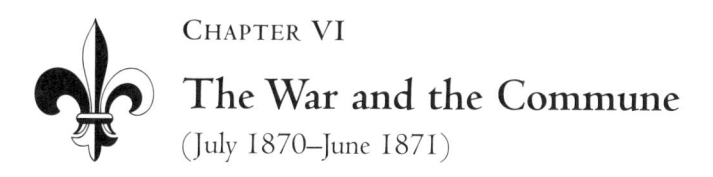

THE 1870 WAR

ON JULY 19, 1870, THE EMPEROR declared war on Prussia. Frenchmen, still dreaming of the epic deeds of the Napoleonic period, were delighted. Even the sisters prayed for victory, according to Sr. Joseph Tranchemer (aged 44), a Breton and supporter of the elder branch of the Bourbons and whose piety was thought by Sr. Dufès to be "of the highest order."[a]

Catherine did not join in with the general enthusiasm. She merely said, "Poor soldiers!"[1]

The serpent in the desert

On August 4, 1870, Fr. Etienne published a circular letter with the aim of inspiring confidence. He conjured up a picture of the extraordinary grace-filled movement that was carrying the Vincentians and the Sisters of Charity along and referred more explicitly than ever to Catherine's first vision: St. Vincent's heart, "deeply afflicted by the great misfortunes that will fall on France." He recalled that both motherhouses had been astonishingly protected in 1830, in accordance with the prediction of the still-unidentified visionary. His enthusiasm for these forty-year-old wonders even prompted him to say:

> In the same way that a bronze serpent was erected in the middle of the desert as a sign of salvation [...], so [God] had placed St. Vincent's body in the very midst of the great capital [...].
>
> This name, for so long forgotten, appears in all the political upheavals which must give birth to a new world, like the Spirit of God hovering over the waters of chaos from which the first world came

forth at the beginning of time. Indeed, it is under his auspices that in the midst of the ruins of the social order is being erected that beautiful institution, the *St. Vincent de Paul Conference,* which is spreading through the whole world.[2]

The siege of Paris

The war went badly–disaster in Alsace from the beginning of August onward, then in Lorraine. Sedan surrendered on September 2. Napoleon III was taken prisoner and the Empire crumbled. A Republic was proclaimed on September 4. The Prussians were nearing Paris. During September 4 to 14, the sisters in the thirty suburban houses, sometimes bringing their poor with them, took refuge in the capital. A medical unit was installed at the motherhouse.

Catherine was working hard in the Reuilly "cook-house" in order to feed not only the elderly residents in the hospice but the starving poor in increasing numbers. More and more helpings had to be provided, up to as many as 1,200 a day.[3] This was rough work for the sisters and a difficult ordeal. On September 11, the superiors made a special exception and permitted them to have daily Communion,[4] which was for them a great source of strength and peace.

On September 18, 1870, the Prussians laid siege to Paris. The sisters placed themselves under Mary's protection; they put up the medal on the doors and windows of the house. "They must be hidden!" said one sister.

"No, no!" protested Catherine. "Put them right in the middle of the front door."[5]

Catherine to be a superior?

During the early days of the siege, Catherine's nephew Philippe, now a Vincentian, came to visit her at Enghien.[6] He found her "in her doorkeeper's office" in the little booth that she kept unencumbered, like a monastic cell.

> She did not discuss the tragic events that were taking place. Her conversation was a little less formal than usual. She spoke to me of her youth, then went on to her life as a religious. I only remember one thing [...]: the Superior General of the Sisters of Charity (I think it was Mother Devos, who died in the odor of sanctity) [had] summoned [Catherine] and [had] told her that she was thinking of nominating her as a Sister Servant [i.e., superior of a house].

"Oh, Mother," Sr. Catherine replied, "you know very well that I'm not capable of doing that!" And (she concluded), "I was sent back to Enghien"–this said in a tone of voice which implied "and a very good thing, too!"[7]

Catherine may not have been a superior in rank, but she was to show herself one in the events that were to come.

Metz surrendered on October 31. As a result, a Revolution broke out but quickly aborted itself. All this did not stop thirty sisters from receiving the habit at the motherhouse on November 14. They were to replace those who had been sent to Bicêtre to care for smallpox patients. Twenty-three others received the habit on November 28 so that experienced reinforcements could be sent to the same hospital.[8]

Famine and "the cook-house"

At Reuilly, "the classrooms and the refuge" were converted to a medical unit and the Val de Grâce military hospital (served by the Sisters of Charity) established an "annex" there. The town hall gave the sisters the job of distributing meat to the small medical units of the area.[9]

Rationing was introduced. Shortage of food became famine and made Catherine's job more complicated in the "economical cookhouse." The forty delivery horses from the Bon Marché shops, "so beautiful, so clean, so sleek and fat," were sold to be slaughtered as there was no more food to give them. The Rue du Bac Sisters learned of this too late–they would have bought the horses!

> Donkey flesh sells at 5 francs a pound [and it is] impossible [to find] any for [...] this extraordinary price. No more smoked herrings, no more hard sausages. Only rice, bread, and wine. We are rationed to 30 grams of meat per person per day.

All this from the Journal for November 10, 1870.[b]

By November 12, a rabbit cost 20 gold francs, a cat 8 gold francs. People started to eat dogs (which many people considered to have an excellent taste)–and rats.[c]

Sr. Catherine, who liked to give decent-sized helpings, was reduced to the kind of parsimony that she could not put up with from Sr. Vincent at the time of her debut in the kitchen. Sr. Mauche, aged 25 and a future Superior General, could not bear to see the wounded so badly fed and found all sorts of ruses to get "supplementary rations" for them. She did so much of this that the sick called her "the Wandering Jew." One day, when the sisters were praying in the chapel, the sick were extolling her virtues with such vigor that the whole community could hear it through the dividing wall—including Sister Mauche herself, who hid her head in her hands. One of the things she had done for her ninety sick people was to make a fruit salad from oranges together with three liters of rum which she had prised out of the doctor and the "commander"—a severe, white-bearded officer.[10] This little luxury concealed the fact that there was not in fact enough for one orange each.

Sr. Catherine went to the same sort of lengths for the medical unit that she was in charge of, Sr. Tranchemer tells us.[d]

Catherine's two nieces, Marthe (aged 6) and Jeanne (aged 4), both of "delicate health," would long remember "the treats" Catherine got for them when they visited Reuilly, "with her superiors' permission." Marthe wrote:

> I remember our childlike joy when she gave us a piece of white bread and a portion of peas including diced bacon—extremely hard to come by at this time. My sister, in her childish simplicity, kept asking my grandmother (Tonine) for "another pea!"[e]

Sweet things were reserved for the sick and the wounded. The sisters' portions were reduced to the bare minimum. Sr. Dufès was worried "on certain days, to see them devouring a piece of black bread and nothing else" after doing backbreaking work.[11] Young Sr. Eugénie would admit later on that before washing up the serving ladle she would look around furtively to see if she was alone and then hungrily lick up the little bits of soup still remaining on it.

True hopes, false hopes

A naïve hope that God would grant the victory was still the predominant one among the sisters. One of them made her young workers recite sixty-three times the invocation *O Mary, conceived without sin...* to obtain success for the French armies. She also got Catherine to pray. Catherine's answer to that was to say: "My children, pray also for our poor soldiers, so unhappy in this terrible war [...]."

When a supposed victory was announced, she would smile with an air of unbelief. "You bird of ill omen," Sr. Tranchemer would chide her. And she would reply, "Don't you worry, the Blessed Virgin is protecting us. She has an eye on us, on the whole community."[12]

Sr. Tranchemer knew that Catherine was the one who had the vision of the medal. She was fascinated by her, but did not understand her attitude. She seemed to see nothing but misfortunes, surrender, and the entry of the Prussians into Paris! And yet she was somehow able to manifest a calm and a complete confidence that she was trying to share with others.

On December 16, two carrier pigeons brought the incredible news that the Prussians had crossed the Loire. Orléans had fallen. New Year's Day 1871 in Paris was dark, with no celebrations; but the *Officiel* on January 2 was quite certain that "we will not surrender at any price." A massed sortie by 400 thousand national guards was being counted on. Clairvoyants were talking of a great combat beneath the very walls of Paris—a bloody and lethal combat, but a victorious one.[f]

The depths of winter

Since December it had been freezing hard: minus 11.5°C (11°F) on January 5, 1871. Shells rained thick and fast on the capital. Street urchins were selling the shell-splinters. One story circulating was of an exchange between a street urchin and his customer:

"How much for a shell-splinter?"

"No more left, Sir. I'm waiting for a fresh delivery!"

People were looking for signs in the sky. On January 17, at about 7:00 P.M., the garden at Reuilly was covered by powdery snow. Young working girls on their way home remarked upon the "extraordinary" color of the "mysterious, veiled horizon." They felt it was an omen.

"The sky is in mourning for all our mourning," said Sr. Tranchemer.[13]

Catherine looked but said nothing. Her companion was soon to learn that this very night the Virgin had appeared in the village of Pontmain, also covered in snow. "Was this what Catherine had been thinking about?" Sr. Tranchemer asked herself, but she never found out.[14]

On February 11, "a display of the Northern Lights [*aurora borealis*] cast terror" on everyone in the house—sisters, children, the wounded.[15] But Catherine remained unmoved.

Going back to January 18, Generals Trochu and Ducrot were secretly preparing a sortie which would make use of all possible forces. People came to Catherine's medical unit, looking for able-bodied men. Some of them had scarcely been declared fit for action again.

"Poor lambs!" said Catherine. "They're being led to the slaughter."

The next day, January 19, the Buzenval sortie took place. The troops stormed the high ground at Montretout, Garches, and La Jonchère, but were swept back in a bloody repulse.[16]

The fall of Paris

On January 26, 1871, seventy-two bombs showered down on the Val de Grâce military hospital at 4:30 A.M. Fire broke out. The nurse on duty—a Sister of Charity—got the sick moved up to a higher floor. Scarcely had the last ones left the room when the ceiling collapsed.[17]

On January 29, an armistice was signed. On March 1, the Germans marched into Paris.[18]

THE COMMUNE (MARCH–MAY 1871)[19]

Another war

It was a humiliating but also a rumbling, threatening peace. While on her way with Sr. Catherine to pray before "the Virgin in the garden," Sr. Tranchemer said to her, "Do you understand that, Sr. Catherine? We have surrendered and all our military men say that we are going to have a war—a war even worse than the last one!"

Although apparently pessimistic with regard to events, Catherine radiated a peace and confidence in the face of the new shocks that took place almost daily.[20] Sr. Tranchemer thought she remembered Catherine predicting "the civil war."[21] In fact, if the date she gives to this conversation (March 21) is correct, the Commune was no longer a question of prediction. It had been in existence since March 2, after a long process of fermentation and the creation of various obscure committees. This movement of popular, anarchical, and lay resistance was hostile to anything connected with the *Ancient Régime*—that is, the clergy and the royal family who subsidized the Enghien hospice. The sisters were thus "on the wrong side." However, their unstinting service to those in any kind of distress ensured that they still had much popular support. It would be impossible to calculate their contribution to this suburb where the Commune would try to awaken a new ideal. Between the "communards," with their red scarves and their brave words, and the sisters, with their sureness of faith and the certainty of their mission—strangers to the political climate in which everything was immersed willy-nilly—there would be a gradual unfolding of psychological dramas which more often than not would end up without anyone losing or winning.

The new Revolution was an adolescent explosion where violence and kindness, utopianism and organization, ideology and humanity found themselves side by side. The humble were not always the stuff of which the power and speech to which they had been elevated were made. The waters of the movement would often overflow because of temperamental problems of this kind, with which it was necessary to deal severely.

On the night of March 17–18, the "Vigil of St. Joseph," the rebels assaulted and captured the Montmartre hill. There was a rumbling of cannons audible from Reuilly.[22] The seat of the Commune was now the Hôtel de Ville and from there the elections of March 22 were prepared.

The day before, Sr. Tranchemer had seized a moment or two of repose to "grill" Catherine, whose obvious pessimism was such an affront to her own patriotism.

"But, Sr. Catherine, how did you know what was going to happen? Who told you? Was it your guardian angel? Was it our Lord?... Well, if it wasn't either of those, it must have been the Blessed Virgin!"

Catherine avoided making a reply, but remained darkly brooding. "My God! So much blood, so much ruin!"

Sr. Tranchemer was excited by this somber view and went to find the superior, who got upset. She had been talking to Fr. Chinchon, confessor to the house, who had come straight to Enghien from Dax[23] that very day, March 21.

"What's the matter?" asked the superior dryly. She knew how this tiresome sister tended to exaggerate things in her excitement.

Fr. Chinchon remained silent during the explanation that followed. Sr. Dufès then grumbled:

"So, then! You're going off your head and Sister Catherine, too! Why don't you go and tell these predictions to your companions. Is that what you were going to do?"

"Oh no, Sister, certainly not!"

"Very well, then. Keep quiet about it!"

"Yes, Sister," said Sr. Tranchemer.

She left, feeling rather small, but impressed by Catherine's calm and her strong hope in spite of such a dismal backdrop to everything.

One result of this was a conversation between Catherine and Fr. Chinchon, her confessor, who had been intrigued by what Sr. Tranchemer had said. It is on this occasion that he would have asked Catherine to make a written version of the predictions received by her during the night of July 18–19, 1830, including the death of the Archbishop, only to be fulfilled forty years later.[24]

The elections decided upon by the Commune were having a rough ride. The whole undertaking was a risky one. But the new régime had the prestige of resistance to the Prussians and of its generous-minded ideas for a new society to arise from the ruins of an Empire whose collapse had been nothing short of catastrophic. The turnout was higher than expected—229,000 voted, compared with 480,000 on the electoral roll—and a large proportion of these were from working-class areas. On March 26, the new government began its legislative program. Despite the counter propaganda emanating from Versailles, it put the public services back to work, imposed a tax on bread and meat, introduced controls on wholesale and retail markets, reorganized the health service (April 13), suppressed night work for bakers, and also (May 20) the right to make stoppages out of wages—a right that employers had hitherto enjoyed. It prepared for elections to a federal chamber of the working classes. Revolutionary committees proliferated.

The reaction against the old order included anticlericalism. Neither did the sisters have any place in this society. They were threatened, and pessimism was rife among them. Catherine, however, reassured them. "The Virgin will keep watch; she will look after everything. Nothing bad will happen to us," she said. And further: "We must pray to God to shorten these bad times."[25]

A dream?[26]

In the early part of April, a preoccupied Sr. Dufès was visited in her office by Catherine.

With her customary simplicity, Catherine began:

"Sister, the Blessed Virgin came to see you, but she did not find you."

"What?" I said—"the Blessed Virgin came?"

"Yes, Sister, she went into the community room and asked for you. As you weren't there, she went into your office. She sat down in your seat and said to me, 'Tell Sr. Dufès to be calm. Nothing will happen to this house; she can go; I myself will stand in for her.'"

Then Sr. Catherine told me that I would have to leave the house, that I would go with Sr. d'Aragon, whose family was very willing to offer us hospitality, and that I would not get back until May 31.

Sr. Dufès shrugged her shoulders. What a dream!

But the "dream" was a striking one, nonetheless. At recreation, Catherine was questioned about it. Sr. Maurel d'Aragon was not present, but questioned her the next day and was given another version, the basic essentials of which were as follows:

> When I saw the Blessed Virgin, I went to look for you so that you could do the honors of showing the house to her and it was you who led her to Sr. Dufès' office. She sat down at the desk, saying that she would look after the house, after which she disappeared.

Catherine's statement was not taken seriously, but simply seen as a symptom of the troubled times. She was treated more with good humor than the reverse. Not normally a "gabber," Catherine herself was rather astonished at having imparted this confidence. Coming across Sr. Dufès later on the same day, she said to her, "Sister, don't take too much notice of what I was telling you." "Sister, I haven't given it another thought!" replied the Sister Servant.[27]

As far as everyone else was concerned, it was all just a fantastic dream. But later on, when it actually happened, Sr. Dufès took it to have been a vision.[28]

Catherine would confirm that later. Sr. Claire d'Aragon remained convinced that if Catherine spoke of a "dream," it was on the spur of the moment and "prompted by humility." However, most of the witnesses speak of it as a dream.[29]

Good Friday (April 7)

The situation took a turn for the worse during the hot springtime.

On April 7, Good Friday, there was an alert in the improvised hospital where the sisters were looking after 200 soldiers. Two of them "claimed that there were two *gendarmes* in the medical unit. It was true."[30] They were both wounded. This news was explosive, for it was well known that "the Versailles gendarmes shoot and assassinate patriots"–the Commune's posters said so.

> The mob came to the sisters' house to seize these two men and shoot them. They could not escape and were escorted off to the guardhouse.

The outcome seemed inevitable. But Sr. Dufès ran "to the Reuilly barracks" and pleaded tenaciously. "These gendarmes have taken no part in operations against the people. They are sick–they're in the medical unit on doctor's orders."

Her authority obtained the impossible—the two men were returned to her. "Be it on your own head!" Nothing happened that day.

Violent Easter (April 9)

Two days later, Easter Sunday, another and final visit was made by Fr. Chinchon,[31] for bold people could still travel in those troubled times. He was on his way to Brussels before going back to Dax. He heard confessions while he was there and Catherine, who had been his penitent for twenty years, certainly profited from the occasion. Was it at this time that he received from her the "black exercise book of prophecies, 15 x 21 cm," the contents of which would make such an impression on Fr. Serpette when Chinchon finally got to Dax?

At any rate, Fr. Chinchon celebrated Mass—and it was a long time since there had been Mass there. How wonderful to be able to celebrate Easter in this way! In the midst of all the plundering and uncertainty, the Eucharist assumed all its transcendent value in the death and resurrection of Christ; its effect on those present was so extraordinary that one would not have thought it possible. The everyday dramas, problems, and privations were put into proportion by the gift of joy and peace.

Fr. Chinchon left at the house a seminarian whom he had brought up from Dax: Abbé Blanchet, a subdeacon. He had a large bald tonsure on the back of his head and had the air of a lamb marked out to be slaughtered. The sisters feared for this youth, so they disguised him in mufti in the style of the suburb, with smock and trousers. They even whitened his shoes to make him look like a workman and gave him a voucher for the soup kitchen. With a cap on his head, the Abbé joined the line. A sister gave him a large piece of bread. He walked through the crowd and the guards with his bread under his arm without being molested, and then made for the Eugène Napoléon house nearby, where he picked up some traveling clothes and wore them back to Reuilly.[32] From there, he set out again to find shelter with Fr. Meugniot, who had become the chaplain to the sisters at Les Invalides.

During recreation on this Easter evening, an armed mob of 100 "communards" invaded the house again. This time they were led by the man who had been made mayor of the twelfth *arrondissement*.[g]

The release of the gendarmes had not gone uncontested. How could representatives of the people allow themselves to be pushed around by a sister, who was doubtless involved in the plot up to her neck? Those who had given in that morning had lost face because of it. Noisily, the mob cried for the two gendarmes.

The War and the Commune 133

The sisters resisted. One of them recognized a man whom she had fed–him and his family–during the siege: there he was in the front row of the crowd. "You!" She exclaimed. He tried to hide himself behind the others, but did not dare to try and calm his companions down.

"Give us our two gendarmes!"

"Never," replied Sr. Dufès. Sabers were lifted and fists raised toward her, but no one actually dared to touch her.

One of the Paris militiamen who had exposed the two gendarmes forced his way through the line of sisters, "followed by guards," and began

> a search of the house, looking for the two "outlaws" whom he knew perfectly, having spent more than two months with them. One of them was well hidden and he did not find him. The other was in his bed, and God arranged that the militiaman should see him, pass in front of him, and not recognize him.[33]

The lack of success exacerbated the situation. Sr. Dufès swallowed her surprise without weakening, but her authority drained away in the turmoil. One of the "winders" laid his hand on her, wanting to remove her by force. "It's either the gendarmes or the superior!" he shouted. "She took it all on her own head!"

But the sick attendants and the wounded soldiers supported Sr. Dufès.[34] Then the thirty sisters (of whom Catherine was one) arrived and stood side by side with their Sister Servant. They would arrest the whole lot or no one at all! The solid phalanx of thirty *cornettes* pointed out the problem, for the hospital could not be left without anyone to run it. The confrontation turned into humor.

"What do you expect me to do with all these frightened swallows?"[35] asked the mayor of the twelfth *arrondissement,* roaring with laughter. His flash of wit had saved the situation, but he added, "You'll be hearing from me tomorrow!"

No one had lost face. It was 10:00 P.M. The sisters were flabbergasted by these violent outbursts on their own "territory." The commandant had used earthy, not to say improper, language! Never had the sisters heard anything like it, even those who had been to the Middle East or to the United States![36]

Easter Monday (April 10)

The sisters had plenty of friends in the locality and they were soon discreetly informed that a formal "arrest warrant" had been made out in the name of Sr. Dufès, for "conspiracy with the d'Orléans," founders of the Enghien hospice.[37] Two Picpus Sisters and two other Sisters of Charity had already been taken to the St. Lazare prison. Sr. Dufès would not avoid a similar fate: she was urged to disappear.

On Easter Monday, April 10 at 11:00 A.M., she fled, taking advantage of the absence of the national guards who had gone to the tavern.[38] With her she took not Sr. d'Aragon, as Sr. Catherine had predicted, but Sr. Tanguy. On the evening of the same day she reached Versailles, where the regular army was quartered. But as soon as she got there, she was filled with anxiety. What had she been thinking of to bring Sr. Tanguy with her? By so doing, she was leaving the community without a leader and in a difficult situation!

In fact the community had already reacted well to the dramatic situation and had found itself another leader....

Catherine goes to the rebels' headquarters

While Sr. Dufès was making herself scarce, "Sister" (the *Journal* of the Commune leaves her anonymous) had the bright idea of taking the bull by the horns, so off she went to the rebels' Reuilly headquarters. It would be better to thrash things out on their territory rather than on one's own. Moreover, this diversionary tactic would serve to conceal Sr. Dufès' flight from danger.

Who was the anonymous sister? Not Sr. Tanguy, who had just left with her superior, nor little Sr. Mauche, who was too young. It was Catherine, an "elder," already in charge of the Enghien hospice[39] and the superior's deputy during her absence. The anonymity maintained by the records of the period is very easily explained by the discretion that was always the rule whenever Catherine was involved–for her secret was already known too widely as it was.

She calmly went to plead her superior's cause before the new mayor of the twelfth *arrondisssement*. That made him think of the time when her father was mayor of Fain. But what could he do, surrounded by nothing but red-belted, strapping young men–who would give a lot of trouble to anyone less solid than Catherine?

Her visit did not make things any easier for the "communards," already unhappy about their relationship with these sisters who had public opinion on their side and, moreover, were acknowledged to be performing a valuable public service. Catherine was amazed at the ease with which she "was able to penetrate this sanctuary."

The account in the *Journal* says with slight exaggeration:

She found herself faced by about sixty individuals, some sitting around a table, some armed with guns, others eating or smoking and all covered in red belts right up to their necks.

The Commune was up-to-date on the matter. Scarcely had Catherine stated her plea regarding Sr. Dufès' rights than she was greeted by a torrent of abuse. Upright and calm, she stood up to the assault without flinching for as long as it lasted. When they had finished and silence was restored, she requested: "Kindly allow me to explain."

She had timed it nicely. Instinctively, Catherine had absorbed the ancient dictum of the Gospel: when you are summoned before tribunals, do not worry about what you are to say; the Holy Spirit will give you the words. So Catherine explained, "courageously and briefly." The lack of "waffle" was to her advantage. According to the chronicler, the basis of her argument was this:

> The superior had been released from her promise, seeing as she had received safe-conducts for the gendarmes: these documents had come from the Commune itself and bore the official stamp; naturally, the gendarmes had made use of them.

"Lies, all lies!" they cried. "And anyway, you should have told us that before."

The peasant in Catherine flared up immediately. "What? Is it our job to be the police? And since when has it been the practice to suspect trickery in a safe-conduct bearing your official stamp?"

They wanted to arrest her then, but she invoked the documents that the Commune set such store by. "Show me your orders, show me your warrant!" she demanded.

At this, the commandant of the detachment drew his saber. "Here are my orders! This is my warrant!"

Several red-belted men surrounded her. But one of the soldiers, who had not forgotten that Catherine had looked after him in the medical unit, got up more quickly than the others. As the chronicler tells us:

> Seizing the sister by both arms, he tore her away from their furious clutches. Such was his enthusiasm that the sister still has bruises all over her arms.[40]

Perhaps she had already been treated even more roughly. At any rate, she left the place, free. She had won!

That evening, the national guards occupying the house at Reuilly were ordered to leave.[41]

Would the communards return, the trembling sisters asked themselves. The description of the bared saber had strongly affected them, as had Catherine's arms, "covered with bruises," which she had to show them when she got back.

The Commune envisaged a long existence for itself—and this would mean putting up with sisters living fearlessly in the area.

Medals and insecurity

On April 23, the fighting got worse. One morning there was a hubbub of activity—there would be a battle the next day. The communards rushed to the house, but this time it was to ask Sr. Catherine for medals. Those she had given previously had produced belief in their protection. One young man who wanted one was swearing and cursing away.

"Where are you going like that?" asked Sr. Tranchemer.

"Looking for a medal!"

"But you don't believe in God or the devil! What will you do with it?"

"True enough," he said, "but tomorrow we'll be under fire. The medal will protect me!"

"Off you go then, and let's hope it will convert you," replied Sr. Tranchemer, for the young man was ready to do anything to get what he wanted, and Catherine was distributing medals generously to anyone, no matter what creed or what sort of persons they were. The Virgin would recognize her own and convert the others. Catherine put everything in her hands.[42]

Life went on at Enghien-Reuilly. Catherine was busy with her work, even more crushing now that the "troubles" had reduced the number of sisters.[43] From thirty-three they were down to fourteen.

It made one get out of breath, with all the work to do, the "cookhouse," the pressures of the Commune, the insecurity of the elderly and the children. A way was found to send the elderly women to Sr. Mettavent's place in Ballainvilliers, in a peaceful area. As for the orphans, they were sent back to their families, wherever they were, if the children had families. But there were still about thirty left. What could be done? Dr. Marjolin of Ste-Eugénie (today the Trousseau) Hospital, seeing the situation, "on his own initiative, suggested" that he "take them into his convalescent home at Epinaysous-Bois (Seine-et-

Marne)." Sr. Millon took the children there, to a place "sheltered from all danger."

"I am convinced that we owe this happy event to the protection of the Blessed Virgin," she said during the canonization process,[h] "and that Sr. Catherine was not unconnected with it."

The accomplishment of the prophecy

Meanwhile at Versailles, Sr. Dufès, torn away from her responsibilities, was being gnawed by anxiety. The day after her arrival, April 11, battle was joined between the "versaillists" and the communards. What would happen to the house? And what had she been thinking of to bring with her the most solid and most dynamic person in the community: Sr. Angélique Tanguy? It would not have taken much for Sr. Dufès to go straight back again! However, Sr. Tanguy forestalled this suicidal plan—she would go back to Enghien herself. Relieved, Sr. Dufès agreed.

"Send Sr. Claire d'Aragon. If the situation is prolonged, I'll go to the south of France with her."

Sr. Claire's family lived near Toulouse and had offered hospitality. It was also to Toulouse (the St. Michael house) that Sr. Dufès had been assigned when she left the seminary thirty years earlier.

So on April 17 or 18, Sr. Tanguy left to return to Enghien. She arrived without any trouble and immediately sent Sr. Claire to Versailles.[44] Sr. Dufès left straight away for Toulouse with her new companion and got there about April 20. She stayed for more than a month. Thus Catherine's prediction came to pass. "It didn't even cross my mind at the time," Sr. Dufès was to say later on. "But afterward I was very struck by the unexpected similarity."[i]

As soon as she returned, Sr. Tanguy took in hand the organization of the school. It was carrying on as best it could, given a lack of personnel and, above all, a lack of anywhere to conduct classes due to the influx of wounded. About April 18, apparently two *citoyennes* [woman "citizens"] arrived wearing red belts.

"We've come to replace the sisters."

They had an operational warrant. What it involved was the education of the children according to "the new spirit," avoiding "anything which could do violence to young consciences." This included "no more talk of God," "taking away the crucifix, no more catechism," etc.[45]

That day, the two women got no further; but they left, saying, "We'll be back!"

There was not long to wait. One of Sr. Angélique's former pupils turned up to take "the headmistress's place."

"Well, well—it's you, *citoyenne!*" said the former mistress to her old pupil who was now trying to supplant her. "Have you really accepted these orders? You have no shame!"

But the old pupil would not listen, sat herself down at the desk as she had seen Sr. Tanguy do in bygone days, and set about giving the children an exercise to do. However, one of the little girls knelt down and all the others followed suit.

"Excuse me, Miss, but we haven't said the prayer. Our teacher always used to make us start off with it."[46]

Once again, solidarity was at cross-purposes with edict. The Children of Mary kept an eye on the house to make sure that nothing was stolen. Bit by bit, they hid whatever looked to be at risk.[47]

These *citoyennes* became the number-one problem. There they were, women among women, on the sisters' property, trying to oust them. One of them was the terrible Valentin, whom witnesses describe as having been "a monstrous woman" without going into further detail.[48]

Catherine and the "monstrous Valentin"

Some time a little after mid-April, two armed communards crossed the Reuilly garden. They entered the small Enghien refectory and asked for Sr. Catherine. Two sisters were there, in no hurry to answer their question. The men placed a revolver against the throat of one of them. Sr. Tranchemer intervened:

"You wretched man! That isn't Sister Catherine! Put your weapon back in its holster and I'll tell you where she is, if you promise me that no harm will come to her."

"I've come to fetch her to Reuilly. Citizen Philippe wants her, but no one will harm her. I'll bring her back to you."

"Well, here she is! But put your weapons away. The sisters don't need that to help them to walk, if what they are being asked doesn't go against their conscience."

Hearts in their mouths, the sisters watched Catherine go. There was talk of hostages and executions. The sisters began to pray, leaving "the windows open," listening for the sound of a "detonation." Two hours passed; it seemed like an eternity.

And suddenly there was Catherine back again, escorted by her two bodyguards. They had been very attentive to her. She had not been summoned for a sister's trial but for Valentin's trial—and as a prosecution witness![49] The Commune had had more than enough of this hot-headed woman and her demands. They wanted to make an example of her. Why did they call Catherine? Was it because of the confidence she inspired? Or because she especially had suffered at the hands of the *citoyenne?*

What the tribunal wanted was a firm accusation from this sister who knew how to talk about justice. What a surprise! Catherine in fact testified in Valentin's defense, "whitewashing" her. It was always something unexpected with the sisters, that's for sure! One never knew what side they were on. And so there were the judges, faced with having to show mercy on this occasion.

Last Mass at Reuilly

On the evening of April 23, the second Sunday of Easter, Fr. Mailly, Procurator at St. Lazare and an intrepid expert at "slipping through," arrived to get the latest news. They had had "neither Mass nor Communion" for two weeks. He promised to return the next day and kept his promise. He had become adept at getting through the sectors he had to cross. That Monday morning, April 24, there he was again in a new disguise that made the sisters laugh. They found it "about as attractive as a third-rate interior decorator." But he had brought a parcel with a cassock in it and put this on as soon as he arrived. He celebrated Mass, heard confessions until 9:00 A.M., and then slipped away.[50]

It was just as well that he did, for someone had noticed this Mass taking place. Furthermore, he had left the sisters with a complete load of provisions sent by the English for poor families. Distribution began shortly after his departure.

Distribution—perturbation

"At ten o'clock"[51] the Commune's delegates arrived. More than 200 people were lining up in the street. The sisters had begun their work. Fr. Mailly was anxious to prevent both a crush and anger on the part of those who would end up disappointed; and on his advice the sisters had warned the crowd: "Good folk, there will only be enough for those who arrive first!"

They all waited patiently, if anxiously.

"Stop the distribution!" ordered the delegates.

"Sirs, you can announce that yourselves; the women in this locality will tear our eyes out if we send them away empty-handed!"

"Certainly!" replied the delegates.

No sooner said than done.

"The Commune has requisitioned the provisions," they announced. There was a colossal uproar. The delegates had to get help from a squad of armed national guards to take away the barrels of biscuits and salted pork. This display of force achieved nothing. The people's "irritation" assumed the proportions of a riot. The delegates gave in.

"The distribution will continue!"

"Citizens, you can do it yourselves," said the sisters politely.

The men were pleased to be given this opportunity to appear generous. But it was not easy to distribute a limited amount of supplies to a starving crowd. Anxious to make amends for the bad impression they had previously given, they tried to make themselves loved by attempting to deal with everybody at once. Disorder broke out again; a "chorus of shouts and screams" filled "the whole street."

"Look at that thief!" screeched one ragamuffin. "That's the third time she's come up; each time she hides away what she's been given and comes back for more!"

The ruckus got louder until no one could hear him- or herself speak. Overwhelmed and totally breathless, the delegates asked the sisters' advice on calming the multitude. The sisters did what was necessary and order was soon restored as confidence returned. The men were astounded.

"Do you often have scenes like this?" one of them asked, when the distribution was finished.

"Every day, sir, at the 'cook-house'!"

"Well, I wish you joy of it."[52]

And off they went.

Catherine had remained calm throughout. She said, "Don't worry, nothing will happen."[53] And she carried on looking after the elderly and the wounded. Growing poverty grieved her sorely, but she knew how to accept it without panicking.

Medals and red belts

Catherine was often "on the door" at 12 Rue de Picpus, at the Enghien side of the property[54] where a watchful eye was needed. Her medals were successful. The communard guards got their comrades to relieve them so that they could come and get some. Catherine gave medals to all comers, with an individual word of encouragement for each one.[55] Even Siron, the commander of the "occupying forces" and a former convict, came to ask for a medal. Catherine did not refuse anyone; and the former bandit said openly, without pretending, "I'm quite changed by it!"

He would later become the sisters' defender.[56]

Crisis

And they certainly needed a defender, for the struggle between Versailles and Paris became tougher. Exasperation found a "safety valve" in the violence of hopeless fighting. On April 28, a group voted for the death of the Archbishop of Paris.[57]

At Reuilly, accusations were hurled at the sisters. People's imaginations ran riot at this point in time, when one of the oldest social needs in the world was growing: the need to find scapegoats.[58] The sisters were accused of having killed three local women.[59] Catherine was summoned by Citizen Philippe to an interrogation from which she extricated herself by dint of sheer calm.[j] On the 28th, a group of angry men arrived, guns at the ready. They broke into the community room. Fourteen sisters were sheltering together on the first floor of the linen room, just above. The sound of shouts and threats wafted up to them through the floorboards.

Viaticum

The next day one of them, fearing sacrilege, went and rescued the ciborium from the chapel. She placed it on a small table between two lighted candles. Still left in peace, the sisters adored the Eucharist and prayed while awaiting what was to happen next. The priesthood of the faithful assumes its true dimensions at times of crisis.

Down below, the "invaders" had discovered bottles of wine intended for the medical unit. Perhaps they were down in that famous "cellar" which was to be Catherine's last resting place. The bottles had not been hidden by the Children of Mary, and soon the corks were drawn. Encouraged by this windfall, the search continued amid a kind of excited euphoria, in the midst of which threats of death to the sisters could be heard. The men climbed upstairs noisily and came to a hesitant halt in front of the linen room door. "Shall we go in?" they asked each other.

Siron was there. He stopped them and shouted through the door, "Don't be afraid, sisters, they'll only get to you over my dead body!" Immediately he lay down across the doorway and, made drowsy by the effects of the heavy drinking, went to sleep. The others did the same.

What were the sisters to do? At midnight, April 29–30, they gave themselves Communion.[60] Was this to be their Viaticum? They felt as strong as Elijah, capable of walking for forty days and forty nights. Silence had fallen again and they opened the door a tiny crack. The communards were still fast asleep. On tiptoe, the sisters stepped over the recumbent bodies.[61]

Having reached another part of the house, they got ready to depart. It cost Catherine much to leave her elderly people. If it had only been her, she would have stayed. But she was not in charge anymore; she had to obey.

The crown

Before leaving the property, Catherine went to kneel one final time before the statue of our Lady. The next day would be May 1–so it was the vigil of the month of Mary. "We'll be back before the month is out," said Catherine.

The sisters prayed and sang a hymn. "No communard woman dared to intervene–not even Valentin!" Catherine took the crown off the statue to preserve it from sacrilege.[62]

"I will give it back to thee," she promised our Lady.

The "occupiers" let the sisters go after having submitted them to a vigorous search. Their blue bags were emptied on the ground, not without much jeering.[63]

"Don't get upset, nothing serious will happen," said Catherine to the worried sisters.[k]

EXODUS

At 6:00 P.M. they began the trip. Along the way, the atmosphere was heated. The crowds, already incited against anything to do with the clergy, insulted the sisters.[64] But the journey was direct and quick: one hour later, at 7:00 P.M., they had arrived at St. Denis where Sr. Randier stayed.

St. Denis

Philippe Meugniot, Catherine's nephew, passed through on the very same day. He had just left, "looking like a commercial traveler, hands in his pockets, without a breviary of course, equipped only with heaven-knows-what sort of foreign passport that he had shown to the 'bitter enders.'"[65]

This is the *Journal's* description of the "agents" of the Commune: "partisans of war to the bitter end" against the Germans.[66] Catherine had narrowly missed seeing her nephew, who was now on his way back to Loos where he would be attempting to teach, virtually without books.[67]

Sr. Randier was most welcoming. She had been Catherine's third superior at Enghien, from 1852 to 1855. Unfortunately, the local administration would only authorize her to keep on a single person out of the new arrivals.

The Reuilly community was dispersing according to what was possible from the point of view of family or community connections.[68] Half of them had gone their separate ways before reaching St. Denis. By the following day, Sr. Angélique would have left to join Sr. Dufès in Toulouse.

By 11:00 A.M. the next day, May 1, only the two "old timers" were left at St. Denis–Sr. Catherine (65) and Sr. Tranchemere (45). Beset by uncertainty, the splitting up of the community, and relaxation from being away from the tension at Reuilly, Catherine felt the whole backlog of tiredness and tension flow out of her. The thought of death came to her, together with concern about everything for which she was still accountable to our Lady, everything that had been refused her. As Sr. Angélique, young and brave, went off to join Sr. Dufès and the others went their own ways, Catherine began to feel the need not to be left alone and perhaps also the need to support Sr. Tranchemer. As the "Versaillists" began their bombardment of the capital, she said to her companion:

"Here we are, old-timers on our own. What are we going to do?"

"Sr. Randier is very willing to let you stay."

"Yes, but only me."

They went down into the garden.

"I'm not well," confided Catherine. "I feel my age. I could die. I'd like to have a companion close at hand. Would you like to stay with me?"

"Certainly, Sr. Catherine. I am at your service."

"Thank you! Don't let's leave each other again!"

And she went to thank Sr. Randier, who urged them to rest until the following day.

Ballainvilliers (May 2–30)

On Tuesday, May 2, the two set off for Ballainvilliers. Catherine was more specific with her companion: "I have something to confide in you at the time when I die. I cannot say it to sisters that I do not know. I would need a companion. And it's you.... Let us go then!"

She started out "with a big smile." The same day, about 5:00 P.M., both of them had been "settled in" at the "château de Ballainvilliers,"[69] run by Sr. Mettavent.[70]

Sr. Mettavent was a formidable woman, just in her fifties. She had spent some time in the Middle East—Constantinople, Alexandria.... Sr. Mettavent had known the worst there is to know: cholera (1865), riots, calumnies, oceans of misery, and appalling death rates. She had been assigned to Ballainvilliers a little before 1870, and had already set up an orphanage, a kindergarten, and a pharmacy in addition to the class that had been there when she arrived. During the war she had organized two medical units and had cared for abandoned elderly people. Her interventions with the Prussians had saved several people condemned to death, including one father with a family. One day she encountered a column of 300 French prisoners dying of cold and hunger, so she took it on herself to requisition everything cookable in all the bakeries she could get at. She distributed the food under the eyes of the Prussians, who were stupefied with admiration. As soon as the gates of Paris were opened after the siege, she went off with a large cart to revictual the motherhouse, where she had been bursar from 1866 to 1868. The German sentries turned her back, like everyone else. But a Prussian officer recognized her, and he took the bridle of the horse and got her through with all her provisions. At Ballainvilliers, she was now protecting the land from being pillaged and was organizing fair distributions of food. She had even been careful to hide a store of corn. This was to be kept for sowing and she would give it to the peasants who had fled, when they returned.

Catherine and her companions helped the mistress of the house wholeheartedly—the more so as she had taken in the old women from Reuilly several weeks previously. This was one of the things which had drawn Catherine here.[71] She felt at home.

She wrote an eight-page letter to Sr. Dufès, which was unfortunately later destroyed. It contained a prediction that seemed insane at the time: "The whole community will be back at Reuilly for the end of the month of Mary!"[72]

May went on and the violence only grew worse. There was no more question of priests going around in cassocks, since they would be arrested.[73] The Vincentians dressed up "in mufti, in civvies, in suits," as the catchphrase went at the time.

"People will believe that all is lost; the churches will be closed," Catherine had said.

In the sixth *arrondissement,* a poster had been stuck up on the door of the boarding school run by the sisters at St. Suplice:

> Notice to Parents:
>
> In this treacherous house, inexperienced young ladies are being detained...having been torn by trickery from the very bosom of their grieving families. It is well known that some of those inside this place are being kept under lock and key, despite denials to their parents and in the face of those parents' legitimate objections and great distress. Wicked nuns! Poor parents! Notify the authorities![74]

On May 16, the Vendôme Column was demolished, in the middle of confused popular festivities.[75]

On May 18, a battalion of "Avengers of the Republic" sacked the church of Notre Dame des Victoires,[76] seat of a worldwide archconfraternity whose insignia was the Miraculous Medal. Catherine, when she heard of it, said: "They have touched our Lady. They'll go no further."

To Cécile Delaporte, Reuilly's linen maid and a laywoman with whom she had often worked, Catherine calmly affirmed: "The Blessed Virgin is guarding our house. We will find it intact."[77]

Death of the Archbishop

On May 21, Versaillist troops penetrated into Paris by the St. Cloud gate.[78] A week of tough fighting began. The hostages taken by the Commune were threatened. On May 24, in La Roquette prison, Monsignor Darboy, Archbishop of Paris, was shot, along with the curé of La Madeleine, five Jesuits, fifteen other priests, and forty-five gendarmes.[79]

Catherine had perceived the Archbishop's death forty years before. Fr. Chinchon, her confessor, had written down this prediction when he passed through Reuilly at the end of March. It was in a black exercise book. Back at Dax on May 19, he had told his brethren about this prediction in confidence: it was in the morning, five days before the massacre of the hostages, according to the young Vincentian, Fr. Serpette (aged 22), a witness to the event. Struck by the statement, Fr. Serpette had sought out Fr. Chinchon (Catherine's confessor) the very same evening. Together they had leafed through the famous black exercise book.[80]

> He read me two lines, predicting Monsignor Darboy's death.[81] He told me that the other priests would also be put to death.... His tears ran

down.... He dismissed me without giving me his blessing, which he normally did at the end of a spiritual meeting–he was too overwrought. From that day on, every time we were able to speak to priests reading the newspaper, I kept asking if there was any news of the Archbishop of Paris. Finally the news arrived–terrible news.[82]

Unfortunately this exercise book has not been traced, nor even precisely identified.

Crises and protection

On May 27, Sr. Tranchemer was on her way back from Longjumeau when she saw the lights of the fire in the center of Paris. She exclaimed: "Paris is burning! What's going to become of the motherhouse?"[83]

Catherine was unruffled. "Do not worry about our houses. The Blessed Virgin is looking after them. They will not be touched."

Nevertheless, the community was living through a real drama. St. Lazare had been surrounded by national guards. The 105th Regiment of the line had set up a permanent post in the parlor. The last of the Vincentian brothers left the capital for Dax. The evacuation of the seminary sisters was also desirable, but the delegates opposed it all day long. Not until 10:00 A.M. that day (May 27) did they take the train for the birthplace of St. Vincent de Paul.

At the motherhouse there had been no Mass for several days. Fr. Mailly carried on celebrating Masses here, there, and everywhere. On May 24, he had risked passing behind the wall of Les Incurables (today Laennec) to say a Mass in the chapel of the Miraculous Medal.[84]

Shells rained down. One of them struck the wall of the seminary and rebounded into the doorway of the St. Joseph refectory. It did not explode. Another landed inside the dormitory and set fire to it. A commando got inside Les Incurables Hospital and let fly with his gun around the house. Federate soldiers returned fire from the sick bay, the kitchens, and the garden. The Superior General gathered the community together in the St. Joseph workroom. She gave her instructions. Inside, the sisters were praying; outside, all was rifle fire. The Council of State, the Tuileries, and the Louvre were all in flames. In the afternoon there were violent explosions: the powder magazine at the Luxembourg was blowing up. During the day of May 24, the fire spread as far as the banks of the Seine. There was fighting everywhere and corpses littered the streets, but *not a single victim* among the sisters.

The drama, the emergencies, the uncertainties doubled and redoubled again. A barricade was erected in the Rue d'Enfer, near the Enfants Trouvés [abandoned children] Refuge, run by the Sisters of Charity. In an untenable position, the rebels gave the order to evacuate so that they could set fire to the house. Seven hundred babies would have to be brought out in a quarter of an hour, into the full blast of the fighting. The situation was manifestly impossible. The Sister Servant threw herself at the knees of the commandant. He reversed his decision, saying, "Sister, I believe in God. Your house will not be burned."

He ordered the bombardiers to take away the cannons already lined up and this order was obeyed. But one doesn't reverse a desperate order with impunity, and the insurgents seized him and shot him on the spot for having weakened the resistance.[85]

Here again, how was it possible for the sisters and all their sick to remain completely unharmed?

On May 28, the Versaillist army conquered Paris.

Return to Enghien (May 31)

Sr. Dufès was recalled from Toulouse by telegram. At Versailles she found her "Ballainvilliers companions"–Catherine and Sr. Tranchemer.[86] They wanted to return home the same day, Tuesday, May 30, but a permit was needed and they were delayed in obtaining one; so the departure was put back to the following day, May 31.

At 5:00 A.M. they all went to the Mass at which Sr. Eugénie Mauche (the sister of the oranges and rum and a future Superior General) made her vows. Early in the morning of May 31, Sr. Dufès was back at Reuilly with her whole community, except for her companion Sr. Claire who had stayed in the south and would not be back until June 4.[87]

Here, then, was the May 31 "appointment" that Catherine had so confidently expected.[88] The statue in the garden had been attacked. It was dressed up in red cloth and (according to some accounts) had been badly damaged.[89] It was to the Virgin in the "chapel at Enghien" that Catherine gave back the crown she had taken on April 30. It was not the particular statue that mattered, but what it represented.

"I told thee, my gracious Mother, that I would come back to crown thee before the end of the month."[90]

The house was in disarray, but the damage was not serious.[91] The Children of Mary brought back the things that they had hidden for safety.[92] Sr. Dufès thought once again of Catherine's dream and our Lady's promise: "I will look after the house. You will have returned before the end of the month of Mary."[93]

The protection given to St. Vincent's two families had been unbelievable. Innumerable stories circulated, together with thanksgivings. They were noted down in great number the same year in the chronicle of those heroic times.[94]

Some of the young Vincentians were disturbed and even scandalized by it all. Why should St. Vincent's two families have all this protection when so many others, including male and female religious, had suffered even to death? Fr. Fiat would later have to use much ingenuity to reassure those who were disappointed at not having "carried their cross."[95]

This was understandable, for peace, when it came, was rough and violent.

At Reuilly, wounded communards had been installed in the orphan girls' dormitory, converted into a medical unit, so that they could be cared for. While waiting for what would be an inexorable judgment, Sr. Dufès entrusted them to Sr. Mauche, who had acquired such a good reputation for looking after the sick during the famine, with her "good chocolate," her "good, milky coffee," and her good heart. She was strengthened by the vows made that morning at Mass before the departure for Reuilly.

When she was entrusted with the communards' care, she was also told what would eventually happen to these thirty or so wounded men. She was already a little frightened by their mistrustful or hostile faces and their worried looks. Now she was crushed by a heavier fear, one with no remedy. What could she do? She turned for help to Sr. Catherine, who had already given so many medals to the rebels.

"Have you got any more?"

She was given a handful, with some encouraging words. "Off you go, my dear. Don't worry about anything."

Sr. Eugénie was afraid of provoking blasphemies and of being the instrument of final impenitence. She waited for two whole days for the right moment. One evening an idea came to her. She took her courage in both hands.

"My friends, I have something to ask you."

"What do you want?"

"Permission to recite a prayer."

"Go ahead, Sister!"

They knew only too well what would happen to them. They had taken off their cotton nightcaps and placed them on their beds. Sr. Euégnie began strongly, but at the end of the Our Father she dissolved into a flood of tears. Everyone looked at her in surprise.

"My friends, it's tomorrow!"

Silence fell. The atmosphere was so tense that Sr. Eugénie did not dare to offer any medals. She went off to a neighboring room and threaded each medal on a cord. Night fell and she prayed and gently laid a medal on each pillow.

When she left the dormitory toward 4:00 A.M. to go to Mass, the wounded were asleep, the medals still on their pillows. When she went back up, they had put the medals around their necks, showed them to her, and thanked her. In the meantime they had made their confessions, following Sr. Dufès' suggestion. A priest had come—a former hostage of the Commune. He went away deeply edified.

At 7:00 A.M., carts and stretchers were brought to take the wounded men to Versailles. They were very calm and thanked the sisters. All of them were executed.[96]

The Versailles army had lost 877 men. They had shot 20,000 in the streets during the bloody week of May 21–28. Some 38,578 suspects were arrested, including 1,064 women and 614 children. Life began anew with a bloodbath.

At Enghien-Reuilly, the sisters put the house in order again. Classes were restarted. Catherine went back to her elderly charges: they had not forgotten her. All during the month of May, they had often said to the male citizen-nurses, "What Sr. Catherine used to do, we will do."[97]

Catherine had only six more years to live.

CHAPTER VII

Declining Years—Ascending Life
(1871–1876)

SR. CATHERINE RETURNED TO HER DUTIES at the hospice, in the chicken run, and as doorkeeper on May 31, 1871. The atmosphere was one of homecoming. The poor, greater in number after all the upheavals, were glad to see her back, manning the door and ready to help. They knew that they were her favorites.

The elderly welcomed her with open arms; for them, "no sister was loved as much as she was," according to Sr. Millon.[1] They loved her fairness, her vigor which kept everything in order for the common good, but above all her considerate care for each person, sometimes a little rough, but always there. They *knew* that she loved them and that they could count on her.

WORK AND DAILY ROUTINE

Catherine was over 65, but she still got up when the bell rang at 4:00 A.M. She was still sturdy in her old age. Her prayer life, too, was both sober and exemplary. She would hold herself upright, motionless, with her hands scarcely pressing on the prie-dieu, her clear eyes fixed on the tabernacle or our Lady's statue.

The senior

On the feast of St. Catherine (November 25, 1871), Catherine, who had four days previously become the "senior" of the Enghien-Reuilly community, was presented with the following "poem" in a doggerel style much practiced in the nineteenth century:

> If glories of a blessed saint are sung through all the heavens above,
> Then here on earth a well-loved sister, too, receives a hymn of praise:

The *Senior of Enghien,* encompassed by our heartfelt love,
We pray will ever stay with us until the end of countless days.

O good and dearest sister, to St. Catherine we pray, that she
May send a heavenly benison to bring you joy, to calm your fears;

Her hand divine guide all your steps, your labors and your charity
And give you grace with us to dwell in quiet and peace for many years.

Catherine was rather more appreciative of this "compliment" from one of her elderly charges (on behalf of all the others): "Sister, you are kind to everyone. When we are eating, you always ask us, 'Have you got enough?'"[a]

Why these compliments? Because Catherine's courage and predictions during the Commune had brought her an hour of glory? No, it is much more likely because the very venerable senior of the community, Sr. Vincent Bergerault, had died a few days before, on November 21, 1871. Aged 75 and, therefore, born in the previous century, she was the last survivor from the foundation of the house in 1819. She was the parsimonious cook who had been such a trial for Catherine; but she had also had a real reputation as a saint. This was not on account of her remarkable gifts which had led her to stumble upon "undiscoverable" benefactors at times when the house was going through difficult times— for example, Madame de Narbonne, who had given 100,000 gold francs to set up the school at Reuilly, or the woman from the Faubourg St. Antoine who had provided 15,000 francs to build the chapel. Rather, it was because her sensitive, ardent, even dramatic piety was much more like the traditional saintly models than Catherine's was, for example. Sr. Vincent was renowned for her outbursts and her spiritual struggles, which were expressed in noble words right up to her death.

"Here I am, on the point of death!" she said two days before she died, on November 19. And then, struck with terror, "My God, what will become of me? I have done nothing for thee; my hands are empty!"

Her heroic fortitude during her long illness had been the subject of much admiration. During the Commune she was already a walking corpse. After receiving Extreme Unction, she had to be dressed again in order to be transported as best as possible to the motherhouse when the sisters were hounded out of Reuilly on April 30.

When they came back to Reuilly, Sr. Dufès fervently brought her in. Indeed, she was much impressed by Sr. Vincent, right through to the "sacred delirium" of her final illness, when she said in the middle of the night, "Go and wake up the sisters. We mustn't sleep; we must get ready for Holy Communion."

The crown of her life was her death on November 21, feast of the Presentation of the Virgin. As the secret was still being kept, there were some people who thought that it was Sr. Vincent who had had the vision of the Miraculous Medal.[2]

An old-timer, not much honored

Catherine thus became the new senior sister, but was not subject to the same veneration as Sr. Vincent Bergerault. Her rough-hewn sort of holiness was misleading. Her simplicity appeared excessive. Her old age did not bring her a halo. "Two or three other aged sisters" seemed more worthy of admiration. The "good-for-anything" side of her personality gave her a subservient air; even though she was in charge of the hospice, she still waxed the floors with the heavy "galley-slaver" polisher, despite arthritic pains and a heart that was beginning to give way under the strain.

Sr. Dufès and others (for example, Sr. de Tréverret, who also became a superior) said that they preferred "a different kind of sanctity to that of Sr. Catherine."[b] They were irritated by her secret which they felt was too well guarded. By way of compensation for their frustration, they "didn't set much store by her."[3]

Catherine had no right to speak at Chapter meetings on community decisions. She accepted this contempt, since it was in fact a protection for her. One day her niece, Léonie Labouré, asked her: "Auntie, how is it that you've been in the same house for more than forty years?" "Only the intelligent sisters get moved," replied Catherine, who was no idiot herself.[c]

Although scarcely consulted by the "higher-ups," she was more than ever an always available reference point, someone to resort to for the young sisters, who were rendered virtually breathless by an overworked house in a poor area, a situation which their inexperience found confusing.

Intuitions and intercessions

Sr. Félicité Hébert (aged 26) had to leave the house for health reasons. She asked Catherine to pray for her and received this comforting reply: "Well, my little one, the Blessed Virgin loves you very much. You can be quite calm: everything will go well."[4]

This was in the midst of the turmoil of 1871. Sr. Félicité was cured, but only learned later of the identity of the older sister whose kindly reassurance she had been privileged to receive.

In December 1871, Sr. Tranchemer told Catherine about something that was grieving her greatly: one of her nephews was ill. He was a young naval officer, well known for being both successful and handsome. He had turned his back on God and rebelled against the thought of death. "What can one do?" she said. "Write to Pontmain," said Catherine, who knew that Sr. Tranchemer came originally from that part of the world, "for the Blessed Virgin revealed herself there...."

A little while afterward, the young man received the sacraments. Sr. Tranchemer states that he was smiling as he breathed his last on the following day, January 12, 1872.[5] With Sr. Dufès' return, things in the house were soon back to their usual hectic pace. Catherine was still treated roughly; as always, she showed no sign of bitterness.[6]

Marie and Gabrielle (1872)

In the spring of 1872, two postulants arrived at Reuilly: on May 10, Gabrielle de Billy, from a well-to-do family; on June 25, Marie Lafon, daughter of an Aurillac smallholder, whose memories of Sr. Catherine were particularly warm.

During the time of "acclimatization" of postulants, the Rule allowed them to go out with their families. Toward the end of June a carriage stopped outside 77 Rue de Reuilly.

Monsieur and Madame de Billy, driven by their coachman, had come to take their daughter out for the afternoon. Marie, the little peasant girl, was therefore left on her own. Catherine was not long in making up her mind and went to see Sr. Dufès with a pretext for going to the Rue du Bac. Of all the places she knew on this earth, it was the best! Permission was granted and Catherine then asked, "May I take the 'little one' with me?"

Perhaps Bibi, the community's horse, was occupied with other work. At any rate, the outing took place on foot, with cheerful zest—the 23-year-old postulant and the 66-year-old sister. They got on like a house on fire. Sr. Cosnard, now working at the seminary, teased Catherine (with perhaps a tinge of jealousy?) when they arrived.

"Well, well, Sr. Labouré, I do believe you're showing a bit of favoritism for Mademoiselle Marie!"

At that, Catherine's Burgundy blood was roused and she immediately retorted, "Heavens above! If Mademoiselle Gabrielle can go out in a carriage, Mademoiselle Marie has every right to go out on foot!"

As Marie said later, "Up until then, I had not realized that there was a connection between the other postulant's outing and mine; but Sr. Catherine out of the kindness of her heart had forestalled any feeling of distress that I might have had from being left out of things."

Sr. Marie's other recollection was of a slightly mad summer's evening with one of those sultry sunsets that seem to go on forever. An elderly man had died at Enghien because of the heat, and there was talk of a lunatic who had escaped the day before from the neighboring asylum. Although a little disturbed by these events, "Mademoiselle Marie" had forgotten them in the course of taking the evening class for young workers at Reuilly. They had chatted with her, and it was not until after 9:00 P.M. that she returned to the Enghien hospice. Activity had put any fears she might have had completely out of her head; nightfall brought them back again. Her long dress rustled in the dead leaves, the noise giving her the impression that she was being followed. The more she hurried, the louder the rustling got. She ran toward the Enghien door nearby; but there, in front of her in the courtyard, was a black figure. Was it a ghost, or the escaped lunatic? Marie took the shortcut up the fire escape leading to the dormitory. Out of luck! The door was locked. The young postulant hammered frantically on it, screaming, "Sister Labouré, Sister Labouré!"

While Catherine rushed down, Marie could make out the dark form approaching her. It was neither ghost nor lunatic, but the chaplain on his way home! Sr. Labouré, candle in hand, opened the door.

"What's the matter, my child?"

Embarrassed, Marie blurted out her story of the dead man, the madman, the leaves.... Would Catherine mock the weak-nerved postulant? Not a bit. She accompanied her to the dormitory, through dark corridors where the candle cast shadows on the ceiling—but shadows that were now no longer threatening. Catherine took off the bedspread and disappeared into the kitchen while Marie got undressed, then came back with a glass of sugared orange-flower water.

After that, "little Marie" slept "like a trooper." At 4:00 A.M. the rising bell rang. Marie tried to open her heavy eyelids, but a soft whisper reassured her. "Ssh, sshh!" Catherine was saying to her companions. "The little one is asleep...."

Postulants were progressively trained to get up at 4:00. They "lay in" three times a week for the first month, twice a week for the second month, and after that could be excused from early rising when circumstances required. Catherine, in charge of the house, had diagnosed Marie's need for a longer rest.[7]

Indeed, Catherine felt closer to the younger ones, for as time went on she saw the branches of her own generation being cut away, while those of middle age were taken up with the main tasks of running the house. More and more, she dreamed of death as of a bill that would soon be presented for payment.

Journey to heaven

Not long after the Commune, Catherine had a dream that she later innocently talked about to her niece Marie-Antoinette.

> I had just died and arrived in heaven, where I went in by a brightly shining door. There I first of all met my father, then my youngest brother [Auguste], and then your mother. I said to my father, "Isn't Louise here, then?" [Louise was her eldest sister]. My father answered, "No, she isn't here, but we're waiting for her!"

A macabre dream? Neither Auguste nor Tonine (Marie-Antoinette's mother) were yet dead. Marie-Antoinette was a realist and a tease. She exclaimed, "But Auntie, one shouldn't believe in dreams; that's superstitious!" "There are dreams and dreams," replied Catherine sententiously.[8]

Did she mean that "there are dreams that one ought to believe in"? What degree of confidence did she attach to this one?

"Alas, she didn't tell me," answered Marie-Antoinette when these questions were put to her.

But the dreamer was haunted by her dream. Later she told it to her nephew Philippe Meugniot, Marie-Antoinette's brother. His version is a little different. When she got to heaven, Catherine said to Tonine, "You're the youngest daughter. How come you got to heaven first?"

"Why not?" Tonine replied.

"This dream affected me deeply," said Catherine, though she pretended not to put too much credence in it.

It was in December 1873 that Philippe came to confide in his aunt with a huge, worrying burden. At the age of 29, he had just been sounded out about becoming superior of the seminary of St. Pons in the Montpellier diocese. Furthermore, the house was "in difficulties."

"Pray that this won't happen!" he said to Catherine. She replied quietly, "I'll pray that God's will be done."

"God's will" confirmed that this heavy burden was to be his.[9]

Neither of them seem to have spoken again about the prediction she had made when he was still a lad–"If you want to join these men...it's possible to become a superior...." He was becoming one before the age of 30, which was quite exceptional. Neither does he seem to have reminded his aunt about what she had told him in confidence in 1871–how she had given him a bad example in *herself* refusing the burden of being a superior....

With age, Catherine became more open for people to confide in. It was around this same time (1873 or 1874) that in the presence of Sr. Cosnard (by now "Sister of Office" [i.e., Assistant to the Directress] at the seminary) she told her sister, Marie-Louise, about the dream which had lit up the path of her vocation: the call from the old man whom she had recognized long after as St. Vincent. Sr. Cosnard was moved by Catherine's accent as she spoke about St. Vincent's *look,* which was still with her.[d]

Farewell to Tonine

Catherine's premonitory dream about deaths in the family began to come true in October 1872, when Tonine fell ill. In April 1873, she was confined to bed for good. She suffered much. Catherine was a frequent visitor during recreation time, for the house was not far away–5 Rue Crozatier in the twelfth *arrondissement.* This was a comfort for Tonine.

In mid-January 1874, Tonine fell into a sort of coma. Turned toward the wall, she no longer seemed to be in a state where her position could be changed. The bed had to be pulled into the middle of the room in order to look after her. She did not speak and seemed unconscious. Word got to Catherine, who arrived on January 16 at 1:00 P.M.–recreation time. She was still accountable to the elderly people for her time.

This was the first time she had found Tonine in such a state. Marie-Antoinette and her two daughters, Marthe and Jeanne, were present; they were silent as Tonine seemed to be "no longer there." Catherine made them leave the room. She shut the door, but they could hear talking inside the room, and this went on for a period of time. After an hour, Catherine reappeared. "Go and see your mother," she said. "She wants to talk to you." And Catherine went straight off to Enghien, to care for the miseries of her elderly charges.

Marie-Antoinette, Marthe (8½ years old), and Jeanne (aged 7) rushed into the room. Tonine greeted them, smiling from her pillow. She seemed happy. She looked affectionately at her two granddaughters. Everything in her heart was conveyed by her commonplace words, "Always be good, won't you!"

"Did Aunt Catherine revive her?" asked one of the two children.

She did not have the time to go into anything more deeply. After an hour, the sick woman fell back into a coma. She gradually became weaker, and the next day at 4:00 A.M. she breathed her last. It was January 20, 1874, the twenty-second anniversary of the Virgin's appearance to Marie-Alphonse Ratisbonne, convert of the Miraculous Medal.[10]

The same year, Catherine got her two grandnieces into the sisters' School at 77 Rue de Reuilly. They tell us:

> There we had the satisfaction of seeing our Aunt Catherine nearly every day. We were especially attached to her because, although having more delicate features, she looked like our grandmother [Tonine] who was no longer with us. During playtime, after the midday meal, we often saw her crossing the courtyard of the Reuilly house to return to the Rue de Picpus house. We would run to her and go with her right down to the end of the garden.[11]

One day she took them out for a walk. It was a special occasion for them; but Catherine also wanted to make someone else happy. She took them to the St. John of God Brothers' Hospital in the Rue Oudinot where her brother Charles Labouré "had come from Burgundy to have an operation for [gall] stones. His condition was sufficiently serious for it to be presumed that he would not live for long [...]. We did not know this great-uncle. She thought it a good thing to introduce us to him," recalled Marthe Duhamel who, thirty years later, retained a clear memory of this unexpected and "conspiratorial" adventure with Catherine.[e]

Visit to the Superior General

Fr. Etienne, Superior General, died on March 12 of the same year, 1874. He breathed his last at exactly 11:00, conscious and free from pain. Three days before he had asked for the Anointing of the Sick, which he had received in the presence of the whole community.

> My mission is ended.... I am going to meet the great family in heaven. I ask pardon of all those that I may have hurt. Yes, I have loved the two families of St. Vincent.[f]

Indeed, he had guided the wonderful advancement of those two families. Not long after his election, apparently, he had finally been told that Catherine was the visionary. She left a handwritten note describing their last meeting. On that occasion she had renewed her request for the chapel at the Rue du Bac to be opened to the public. She had also submitted to him her wish for Mary to be venerated within the community under the title of *Queen of the Universe*. He had replied in an evasive but encouraging fashion:

"Well, Sr. Catherine, did the Blessed Virgin tell you *when* she wished to be honored under this title? When she does tell you, we will do what has to be done. Pray for that. The Blessed Virgin wants something of you."[12]

On September 11, 1874, Fr. Boré became Superior General. Not long after his election, concerned to throw light on her conduct, he summoned Catherine. Together with the "major superiors," he questioned her "about the revelations with which she had been honored in 1830. The result of this was a kind of reflected light around her, which contributed to her reputation for sanctity," Fr. Chinchon, her confessor, assures us. Nevertheless, she appeared disconcerted by this unexpected interrogation and scarcely said a word. She was dissembling.[13]

For France, these were dark and toilsome years. The executions of communards went on until June 6, 1874. But the country was rising out of its ruins. Catherine carried on with her hard work, keeping her ears open.

In the autumn of 1875, the Abbé Olmer rang at the door which Catherine was minding. He was a physically strong person, but also a holy one, and at this time he was preoccupied with building. He was Jewish in origin, almost unheard of for a priest. As a baby, he had seemed to be dying—a hopeless case—so his wet-nurse had thought it best to baptize him. The result was not another Mortara case (1858). Rather, his relatives were affected by the unexpected cure and converted to Christianity one after the other. Abbé Olmer had been renowned during the 1871 Commune for his courage and devotion and for an escape from certain death. The previous year (1874), he had been nominated administrator of the new parish founded in the locality. He already had two curates and was constructing a church. It was to be dedicated to St. Radegunde, but a movement was afoot for our Lady to be the patron saint. This was Catherine's wish—she seemed to have second sight where the Virgin Mary was concerned. Her greeting to the Abbé was cordial and unexpected: "Good morning, Fr. Parish-Priest-of-the-Immaculate Conception!"

"But I am not the parish priest!"
"You will be!"
"All right, but the parish's name is St. Radegunde!"
"It will be called the Immaculate Conception!"[14]

Fr. Olmer was installed there as parish priest two years later on September 29, 1877, and it was the first church in the Paris diocese to be dedicated to the Immaculate Conception.

Catherine continued to feel sorry that the chapel in the Rue du Bac was not open to pilgrims, for she was still being urged by our Lady's promise that "people will know where I have been."[g]

"The problem is still that of opening the chapel to the public in a place where there is a [large] novitiate like ours," explained Sr. Cosnard. However, Catherine would sigh when hearing about the cure of a deaf-mute at Lourdes and say, "You know, all these miracles should have taken place in our chapel!"[15]

"She was also sorry about the neglect of the medal," added Sr. Cosnard. "She said to me, 'There are some sisters in the seminary who are not wearing the medal and no one had thought to give it to them.' I asked her, 'How do you know?' and she replied, 'Ah! Ask around and you'll see!' I had to agree that it was true."[16]

Catherine asked people "to pray a lot," but also "to add [to prayer] the spirit of penitence and sacrifice." "Too much do we ask for what we want, and not enough for what the good Lord wants," she said to Sr. Tranchemer, who too easily took her own legitimist desires for those of God himself.[17]

Marshal MacMahon had been elected President of the Republic on May 24, 1873.[18] His wife became a friend of the house. She was a strong woman, generous and discreet, and she came without fuss.[19] She was let in on the secret of who the visionary sister was, and Sr. Dufès found an excuse to introduce her to Catherine—but nothing more than that. Catherine understood, but did not run away. A few days before, a poor woman had come to ask for 60 francs to pay her rent. Catherine had nothing to give the woman, and she was going to be evicted. When Catherine told this story to the Marshal's wife, she was moved and gave the 60 francs.[20]

Reduced to the ranks

In the same year, 1874, Sr. Dufès decided to replace Catherine and put someone else in charge of the Enghien hospice.

What she needed was a strong arm to tighten the bonds of unity between the two houses and overcome certain tensions that existed. So she put Sr. Angélique Tanguy, aged 36, in charge of the hospice, giving her the title of assistant superior. This was quite an ordeal for Catherine; it is always difficult to return to the ranks in a situation where one has been in control, and Catherine still had the work of the foundation well in hand—even if the foundation had become a side issue next to the busy hive of humanity that the Rue de Reuilly had become. Catherine's responsibilities merited her a place of honor "seated next to the superior" in the refectory and also "during recreation."[h]

Catherine was not in the least concerned about protocol, but she liked her work. Her peasant childhood had taught her to defend her domain and the customs rooted in it. She was imperious and quick-tempered. How would she react?

The sisters asked themselves all this and more when Sr. Dufès announced Sr. Angélique's promotion and her additional status of Assistant, which Catherine had never had even though she had fulfilled the same function. The sisters working with the elderly preferred Catherine to the new "boss," a woman more imbued with the new Reuilly style, less bending and less experienced. But Catherine hastened to tell Sr. Dufès: "Oh, Sister, we will obey her as if she were you yourself!"[21]

This was neither flattery nor diplomacy to get around the new Assistant, for Sr. Tanguy was not even there at the time of the announcement (she made this clear herself during the canonization process). It was with apprehension that she tackled Sr. Catherine, whose place she was taking: "I hope that you'll be all right and that you won't make life miserable for me!" she said the same day.

"Oh, no, my good Sister," replied Catherine, "you'll have nothing to fear from me."[22]

The sacrifice had been made, complete. Now let us throw light on the details of how it was accomplished.

Since Sr. Dufès had been living in the Rue de Reuilly, at the other end of the garden (1868), Catherine held the keys—a symbol of her power over the house. Each day she locked the doors on the Rue de Picpus and took the keys to her bedroom.

"Hang on to the keys," the sisters advised Catherine. They did not see the newcomer from the other house in a good light; she would simply be an arm of the other house and its plans—plans which would hardly be for the good of the elderly residents.

These instruments of temptation would never know that Sr. Tanguy had crept up and overheard the conversation. She did not reveal herself but slipped away while Catherine replied, "But of course: this evening I shall hand them over to Sister Assistant, since she is the superior's representative."

That evening, Sr. Tanguy was on the lookout for Catherine's footsteps. The clicking of the heavy locks reached her, amplified in the silence of the night, as Catherine locked them one by one. After the final click, Sr. Catherine's calm steps came near. She put the bunch of keys down near Sr. Tanguy's bed, the last sound in the Great Silence that would only be broken by the rising bell the next morning.[23]

The next day in the refectory Catherine's place had been laid as usual in the place of honor near Sr. Dufès, the superior. The refectory sister had not moved it out of respect for "the fine old lady," with the object of keeping "her place" for her. Sr. Dufès allowed this to go ahead, out of deference for Catherine, who did not realize what was going on—until the moment when she noticed Sr. Tanguy sitting in a lower place. Catherine did not move then, but after the meal she went to look for the refectory sister, Sr. de le Haye St. Hilaire, aged 28, and said to her: "Please relay my place and give my place to Sister Assistant...I find it tiring to have to go around to that side of the table," she added, to give her request a meaning devoid of implications. Sr. de la Haye St. Hilaire also adds:

> It was said to me with such simplicity that I could have been mistaken, but the problem involved in reaching the place that she had had up to then [...] was too insignificant for me to have any doubt as to her motivation [...]: deference and humility.[24]

Catherine retained freedom of spirit in the responsibilities left to her. One day, helped by Sr. Cantel, she was giving the elderly "some helpings that had been left over." She liked to give generously. The Assistant passed by and reprimanded her. Catherine kept a respectful silence, but her companion was shocked.

"Don't worry about it; I am quite in order; I have permission."

According to Sr. Cantel, this meant that she had received authorization from Sr. Dufès herself; but Catherine had not taken advantage of the fact in order not to provoke loss of face for the young Assistant, still fragile in the exercise of her authority.[25]

Catherine supported the Assistant in every situation. For example, Sr. Jeanne Maurel tells us how "one day, when there was Exposition all day, knowing how happy she would have been to go to the chapel, I said to her, 'Sister, today it's my job to look after the door and yours to go to God's house.' But Sr. Catherine replied: 'Sr. Angélique has ordered it [this way]: that is enough [for me].'"[26]

A final glimpse of what these sacrifices must have cost Catherine comes in a remark she made one day to Sr. Tanguy:

> "I suffered much, I had great problems. There was one moment when I thought of asking to be moved to another house. I prayed, I consulted my confessor, and I stayed."[27]

"Milk soup" and patience

Sr. Jeanne Maurel, who arrived in October 1875, aged 31, gives a unique insight on Catherine, who initiated her into her first jobs: vestment sister and pigeon-keeper.

Coming from a family that had not brought her up to do manual work, she realized that she was scarcely "cut out" for the first job and "even less" for the second. But, she says, Catherine "reprimanded me with so much charity that I was quite overwhelmed by it."[28]

One day Sr. Jeanne allowed a pigeon to die. Catherine was grieved by this, but with much friendliness she made her understand her mistake, for the younger sister would have been prone to discouragement.[29]

Sr. Jeanne was very afraid of looking after the elderly people. Catherine helped her to get over this and said to her sententiously one day: "Whatever you may think of it, you're the one that will replace me."[i] This is precisely what happened. When Catherine started to go downhill a few months later, it was Sr. Jeanne who took over fom her.

On another occasion Sr. Jeanne was very worried about an elderly man who was not a Catholic.

> It looked very much as if he would die without being converted. I shared my anxiety [with Catherine...]. She replied, "You're lacking in confidence. Nothing is impossible for the good Lord."
>
> Her prayer was answered since even this man, before he passed on, asked to see the chaplain.[j]

Sr. Jeanne also experienced the benefits of Catherine's "radiance."

> I loved to be in her place in the chapel when she wasn't there. One of our sisters reproached me for it, saying that it was very arrogant of me to take her place. I wanted that place because, for me, it was a saint who prayed there and there I was able to pray as if I were kneeling on a saint's tomb.[k]

She also relates:

> One day I got very impatient with the sister whose job it was to bring me breakfast to give to the elderly. She was always late and this often prevented me from being at Mass at the beginning. I was angry about it. Sr. Catherine said to me, "You must give everything to the good Lord and not go around grumbling." And she herself lived by this principle.[30]

But what struck Sr. Jeanne more than anything else was Catherine's inexhaustible patience with Blaisine "The Blot," her helper at the door.

She was only kept on through sheer charity; she was very dishonest, even with Sr. Catherine. Several times I wanted to go and give Sr. Dufès the real picture so that she would throw the girl out, but Sr. Catherine always stopped me, "because this person is incapable of doing anything in the world [outside]."[31]

At that time Catherine had to put up with a lot of whimsical teasing from a facetious sister, whom she also teased in her turn, referring to this "character" as "the little imbecile from the asylum." This young sister wanted to probe into Catherine's secrecy regarding the apparition of the medal; so one day during recreation, right in front of Catherine, who was bent over her knitting on the right of Sister Assistant, she said "The one who saw her saw nothing but a picture!"

The last word of that remark in fact merely echoed Fr. Aladel in his pamphlet.[1] But sister said it in a skeptical and deliberately provocative tone of voice. Without thinking, Catherine drew herself up and the blood ran to her face. "My dear, the sister who saw the Blessed Virgin saw her in the flesh, just like you and me!"

Sr. Tanguy was presiding over the recreation period and changed the subject. For once, Catherine had been taken by surprise and had nearly given herself away.[32] She buried herself in her work again with a sort of indifference and did not say another word.

> Normally she was noticeable above all for her humility and her discretion. One day during recreation a young sister was supporting an opposing view to Sr. Catherine's.
>
> As Catherine stood up for her point of view, the superior intervened:

> "I see that you are vigorously upholding your opinions."
>
>   Catherine got down on her knees in the middle of the assembled company and asked pardon.... "I see truly that I am nothing but a proud woman."
>
>   To see this aged sister humbling herself in this way brought tears to the eyes of her companions.[33]

Sr. Jeanne's most remarkable memory is Catherine's advice when faced by problems: "One must have confidence."³⁴

ANONYMITY IN PERIL

Catherine's secret was being penetrated from all sides. She had a great deal to do.

From the seminary

Antoinette Montesquiou de Fezensac (aged 27) entered the seminary in April 1873. She overheard someone telling Sr. Mauche, Sister of Office, that "the visionary" was "supposed to be" Sr. Catherine Labouré. Sr. Antoinette had a burning desire to meet her.... Sr. Mauche found an opportunity to arrange it: "This is the sister I was talking to you about." Sr. Antoinette tells us:

> I was overjoyed at this new knowledge and later I pointed out Sr. Catherine to a companion, saying: "That's the one!" Sr. Catherine noticed it and gave me a severe look. This disconcerted me completely and I no longer dared to look at her.ᵐ

From the Archbishopric

Monsignor Fages, future Vicar General of Paris, was at this time private secretary to the Coadjutor Bishop, Monsignor Richard. Monsignor Fages came to Enghien along with Abbé Odelin in order to delve into the famous secret. He organized things so that he would arrive at the very time when Catherine herself was at the door. He started to broach the subject, but she had "seen him coming," buckled shoes and all, and very quickly she "cut him short, briskly."

"You wanted to know the way, Father; here it is!"

And when the two ecclesiastics tried to persist, she said, "I'll take you to my superior. She will answer your questions."³⁵

Sr. Marie-Louise de la Haye St. Hilaire (30 years old) was one day entertaining her friends the Count and Countess d'Avenel de Nantré. She thought it would be all right to share with them discreetly the "secret of the house."

> At the very moment when I was showing them to the door, we met Sr. Catherine and I whispered to Madame d'Avenel: "This is the sister who had the vision of the Miraculous Medal."

Contrary to all my expectations, Monsieur d'Avenel turned around and said to Sr. Catherine, "Oh, Sister, I am delighted to see and to be able to greet the sister who was granted the great favor of the vision of the Miraculous Medal."

Not knowing what to do, I said to Madame d'Avenel, "Madame, if you only knew what your husband was doing, how far he is running counter to my wishes. The sister does not want anyone to know."

In a very self-composed manner, Madame d'Avenel said to her husband: "Joseph, you're making a mistake. Sister did not say that!"

All this time Sr. Catherine was shaking her head and pretending to be highly amazed. During the day, Sister Superior told me to ask sister's [Catherine's] pardon, which I did straight away.

"Ma petite," said Sr. Catherine, kindly and very gently, "you shouldn't go around talking like that off the top of your head."

And she bore me no grudge whatsoever concerning the incident.

According to Sr. Desmoulins, Sr. de la Haye St. Hilaire said to Catherine, in great embarrassment, "Sister, at the seminary I was told that it was a sister in the house at Enghien who had seen the Most Holy Virgin!"[36]

Mind reading?

Catherine certainly knew how to conceal herself, but did she also have the gift of reading people's minds? This was the impression she gave to Sr. Darlin during one of her visits to her beloved Rue du Bac "about 1875."

> I was supervising in the small parlor in the seminary. Several sisters from Enghien came to see their postulant and an animated conversation began. One of the sisters remained a little isolated, not taking part in the conversation. I had been told that it was the sister who had had the apparitions of the Most Holy Virgin.... I would dearly have liked to talk to the venerable old lady, but I did not dare to. At that very instant she left her seat, came to me at the desk and said, looking kindly at me: "Sister, come with me to the Ste-Marie classroom to say an *Ave Maria* to the Most Holy Virgin."
>
> Now this class was precisely the one that I was in charge of. I got up without a word, very happy. I was flabbergasted by her words, for she had never seen me before.

But Sr. Darlin fell into the trap of allowing the "visionary" to see her devotion to her, she was so overcome. As soon as she saw that, Catherine excused herself and left.[37]

THE GREAT SECRET (SPRING 1876)

Tension with Sr. Dufès

At the beginning of 1876, Sr. Dufès' annual report on Catherine testifies briefly: *very bad health. She does not get up* (i.e., "at four o'clock in the morning," the hour prescribed by the Rule).

In spite of this physical decline, Sr. Dufès pays her this compliment: *Sturdy piety, excellent performance of her duties*.[38] This praise carries some weight, for Sr. Dufès' reports are quite candid and sometimes without pity. Nine sisters are stated to have "bad," "very bad," or "intolerable" characters. Less than half get the same approbation as Catherine, who managed to "perform her duties" despite a weariness that grew heavier as each day passed.

Sr. Dufès nevertheless adds: *Very lively character; sense of judgment passable*. In other words, she sometimes did not see eye to eye with Catherine and still felt impelled to treat her harshly.[n]

The most astonishing thing is the humility with which Catherine put up with Sr. Dufès' especial severity toward her. Not only did she accept all the reproaches and stifle the fires inside her, which made her blush, but, even when the scolding was bad enough to erect a barrier, Catherine would herself make the first move to re-establish contact, just as if nothing had happened. She would think up some permission to ask for (one of those that the superior never refused) and go and knock on the superior's office door: "Sister, would you be kind enough to allow me to...?"

Contact was renewed, permission granted. The superior was happy that everything was smoothed over; it calmed the pricking of her conscience over her "impulsion" to put Catherine to the test in this way. It is amazing that the "Labouré pride" could be squashed to such an extent. Bernadette was not able to act thus with Mother Marie-Thérèse Vauzou.

Catherine loses her confessor

In the spring of 1876, it was not a "small permission" that Catherine went to ask for, knocking on the door of Sr. Dufès' office: "Sister, would you be kind enough to allow me to go and see Fr. Boré?"

She wanted to see the Superior General.

"Are you sure that's all you want?" asked Sr. Dufès, sarcastically.

Catherine went on calmly: "He has withdrawn our confessor, Fr. Chinchon, and I need in conscience to speak to Fr. Chinchon. I would like to ask Fr. Boré's permission to do so."

Fr. Chinchon had been relieved of his outside activities—including Reuilly—in order to devote himself exclusively to his students and his novices. But Catherine felt that her end was near. She began to say that "she wouldn't see the year out."[39] She was seized by a sense of urgency to sort out one of the duties of her mission that had been rebuffed for forty years. It was not that Fr. Chinchon was more open than Aladel had been. Indeed, Sr. Cosnard tells us that he was hard on Catherine.

> Sometime between 1864 and 1873 (I cannot be more exact), Fr. Chinchon [...] publicly—in a sisters' meeting—humiliated Sr. Catherine. He told her off for wanting to pass off her dreams as reality and [for] ridiculing an entire community.
>
> Sr. Catherine remained humble, quiet, in her place, without replying nor showing any sign of discontent. It was very striking [...]. Was he talking about the apparitions [...]? Probably, but he did it in such a way that you could easily misunderstand. I came out of the meeting almost scandalized by Fr. Chinchon's behavior. Afterward, I thought that he had wanted to test Sr. Catherine's virtue, for he never normally talked like that, being the soul of discretion.[p]

In spite of this severity, a sort of dialogue and unspoken confidence sprang up between the confessor and his spiritual pupil. When he was worried by something or other, Fr. Chinchon would ask Catherine to "offer up a Communion for my students and novices!"

Catherine prepared the ground around him to obtain what was still in a state of suspended animation: the altar and the statue of the Virgin with the globe on the spot where the first apparition had taken place.

Fr. Chinchon listened to her more than Aladel. The sisters who knew Catherine's lack of wordiness were astonished at her rather lengthy confessions, which held up the penitents who followed.

"Sr. Catherine," one of them teased her, "you are so brisk with everything. Why then do your confessions take so long? Are you over-scrupulous?"

"My dear, we all take as much time as we need, and that's all there is to it!"[40] This sudden gulf which had opened between her and Chinchon was catastrophic. There was no hope of getting anything from his replacement, Fr. Laurent. Catherine therefore tried to set down on April 10, doubtless for Fr. Chinchon's sake, an account of the third apparition (second apparition of the medal), in which she stressed the point that had failed to be recognized: the Virgin held "in her hand a ball, which represented the globe, surmounted by a little cross."[q]

Top-level refusal

This was why, in the month of May, Catherine asked to see Fr. Boré to get his authorization to speak to her confessor. Sr. Dufès at first was not in favor, but ended by giving her consent. Alas! The interview met with defeat. No exceptions would be made, no precedents existed!

Tomorrow at 10:00

Catherine returned to Reuilly with her eyes still full of tears. Sr. Tanguy was amazed by this—no one had ever seen Catherine cry, even in the deepest of family sorrows.

"Even so, I still need to talk to this confessor!"[41] she said to Sr. Dufès, and added, "I will not live much longer now. I think the time has come to speak—you know what about."

Moved, Sr. Dufès replied, "My good Sr. Catherine, it is true that I suspect very strongly that you received the Miraculous Medal, but, through discretion, I have never spoken to you about it."

"Very good, Sister, tomorrow I will ask the Blessed Virgin's advice in my prayers. If she tells me to tell everything, I will do so. If not, I will keep silence. If the Blessed Virgin allows me to speak, I will get someone to come and fetch you at 10:00. If you come to Enghien, we will be quieter in the parlor."

Sr. Dufès confided this dramatic turn of events to Sr. Tanguy, adding, "You can imagine how I'll be on tenterhooks until tomorrow morning!"[42]

The next morning, Catherine signaled to her. She rushed over. "The interview began at 10:00 and did not end until midday." What Sr. Dufès found so astonishing was the sight of Catherine, normally not much of a talker, expressing herself "concisely and fluently."

She related the first apparitions: St. Vincent's heart, Christ in the Eucharist, and the Virgin on the chair on July 18, 1830–these last quite unknown up till then. She kept to herself the secret of the confidences imparted and the handwritten account of 1856 that no one knew of.

Sr. Dufès, whose harshness toward Catherine had been in the nature of a defense mechanism,

> felt herself several times wanting to throw herself at Catherine's knees, to beg pardon for having known so little of her. [However, she did not

actually do so] but could not prevent herself from murmuring, "You were highly favored." "Oh," Catherine replied, "I was nothing but an instrument. It was not for me that the Blessed Virgin appeared. I did not even know how to write! It is within the community that I learned what I know. And if the Blessed Virgin chose me, an ignoramus, it was in order that no one should be able to doubt her."[43]

Here, as frequently happened, Catherine is an interior echo of St. Vincent, who said, "I was chosen because I was nothing; no one can doubt that such great things are God's work."

The Virgin with the globe

Catherine was getting around to the problem that had troubled her "for so long": the Blessed Virgin had held a globe in her hands. No representation portrayed her in this way. Fr. Aladel had always refused.

Sr. Dufès was perplexed. What new thing was this? And how could such a representation be reconciled with that of the medal—the Virgin with open hands? Really, Catherine was going too far.

"People will say that you're mad!"

"Oh, it won't be the first time! Fr. Aladel called me a 'blasted wasp' when I persisted on this subject!"

Sr. Dufès understood the meaning of the image: the gesture of a mother and the Queen of the Universe. Our Lady protects and offers to God this earthly globe—and yet Sr. Dufès was baffled. "What happened to this ball?" she asked, worried at not being able to reconcile the two images.

"I no longer saw anything but the rays of light falling from her hands," Catherine replied evasively.

Sr. Dufès was more and more bewildered. "What will become of the medal if this is published?"

"Oh, there is no need to touch the Miraculous Medal!"

From 1839 onward, Fr. Aladel had certainly made it clear to her that it would not be appropriate to change what had been established and had proved itself, but that it would be all right to have a complementary portrayal. Fr. Aladel had envisaged a painting by Letaille.[r]

Sr. Dufès pressed harder. "If Aladel refused, he must have had his reasons."

"It was the martyrdom of my life," admitted Catherine, who could not resign herself to the omission.

"Do you know anyone who could confirm what you say?"

"There is Sr. Grand."

At the time, she had been at the Secretariat. Now she was superior at Riom. She had worked with Fr. Aladel.

The same afternoon, bowled over by what she had been told, Sr. Dufès passed on the secrets to Sr. Tanguy. She wanted to be convinced, but was confused by this difference between the apparition and the medal. Wasn't Catherine just laying it on a bit thick in her old age?

The superior recalled to mind several little details which had fed her bewilderment and her aggression with regard to "the visionary." In the time of Fr. Etienne, just after the Commune, hadn't Catherine had the idea that at a depth of "1m 50" [5 feet] a "flat stone like a tombstone" would be found (Sr. Dufès had noted this down without understanding) and also "the wherewithal to build a chapel," or rather "a church"? She had thought of buried treasure, and since the extraordinary fulfillment of Catherine's predictions during the Commune had given her a certain influence, she had informed Fr. Etienne. They had decided to dig. Where? Here, Catherine was in difficulties. Excavations were made in vain. They were tried again under Fr. Boré. Nothing was found except a blocked up well which necessitated digging down to a depth of 18 meters [59 feet].

"Sister, you have got it wrong!" Sr. Dufès had said bluntly. Catherine had not argued. She had humbly replied, "Well, Sister, I have made a mistake. I thought I was correct. I am very glad that the truth is known!"[t] But what a waste of time and effort digging in vain like that![44]

Was Catherine mistaken again this time? To check up, Sr. Dufès wrote to Sr. Grand. Her reply was some time in coming, not being sent off until June 24. Sr. Grand apologized for the delay, due to overwork (there's never any slacking where the poor are concerned!). She confirmed Catherine's amazing version:

> Yes, good Sr. Dufès, our sweet Queen did appear, holding the ball of the world in her virginal and blessed hands, warming it with her love, holding it to her merciful heart, and looking at it with ineffable tenderness. I even still have a sketch produced a long time ago showing her like this.[u] I do not know if it is with our papers or our books, for this goes back many years. The worthy and venerable Fr. Aladel—perhaps at the request of the sister—had thought to preserve this memorable souvenir, while commissioning a second image representing this apparition; but things rested there.

Sr. Grand added a heartfelt but vague plea for harmony between the two visions, with and without the globe.[45]

Visionary and sculptor

On receiving this confirmation, Sr. Dufès took Catherine off to the Rue du Bac, after an "early breakfast." And "while" the community was having "lunch," she took her to the chapel. There, she got Catherine to show her the exact place where the statue and the altar should be put: it was on the right-hand side, looking toward the high altar, on the spot where St. Joseph's picture was mounted.

Sr. Dufès submitted a request to the superiors. There was no question of granting it. That would mean two statues of the Virgin and would cause difficulties in high places. But there was nothing to prevent the plan being brought to fruition as a private project for the Reuilly house.

Sr. Dufès saw to everything. She took precise details on what was required, without, however, leaving us any record of the questioning that this must have entailed. Chevalier alone made some notes (after 1878) about various definite characteristics in the specification, according to Sr. Dufès:

> Neither too young nor too smiling, but with a gravity mingled "with sadness that disappeared during the vision when the face was lit up with the bright light [...] of love, above all at the moment when she prayed."[v]

This gravity had lent to the apparition the face of a woman "about forty years old."[w] Catherine herself, in the autograph of April 10,[x] described how: "The Virgin offered the globe to our Lord. It is impossible to reproduce that. It would be impossible for me to describe it."

Sr. Dufès ordered the statue from Froc-Robert and sent Catherine to the workshop to inspect the model. Her assurance and her criticisms rang a bell with the sculptor: "Aren't you the sister who had the apparitions?"[y] This was sufficient to cut short the conversation. Catherine slipped away with the confused look that she adopted on such occasions. This kind of interference by a peasant woman in the work of an artist made her companion roar with laughter. "What's it got to do with her? Has she gone off her head?"

Catherine could not hide her disappointment. No, the statue was not accurate. Sr. Dufès took her to the shops in St. Suplice to see if a good model could be found there–but without success.

A few weeks later the statue was delivered to Reuilly. Sr. Dufès would not put it in the chapel, but had it discreetly placed in her office. There, Catherine was invited to come and see it. She looked at it carefully. Several details from her description had been scrupulously carried out: the golden globe surmounted by a cross, the "greenish serpent" beneath the feet of the apparition, but still she could not show any enthusiasm for it. Rather, she "pulled a face."

A little disappointed herself, Sr. Dufès lectured her: "Don't be too difficult over it. Earthly artists cannot realize what they have not seen!"[46]

End to martyrdom

The imparting of the confidences and the realization of the statue were a great relief for Catherine and brought her much peace. Too many obstacles had bruised her, too many refusals had torn her between obedience to the Virgin, whose messenger she was, and obedience to the confessors who rejected her requests. Her conscience had suffered violently. But now anxiety disappeared, wounds started to heal. This unlooked-for sign gave her hope that the statue would one day find a place in the chapel on the spot where she wanted it, on the spot she had pointed out with complete confidentiality to Sr. Dufès. And Catherine's hope was not misplaced. Four years later, after her death, Fr. Fiat, the new Superior General, had a larger version made of the statue produced by Sr. Dufès. He put it on an altar erected on the spot indicated by Catherine. (The statue is preserved today in the Rue du Bac in the *Sale des Retraites* [Retreat Room].)

How important was it?

Accountable to our Lady for what had not been done, Catherine now felt discharged of her obligation and ready for the departure from earthly life which she now felt was coming close. At the time when her body was abandoning her, the serenity in the depths of her being rose up to the surface. Her old age became the beautiful autumn of her life, but the peasant in her knew very well that these last joys were but the prelude to winter and death. It cost her nothing to see death approach in this way—she simply let herself be carried along toward this unknown encounter, as if on a journey toward the one loved.

What might follow was no longer her concern. Heaven and the superiors would look after that side of things.

How important was it to have this complementary portrayal of the Virgin with the globe? It is difficult to say. This statue has not had the tiniest influence compared with that of the Miraculous Medal, which came about at just the right time to awaken within the Church a new springtime of gifts and conversions. If Fr. Aladel had not been too scrupulous over details, he had certainly respected the basic essentials: the invocation to *Mary, conceived without sin,* the most classic representation of the Immaculate Conception, and the rays of light coming from the hands—a new symbol of the light of God through the medium of her who gave birth to the Word. He had succeeded in getting this new idea through by choosing the most well known, the most accepted, the most traditional form of Mary Immaculate, following the exact advice of the Archbishop. In this way he had rendered the image clearer and more acceptable to the people of God, which was certainly beneficial twenty-two years before this doctrine was defined by Pius IX. He had also avoided the problems that would be encountered by the Virgin with the globe: less than a year after its installation in the Rue du Bac in 1880, Rome had this statue removed on January 22, 1881. It would take four years and an intervention with Pope Leo XIII himself, by a Vincentian Bishop, to re-establish in the chapel the Virgin with the globe—but with the proviso that no reference was made to the apparition.[z]

Aladel had also skirted the problem of portraying in a single image two different balls representing the world: the one in the hands and the one beneath the feet, and the obscure indication that the first of these in some way disappeared in the rays of light—a detail difficult to represent materially, especially in the tiny format of a medal.

But it was legitimate that Catherine would want to see this complementary element portrayed—an element, moreover, that was not without a basis in tradition. In the history of religious images, the Virgin with the globe is rare but not unknown.

The gesture of protection and offering fit in well with the message of the Miraculous Medal. The globe between the hands also signified that our good Mother was Queen of the Universe.

A word here about the "relativity" of visions in general. The Church has always insisted on this, stressing the contrast between private revelations of this sort and the revelation of the Gospel. They are only one kind of special gift, destined to awaken new hope in people.

It's the last time

Without anxiety, at each liturgical festival Catherine would repeat what eventually became a constant refrain: "It's the last time that I shall celebrate this feast."[aa] People thought she was rambling on, for she did not seem to be getting any worse. But she persisted in saying it all the same. For example, on August 15, feast of the Assumption, when Marie-Antoinette Duhamel brought Catherine's two grandnieces to see her, Marie-Antoinette relates:

> She gave them holy pictures as a reminder of the elder niece's First Communion.
> I remarked that there was no hurry, since [the younger one] was not due to make her First Communion until the following year. She answered,
> "Oh, my dear child, next year I shan't be there."
> "But it's still too early," persisted Marthe. "I don't make my First Communion until May!"
> "I know, but I won't be here by then. I would prefer to give [them] to you straight away."

She gave her a picture showing a girl making her First Communion, together with some souvenirs.

"But you're as well as ever," Marie-Antoinette Duhamel pursued.

"You don't want to believe me!" said Catherine pleasantly, without any loss of conviction. "You'll see!"[47]

On September 8, Philippe Meugniot visited Catherine. He did not know that it was the last time that he would see her. Sr. Dufès let him in on Catherine's secret. He had known nothing about it. But he did not dare to speak to her concerning it and was amazed to find her as discreet as ever.

Catherine's heart and her breathing were now giving her trouble, but she still managed to sit up in bed. He was struck by her calm and her "tranquility"; she was "ready to appear before God."

Catherine tried to make a joke of her enforced rest, which she found trying: "Here I am, lying here like a queen...."[48] Bernadette Soubirous would use the same simile in a letter to Mother Sophie Cresseil in 1876.

Toward the end of the month, Catherine was confined to bed again. Sr. Henriot came to see her and look after her in the absence of the usual sister infirmarian.

"Pray for me," she asked.

"Think of me and I'll pray for you," replied Catherine.

The following March, Sr. Henriot would remember this promise. She would keep vigil at Catherine's tomb, praying for another very sick sister. That sister would recover.[49]

A Radiant Autumn

Declining

Catherine was able to get up in October. Her decline was gradual: "weakening, listless, aged, worn out, exhausted" was how contemporary witnesses put it.[50] Sr. Henriot said that it seemed to her "that she was dying of listlessness." [bb]

"She no longer has her wits about her," said those who saw her sinking. [51]

"People have said that about plenty of others belonging to our Lord,"[52] replied Catherine, whose hearing was unimpaired and whose blue eyes still shone brightly behind her metal-rimmed spectacles.

Her heart weakened, her breathing became stifled. Leeches were applied to the small of her back to relieve her pain.[53] Her patience grew in proportion with the pains in her legs.

Sr. Combes was constantly amazed to see her "the whole time as if she were not suffering at all." When pain did show itself and those around her showed pity for her, she would say, "Isn't the good Lord worth a lot of suffering?"[54]

Final bouts of activity

Catherine had by now stopped waxing the floors with the heavy "galley-slaver" polisher;[55] she was excused from regular chores altogether. But when she was able to get up she would look after the door,[56] do little bits of extra washing, check through the elderly residents' lockers, and keep an eye on their diet—after all, she had been dealing with their problems for forty-six years and was very familiar with them![57] Her guiding principle was that everybody should have what he or she needed.

"In the final months of 1876," Catherine instructed the young sisters in the chores she was giving up. Sr. Cabanes, who worked in the kitchen, used to see Catherine arriving "every day, before each meal, to make sure that everything was just so." Catherine gave her lots of "little hints" with the greatest of "charity."[58]

"This is what I used to do," Catherine would say, "and those who preceded me. If you run into any difficulties, don't worry—I encountered others!"

On October 30, 1876, Catherine took up her pen and set down what our Lady had confided to her while seated in her mysterious chair in the Rue du Bac. "My child, the good Lord wants to entrust you with a mission."[59]

Around the same time, she said to Sr. Millon: "I shall die before next year and no hearse will be needed to take me to the cemetery!"

"You must be joking, Sister Catherine!"

"You'll see, my dear!"[cc]

November retreat

On November 5, 1876, Catherine was still strong enough to go to the motherhouse to make her retreat. She was taken there by carriage. The place was decorated with golden autumn leaves and Catherine showed her bravery there, following all the spiritual exercises. She would stay on her knees like the youngest sisters, in spite of her painful arthritis and swollen knees. She even refused a cushion she was offered to make it less painful for her.

Here, too, her "babbling" continued. "It's my last retreat, you know," she said to Sr. Pineau.[dd] Hardly anyone believed her. They thought it was an old lady's affectation, looking for sympathy...although she had said it quite simply.

When Catherine arrived, she went to see her older sister, Marie-Louise, and was not too pleased to find her in bed, even though she was in her eighties. "You coddle yourself too much," she said. "I think you could perfectly well get up if you wanted to!"[ee]

It was not a lack of compassion for physical disability. A little while before, she had been visiting a sick brother in the Lariboisière Hospital and had rushed to get out of the carriage first in order to help her aged sister; but in her haste she had sprained her wrist, not that this had prevented her from going through with the visit in good heart, with her hand all wrapped up. No, Catherine was now in her old age and knew very well what it cost in terms of effort to make one's old bones get up each morning. It wasn't like Fain anymore–she had been young then.[ff]

On this visit to the motherhouse, Catherine talked to Sr. Cosnard above all, her former companion at Reuilly between 1864 and 1873, who was now working in the seminary. There was a real empathy between her and Sr. Catherine, and Catherine hoped that through her she could transmit our Lady's message–still too little recognized.

Sr. Cosnard was one of those "in the know." Contained and discreet, although very fervent, Sr. Cosnard knew about sharing things on a deep level. In this way she managed to get Catherine to talk about the apparitions by means of large hints without Catherine having to reveal herself. Thus Catherine was able to confide in her the message which was so close to her heart.

> When she appeared to ONE OF OUR SISTERS [...], the Most Holy Virgin held a globe of the world in her hands. She was offering it [...]. No engraving of the apparitions portrays her like this. But she wants it and she wants an altar on the spot where she appeared.

And then again, regarding the seminary and the sisters' process of formation, it grieved Catherine that some of them did not even wear the medal and that the chapel at the Rue du Bac was still not open as a place of pilgrimage.

On the last day (November 14), Catherine asked Sr. Cosnard: "Take me to the seminary."

It was recreation time and no one was about. Catherine wanted to have one last sight of the two pictures of the apparitions painted by Lecerf in 1835—the first and the most carefully carried out of the pictures painted to commemorate our Lady's message given in the house of the Sisters of Charity. Catherine knelt down to pray. Then she got up (with considerable difficulty) and spent a long time gazing at the pictures that Aladel had shown her thirty-one years before. She lingered there too long. The bell rang for the end of recreation and the young sisters came back to the seminary. They watched the blue-eyed visitor, and suddenly one of them guessed: "Oh! It's the sister who saw the Blessed Virgin!"

Catherine came to, rapidly. "All right, Sister, all right!" she said dryly.

Had the whole thing been designed to "show her off"? Had Sr. Cosnard revealed her secret? Catherine left abruptly and went back to Reuilly without going to say goodbye. Sr. Cosnard was unhappy. Did Catherine think it was her fault? Was she cross? What a sad ending to so many happy meetings![60]

"Our jewels!"

Despite this incident, Catherine's stay at the Rue du Bac had turned out well. She valiantly took up her work again. On November 24, the eve of St. Catherine's feastday, Sr. Tranchemer, who was still always on hand, brought some children along to wish Catherine a happy feastday. Catherine was kneeling by the wash place in the courtyard. All by herself, she was washing the "old people's chairs"—the commodes, used for nighttime necessities at a time when there were no upstairs lavatories. It was not a very savory occupation. The children held their noses. Catherine smiled at their discomfiture and said, "That, my children, is what the Sisters of Charity are all about; these are *our* jewels!"

She washed her hands, took off her apron and—all clean and tidy again—said, "Now come here so that I can embrace you!"

This was a rare occurrence for, as Sr. Tranchemer relates elsewhere, Catherine "was not normally in the habit of embracing children; she would bob down and give them a light caress." But on a feastday, in traditional peasant style, embracing was the rule.

"Be really good, really obedient, and the Blessed Virgin will love you very much. I'll pray for you," she said, before going back to her work.[61]

On November 30, Auguste died. He was Catherine's "little crippled brother" whom she had looked after when they were both young. All his life he had remained handicapped, looked after by different people. On September 1, 1867, one of his brothers had put him in the Chartreuse at Dijon; in the Route de Plombières, this was the regional asylum. After nine years' confinement there, he died of an attack of pneumonia. Catherine had not seen him for a long time. The Benjamin of the family was 67 when he died.[62]

Last feast of the Immaculate Conception

On December 8, Sr. Dufès arranged a joyful experience for Catherine—she took her to the motherhouse for the feast of the Immaculate Conception. This was in fact killing two birds with one stone, for Sr. Cosnard was still moping in the wake of Catherine's brusque departure after the retreat.

> She was a little cross with me, being convinced that it was I myself who had provoked the novices' exclamations. We embraced each other as a sign of reconciliation, without going into any other explanation.[gg]

Catherine's secret was leaking out more and more, but people avoided provoking her. The fervor surrounding her kept itself at a distance.

Was it a mistake to help her up into the carriage? When leaving the motherhouse, Catherine fell and dislocated her wrist. She did not say a word and no one noticed. Somehow or other, she wrapped her bruised arm in her handkerchief.

*Marie-Louise Labouré,
Catherine's sister
(1795–1877).*

*Catherine's letter to
Marie-Louise dated
September 15, 1844.
(No. 531 in the archives
of the Sisters of Charity.)*

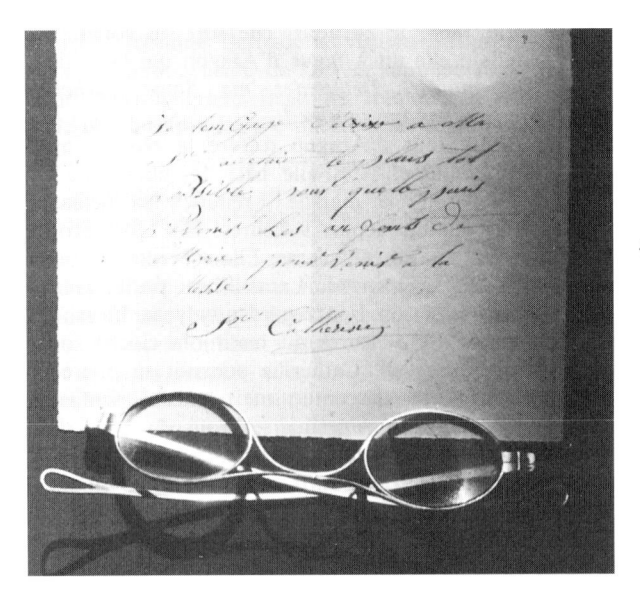

This note signed by Catherine shows her concern for the Children of Mary. She galvanized their contacts and plans. Beneath, Catherine's spectacles, preserved by her family.

J. B. Etienne, Superior General from 1843 to 1874. At the time of his election on August 4, 1843, he was 42.

Chapel at the rue du Bac as it is today with the marble statue of the Virgin with rays of light coming from her hands in the center and the Virgin with the globe (by Real del Sarte) on the right.

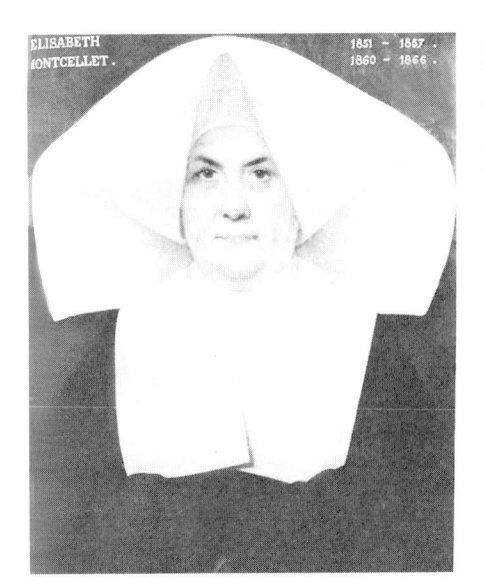

*Two of Reuilly's Superiors:
Sr. Montcellet and Sr. Mazin (a future Superior General).*

Catherine distributing medals during the Commune. A painting by J. M. Durand, given by the Meugniot family to the motherhouse of the Daughters of Charity.

Sister Jeanne Dufès (1822–1908), Catherine's superior from 1860 until her death, who received the decisive confidence in the spring of 1876.

Jules Chinchon, C.M., Catherine's confessor from 1851 to 1875. Losing him was a great blow for Catherine.

The only photograph of Catherine taken during her lifetime, in 1876, doubtless at the beginning of winter. Catherine appears old and suspicious of the camera lens. The cornette, white on a white background, is not visible in the original but has been touched up in this photograph.

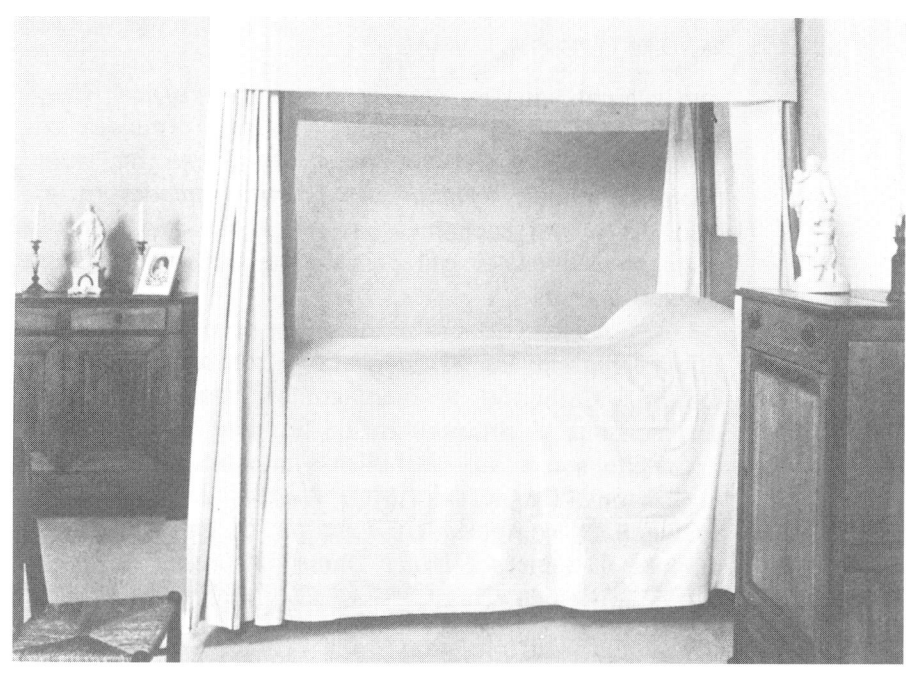

Catherine's deathbed, preserved at Reuilly.

*The first photo of the deceased taken on January 1.
Catherine is wearing her seminary coif.*

The burial vault at Reuilly, which was transformed into a chapel by the addition of an altar around 1900.

"What's happened to you, Sr. Catherine?" asked Sr. Dufès.

Catherine held up her bound wrist, which she was holding with her other hand, and gaily answered, "Oh, Sister, I'm holding my bouquet of flowers. Every year the Blessed Virgin sends me one like this!"

She accepted the rough with the smooth as gifts of equal value. Her explanation was no less surprising for Sr. Charvier, who exclaimed (sarcastically), "She certainly does look after you, the Blessed Virgin! Look what happens to you when you take the trouble to go to pray to her at the motherhouse!"

Catherine replied very calmly, "When the Blessed Virgin sends suffering, she is imparting a grace to us."[63hh]

Yes, everything was grace for Catherine.

The same day, Sr. Tranchemer, who was herself ill, dragged herself up to the Enghien dormitory, leaning on her umbrella. She found Catherine "standing in front of the mantelpiece, her eyes fixed on the statue of the Blessed Virgin, leaning with one hand on the back of her armchair"...motionless, smiling. She thought Catherine was "luminous." However, Catherine was not in a state of ecstasy or anything of the kind. She greeted Sr. Tranchemer with her usual cordiality.

"Oh, it's you! Come over here and sit yourself down!"

Catherine made her sit down in the armchair. Then she drew up an ordinary chair for herself. Once again, Sr. Tranchemer had come to confide to Catherine what was on her mind: the future of three of her pupils—Maria, Béatrix, and Christine. She was afraid that their beauty would be their downfall. Catherine reassured her in the face of her anxieties—now, as so often, exaggerated.[64]

Onset of Winter

The final decline began for Catherine. Her wrist was no longer usable. She was often confined to her bed. From time to time she got up as she felt able to, even if it was just to stay in her room.[65] She was a more tired than pitiful figure, with a never-failing courage. In her "well-worn" state, she did not need a lot of looking after.

"Whatever you like"

Catherine was not difficult to feed, but she ate less and less. In the mornings, she could not eat anything at all. In the evenings, when asked what she wanted to eat, she would reply, "Whatever you like." And if pressed, she would invariably end up with "scrambled eggs."

Self-indulgences?

However, one day she changed her tune. She felt weak; she had not eaten for several days, and concern with getting her strength back prompted her to ask for "a baked apple"!

Normally seeming so indifferent, she was quite obviously anxious when the apple took some time in coming. Was she hungry? Yes, with the sudden hunger of the dying, the sudden spurt of life in an exhausted organism.

"How is it that a sister who is said to have seen the Blessed Virgin is able to let herself go to the point of wanting such self-indulgences?" exclaimed Sr. Tanguy.

This was in the presence of Fr. Chinchon, Catherine's former confessor, who astonished Sr. Tanguy by leaping to Catherine's defense: "Oh, I could cite a canonized saint [the name has been forgotten by the witness] who asked for strawberries on his deathbed."[ii]

Like all people who are getting weaker, Catherine sometimes felt the need for more stimulating nourishment. In her final days, when she could no longer eat anything in the mornings, she kept up her strength by taking "clear soup, milk infusions, or even dried raisins"[66] in the evening.

She did not suspect that these minute details would soon be scrupulously examined in the course of the canonization process. The Devil's Advocate, astonished by such "partialities" in a candidate for sanctity, wondered if gluttony had not been the besetting sin of her old age. This was also the view of the Vincentian, Fr. Hamard, whose critical and facetious spirit delighted in debunking fervors which seemed to him excessive.

"Sr. Catherine was a good girl," he used to say to the sisters at Reuilly, "but she let herself go when she was ill and slid into a little sensuality!"

Sr. Lenorm would later feel obliged in conscience to report these words, since she had sworn an oath to tell everything. Long dissertations were necessary to dissipate these deceptive criticisms—a task which would end up with the proper placement of Catherine's modest desires in their correct proportion. They would be found to be in conformity with St. Vincent's Rules and able to stand comparison with the sometimes more refined tastes shown by certain saints during their final illnesses. During the summer of 1896, twenty years later, Thérèse of Lisieux, on her deathbed, would ask for rather more expensive things: roast meat or chocolate éclairs.[ii]

Sanctity does not exclude innocent natural desires, nor simplicity of heart.

A negligent infirmarian

Catherine was sometimes obliged to nibble between meals because her negligent nurse, Sr. Maria, would forget her dinner when the sick "senior" was unable to come down for it. Catherine would not have complained for all the world, but when this happened she would find whatever she could to eat. This gave rise to frugal and irregular meals which were taken to be extras.

Sr. Tanguy, the Assistant, recognized this herself, as did Sr. Olalde.

> Catherine did not grumble and put up with everything. [...] Having noticed what was going on, I wanted to know what the venerable old lady thought of it. Calmly and simply she answered me, "Sister [Maria] is not a worker."[67]

Abandoned but uncomplaining, Catherine received nothing but fairly sharp tellings-off, including some from Sr. Tanguy herself. Sr. Cabanes tells us:

> I myself saw Sister Assistant giving Sr. Catherine a good dressing-down because she had not taken the medicines that the pharmacy sister had brought her when she was sick and confined to bed. [...] She made no excuses and [...] remained silent [...]. When Sister Assistant had gone, Sr. Catherine turned to me and said with great gentleness, "I haven't seen her all day, and look how she treats me when she comes!" She *had* taken her medicine![68]

One day Sr. Tranchemer discovered Catherine with no fire lit in the middle of December.

"You must be very cold, Sr. Catherine. I'll re-light it...."

"No, don't bother. It's nothing!"[69]

For Catherine, everything was grace during those long nights without electricity. Around mid-December, Sr. Maurel tells us, "She could take no food, her digestion was so out of order. [...] We were lucky if we could get her to take a little clear soup at about 9:00 in the morning."[70]

On December 18, Sr. Cessac, a postulant about to leave for the seminary, came to say goodbye to Catherine.

"She was very calm and said to me, 'I am leaving on my way to heaven.'"[71]

I shall go to Reuilly

Around December 20, Sr. Maria Thomas (the negligent infirmarian, according to Sr. Pineau[kk]) found Catherine to be as benevolent as ever.

"How good my superior is!" Catherine exclaimed.

Later, after her well-known refrain about being dead "before next year," Sr. Maria was amazed to hear her say, "and a hearse won't be needed!"[72]

Sr. Maria exclaimed, "But what will we do with such a large body?"

She replied, "Well, it will be like this: I shall come to live with you at Reuilly." And she added, "There'll be no need for ribbons."[73]

She was referring to what were at that time called "pall strings"—ribbons attached to the funeral pall and held ceremonially by friends at the four corners of the funeral carriage.

Sr. Maria rushed off to tell these strange remarks to Sr. Dufès, who replied, "Keep that to yourself!"[ll]

The Marshal's wife and other visitors

Sr. Tranchemer was still "hovering" around Catherine to be able to talk to her of her intentions and about the medal.

"I will pray for you in heaven," Catherine said to her.[74]

She was now confined to bed more often than not. This produced a steady flow of visitors—those who *knew,* notably Marshal MacMahon's wife. Catherine gave her rosaries and medals.[75] But Léonie Labouré, who came to visit her aunt some weeks before her death, was not given permission to go up to the dormitory. Catherine was no longer in a state to come down.[76]

Among the daily visitors, apart from Sr. Tranchemer[77] there was Sr. Charvier, who tells us:

> I went to see her every day and sometimes several times a day. She was brought Holy Communion from time to time. [...] One day I asked her why she did not request this privilege more frequently. She replied: "I am happy when the good Lord is brought to me, but I like to do as everyone else. I don't want to draw attention to myself."[78]

There was also Sr. Cabanes.

I saw her every day from the time she was bedridden, and I was very edified by her admirable patience. I said to her, "Sister, dear, you are all alone!" She answered me, "Get along with you. I don't like people feeling sorry for me. I've got everything I need."[79]

Finally, her confessor

Although she had long since gone beyond the stage of frustration at the non-fulfillment of her wishes, Catherine had nevertheless expressed one desire—to see Fr. Chinchon again, the confessor that she had been refused permission to see the previous year, after a quarter of a century during which so many things had gotten under way. It was a calm request. Now that she had passed on her secrets, Catherine felt herself to be beyond the possibility of being hurt anymore. This was a last exchange of ideas, a final encounter, a farewell.[80]

On December 29, Sr. Tranchemer paid Catherine a final visit—Sr. Dufès was at her bedside. Sr. Tranchemer was dazzled by the serenity on Catherine's face.[81]

Anointing of the Sick

In the final days of December, Catherine asked to be anointed. This seemed a little premature. As she seemed to be getting weaker, the suggestion was made that a neighboring priest should be fetched from the Picpus Fathers.

"I can wait for a Vincentian to hear my confession...."

Paradoxically, the Vincentian was Fr. Hamard. Catherine received the last sacraments at the hands of the one who would later be the most dangerous Devil's Advocate when her canonization process was just under way—not because he was hostile, but because he enjoyed paradoxes....

Several of Catherine's companions were present.

"I ask you pardon for all the wrongs I have done you," Catherine said to them, following the custom. In a state of total consciousness, she received the anointing on each of the five senses, beginning with her blue eyes.

"May the Lord grant remission of all the sins you have committed with the sense of sight."

The ritual formula appeared a little odd in light of Catherine's transparency.[82] Catherine renewed her vows with a calm intensity.

Imparting her final confidences

On December 30, Sr. Cosnard came to see Catherine. Other sisters were present. After the reconciliation on December 8, Sr. Cosnard wanted a more intimate meeting with Catherine, but how could this be achieved? Sr. Cosnard drew close to the bed and murmured, "Sr. Catherine, are you going to leave me without saying a word about the Blessed Virgin?"[83]

Catherine signaled to her to come closer, right up beside her (Sr. Pineau records). Catherine bent toward Sr. Cosnard and whispered in her ear. The others heard nothing of what was said.

Catherine certainly had something to say to Sr. Cosnard since she was the "Sister of Office," in charge of formation in the seminary. Catherine still had great desires—and great sorrows, too—regarding St. Vincent's two families. She spoke with a sense of realism, but above all with great peace and love.

"Make sure everyone prays properly; may the good Lord inspire our superiors to honor Mary Immaculate. She is the community's treasure. The rosary should be said often. Vocations will be plenteous...if all these things are done and profited from."

Catherine spared a thought for the young sisters whom she had helped to conquer their distaste at various things—most recently Sr. Maurel, who had replaced her: "The postulants must go into the hospitals: to learn MASTERY OF SELF." She stopped herself, afraid of going "beyond her brief."

"It is not my place to talk about these things. Fr. Chavalier [Spiritual Director of the Sisters of Charity] is the one whose task this is!"

Perhaps Catherine also remembered the sister who treated her as a simpleton and looked for more exalted tasks, for she also said, "We bring *up* the young sisters too well, instead of maintaining them in a state of humility. They should listen to the older sisters and should learn the spirit of St. Vincent....

"The Blessed Virgin has promised graces every time that someone prays in the chapel—above all, purity of spirit, purity of heart, purity of will...pure love."

Prayers for the dying

Catherine was weakening. Around her bed, prayers for the dying were being recited, at her own request.

"Aren't you afraid of dying?" asked Sr. Dufès.

Catherine's blue eyes seemed to fill with wonder, like a cloudless sky. "Why be afraid of going to meet our Lord, his Mother, and St. Vincent?"

CHAPTER VIII

Catherine's Death
(December 31, 1876)

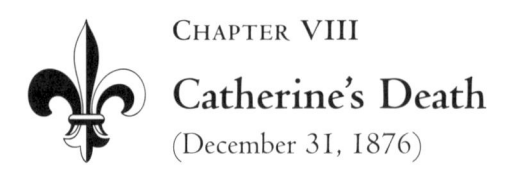

CONSCIOUS AND AT PEACE

IT WAS DECEMBER 31, 1876. The year was coming to an end and still Catherine was not dead. She did not seem ready to go. Sr. Dufès teased her about this "stubbornness." Catherine quietly said to her, "I shall not see tomorrow."

Sr. Dufès rejoined, "But tomorrow is New Year's Day! This is no time to be leaving us!"

But Catherine, imperturbable, merely reiterated, "No, I shall not see tomorrow."[1]

Visit by her biographer

In the afternoon, Fr. Chevalier, sub-director of the Sisters of Charity, came to give her his blessing.[2] She had seen him several times that year,[3] for he was finishing a new edition, revised and reset, of the booklet about the medal whose eighth edition had been published by Fr. Aladel in 1842. He was concerned about the Virgin with the globe.

"Didn't you dream it?"

"No, I certainly saw the globe!"

"Why did Fr. Aladel suppress it?"[4]

Catherine had no answer. He would look for one for a long time to come. He was counting on being able to publish it that year, but Catherine gaily said to him, "I shall be dead when this booklet comes out!"[5]

"It's ready!" he retorted, at his previous visit.

"I'll show you, you'll see! In 1842, too, I told Fr. Aladel that neither he nor I would see the following edition."

Catherine was also still very concerned about the Rue du Bac—an unrecognized fountain and a sealed-off one.

> The pilgrimages that the sisters make to other places are not helpful to their piety. The Blessed Virgin did not say that you had to go and pray so far away. It's in the chapel of the community that she wants the sisters to invoke her. There is THEIR pilgrimage.[6]

The future historian gave her his blessing before leaving. She seemed happy.

First Alarm

About 3:00 P.M. Catherine had a welcomed visit—Marie-Antoinette Duhamel (Tonine's daughter) with her two little daughters, Marthe and Jeanne, together with another niece.[7] Luckier than Lèonie Labouré, who had been kept at a distance in mid-December, they were given the privilege of going up to Catherine's "dormitory." Her breathing was difficult; "sweat stood out on her forehead," but her heart was ready to welcome them. She sat, "legs dangling," at the head of her iron bedstead, cornette badly adjusted by her negligent nurse. Catherine had prepared New Year's gifts for the children and sent a sister to look for them in the cupboard: sweets, chocolate...and a handful of medals for their mother. The visit did not last too long so that Catherine would not be tired by it.

"I will come back tomorrow to wish you a happy New Year," said Marie-Antoinette, getting up to go.

"If you come back, you will see me, but *I* shall not see *you* because I will have gone," Catherine answered sententiously. She seemed to be dozing off, her blue eyes becoming misty.

Scarcely had Marie-Antoinette and Catherine's nieces reached the end of the garden than Catherine collapsed on her pillow. She had been in the course of preparing gifts for the sisters—little packets of medals. They fell from her hands and scattered all over the bed. The nurse alerted Sr. Dufès. The community ran to the dormitory and began to pray, but Catherine opened her eyes again. False alarm![8]

"My dear Sr. Catherine," Sr. Dufès teased her, "don't you know it's December 31? Now I ask you, is this the sort of day on which you ought to be frightening us like this?!"

"But, Sister, I did not want you to be disturbed. It is not over yet."[9]

Nevertheless, they decided to bring her Viaticum. The sisters went downstairs to bring the Blessed Sacrament in procession. At this point, Sr. d'Aragon arrived–Sr. Dufès' companion during the "exodus" during the Commune.[10] She took advantage of the fact that no one was present to draw near Catherine's bed.

"Sister Catherine, pray for me...for my new responsibilities." (She had just been nominated Sister Servant at Blancs-Manteaux.) Catherine promised her and then added, "I have seen Fr. Chevalier. I am happy!" She received Viaticum.

A sister asked her, "Will you take any messages to heaven with you?" Catherine replied in her down-to-earth way, "I don't know how these things work up there!"

In life as in death, one must never make a promise that one cannot keep! "Did she see heaven as a kind of majestic court?" Sr. Dufès asked herself.

"Come now, Sr. Catherine! In heaven, there's no need to put on airs and graces. You tell the good Lord what you want simply by looking at him!"

"Oh well, in that case I will pray to him [for you]!" replied Catherine, who could feel at home in this way of thinking.[11]

Sr. Dufès received a message to go to the parlor: "Some youngsters have arrived who want to wish you a Happy New Year." She hesitated, but Catherine said to her, "You've got plenty of time. You can go. I'll make sure you are warned."[12]

About 5:00 P.M., Sr. Dufès sent Sr. Clavel to Catherine's bedside. "I don't think she's as close to the end as that, but if you see her sinking, come and tell me."[13]

At about 5:30, Sr. Combes joined Sr. Clavel.[14]

At 6:00 she suddenly had the impression that Catherine was slipping away.[15] She went down to fetch the superior.

Sr. Dufès rushed up as quickly as she could, but, seeing her, Catherine began to move again and was able to speak once more. Sr. Dufès had begun to believe that Catherine really was going to die and smiled at her, saying the sort of encouraging words that one finds in such situations. "Come on, don't worry. You're on the mend!"

Catherine was not worried, but calmly repeated her refrain: "I shall die this very day."

Departure from This World

Sr. Dufès went downstairs to eat. Another sister arrived, bringing some medals with her. (Catherine had started again preparing little packets for the community and for Sr. Cosnard. She had now run out of medals and had asked for some more.)

"Sr. Catherine—here are your medals!"

Catherine did not answer or give any sign of life. Sr. Tranchemer put them in her hands. They fell on the sheet.[16] It was 6:30 P.M. This time, she really was going.

Sr. Dufès abandoned her meal and hastened upstairs.[17] The bell was rung.[18] It was not customary to do this for the dying, but this was for Catherine!

The community came running. This was not usual either, but this was for Catherine![19]

She had already made her request for the liturgy of her death: sixty-three children, with each child reciting one of the invocations in the litany.[20] Sr. Dufès had winced at this unusual demand. "There aren't sixty-three invocations in the Litany of the Blessed Virgin!"

"Yes, there are, in the *Office of the Immaculate Conception*... in our prayer-book!"

The *Litany of Mary Immaculate in the Manual of Prayers for the Use of the Sisters of Charity* was consulted. Only thirty-seven invocations! But Catherine had not said *litany,* she had said *office*. And, in fact, the *Little Office* published in the same manual contained exactly sixty-three litany titles, from "Queen of the World" (*Domina mundi*) to "Refuge of the poor sick." They were set out one after the other, without the intervening "pray for us," which was not calculated to make them easy for children to recite!

Catherine's admirers had not quite gotten to that. They prepared the sixty-three invocations on sixty-three little pieces of cardboard. Catherine had been as exact in her reckoning of the number of invocations in the litany as in her days of handling the farm accounts.

Had she thought about the intentional symbolism of the number sixty-three? We do not know. But the compiler of the *Office* had apparently chosen that number because of the tradition that our Lady lived for 63 years—fifteen *before* and fifteen *after* Christ's 33 years.

The little pieces of cardboard were thus present, but on the eve of January 1, there were no children! The orphan girls had been dispersed among host families for the celebrations of the New Year.[21]

Only two or three were to be found, and they were in no state to do the recitation. At least Catherine would not die far from children. She had seen her three nieces that afternoon (and they would keep the sweets she had given them as if they were relics[22]). Three little orphan girls were still there and they came along willingly to this last ceremony.

The sisters recited the litany.[23] Catherine had asked that the eighteenth invocation, "Terror of demons," be emphasized. They repeated it three times. She seemed to be joining herself to the prayer, but her voice made no sound.[24]

Sr. Dufès sweetly and tenderly said to her, "So you want to leave us." Catherine did not reply, "silent at the hour of her death as she had been during her life."[25] The sisters continued with the prayers for the dying.[26]

Sr. Tanguy, the Assistant, had to go downstairs while the prayers were being said.[27] When she came back, and when Sr. de la Haye St. Hilaire arrived (the last to do so), Catherine gave no further sign of life.

The sisters repeated the medal invocation: *O Mary, conceived without sin....*"[28] Gently, Catherine dozed off and went to sleep, without the death agony.[29]

Sr. Cantel was amazed that "none of the signs that you normally notice on the face of people who are dying appeared on her face." She had "never seen anything like that."[30]

Catherine accepted death quietly and in a dual sense—as a country woman, used to espousing the rhythm of life and as a Christian, happy to be going to meet (according to one of her last pronouncements) "our Lord, his Mother, and St. Vincent."[31]

A smile crept across her face...two large tears rolled down her cheeks.[32] It was the end. Someone closed Catherine's eyes. It was just 7:00.

Thirty-three years before, during the May 1843 retreat, Catherine had glimpsed the kind of death she would die. She had seen it solely in the light of the poor and the Blessed Virgin, and she had written:

> *Mary* loved the *poor,* and a Sister of Charity who loves the poor [...] will have no fear of death. No one has ever heard that Sisters of Charity who really loved the poor had terrifying fears of death. Quite the opposite [...] such sisters have been seen to die the gentlest of deaths.[a]

This is precisely what had been seen of Catherine herself, in death as in life, that evening of December 31, 1876.

The Light

"Yes, it was certainly she who saw the Blessed Virgin!"

There was no longer any reason for a conspiracy of silence, now that she who had so valiantly defended her secret had departed her earthly life.

You will have grace

In the refectory that same evening, Sr. Dufès made a declaration. "Since Sister Catherine is dead, there is nothing left to hide. I am going to read to you what she wrote."[33]

She went to her desk to look for the autobiographical account of the first apparition of the Virgin that Catherine had written down for her on October 30, after having confided in her. The dates had lost none of their exactitude in her mind.

> July 18, 1830. Conversation with the Blessed Virgin from eleven o'clock until half past one in the morning, July 19, St. Vincent's feast day: My child, the good Lord wants to entrust you with a mission. You will have plenty of suffering, but you will overcome yourself by remembering that you are doing it for the glory of God [...]. You will be tormented [...], you will be contradicted, but you will have grace [...]. Misfortunes will come crashing down on France [...], but St. Vincent will protect the community [...]. I shall be with you. Have confidence.[b]

That evening, this formed the community's spiritual reading.

Keeping vigil

From that evening onward, rumors were rife.

There was arguing over the happy task of preparing, then of watching over, the body that night.[34] Even those sisters who were frightened of being in close proximity to a corpse did it with joy and enthusiasm. Catherine was laid out in "the room of the dead," which the architect had provided in the hospice next to the chapel on the left of the entrance. In her hands were placed a rosary and the medal. Above her head was a statue of our Lady, bedecked with a lily and some wild roses from no-one-knew-where at that time of year.

"How beautiful she is in death," marveled Sr. Madeleine. (She had found Catherine "not beautiful" while she was alive.)

Photographs[35]

Photographs were wanted of this face that would not be seen again, so first thing next morning, January 1, a photographer was summoned.

"She should be photographed wearing her clothes as at the time of the apparition," suggested one sister.

They dressed Catherine's body in a seminary coif, which made the death mask look strangely much younger. Then the winged cornette was put back on for a second photograph.

Rumors and crowds

Already on this same morning, January 1, rumors had produced an endless stream of visitors—from the locality, from the motherhouse, from St. Lazare, and elsewhere.

"The crowd seemed to come from out of the ground itself," said Marie-Antoinette Duhamel, amazed.

The multitude had to be controlled in order to protect the object of the visitation. Two sisters took up positions, one at Catherine's head, the other at her feet. They intervened and took objects with which the visitors wanted to touch the body—rosaries and medals. Even the men were affected by the prevailing atmosphere. Having nothing else, they handed their pocket watches over to the two sisters and received them back fervently.[36]

The little Duhamel girls were there. They helped to act as relays between the crowds and this body, temple of God. Catherine drew the crowds "like a saint," said little Marthe.

Sr. Angélique relates: "When one of our sisters dies, we are filled with sadness, quite naturally. But when Sister Catherine died, no one cried and we did not feel sad at all."[c]

Catherine had been a joyful person and had had to use her joyfulness to overcome plenty of torments. The last thing she would have wished to leave behind her was sadness.[37]

She had the appearance of someone who was asleep. Her limbs remained supple. Marie-Antoinette Duhamel went so far as to ask, "Is she really dead?"[38]

Rue du Bac

The community did not think they could "abandon" Catherine to the cemetery. Sr. Dufès wrote:

> To have been dispossessed of her presence would have broken our hearts. It seemed to us that from that point onward the Immaculate Virgin's protection would no longer enfold us.[d]

But to keep her also appeared to be impossible.

Sr. Clavel and Sr. Charvier had set out that same morning for the motherhouse to break the news of Catherine's death—a strange way of beginning the New Year! Léonie Labouré had called on Marie-Louise to give her her best wishes. On hearing the news, Catherine's elder sister said, "She was a saint," knowing full well what she personally owed her. "I'm going to pray to her to summon me before the good Lord this year. At my age, I'm only a burden on the community." (She would indeed die that very year, on July 25, at the age of 82.[39])

Sr. Clavel and Sr. Charvier went to the Secretariat. Rashly but hesitantly, they broached the idea of having a tomb at Reuilly. To their surprise, Sr. de Geoffre found the idea very attractive. She would look into getting permission from the superiors.

Encouraged by their success, the two emissaries then went to the Rue du Sèvres to speak about it to Fr. Boré, Superior General. He authorized them to "do the necessary."

On their return, the two sisters did not dare to disclose their (indiscreet?) initiative to Sr. Dufès, so it was a great surprise for her when two superiors from the motherhouse arrived at Enghien in the afternoon to pray at the dead woman's coffin and said to her, "Yes, certainly. We authorize you to take the necessary steps for keeping Sr. Catherine's body."

Sr. Dufès turned to the morning's messengers and said, "Well, since you committed the sin, you can carry out the penance. I'm instructing you to take the necessary steps yourselves!" As if on wings, they flew to the nearest police inspector, who replied, "What you are asking is rather difficult and outside my competence to deal with, but I think you have friends at the Elysée Palace."[40]

The hint was no sooner dropped than acted upon. The next morning, January 2, the two sisters were at the presidential palace. Marshal MacMahon's wife telegraphed the Chief of Police for the warrant and came to deliver it in person that evening. She prayed by the body of the Servant of God.[41]

It was a "temporary warrant," but guaranteed to become permanent as soon as the location and ways and means of the burial place had been worked out. And therein lay the problem: where to put her?

The vault is under the chapel

And that was where matters rested on the evening of January 1, according to Sr. Dufès, who was at a total loss faced with the problem.

"Let us pray," I said to our sisters. They spent the night imploring Mary Immaculate not to allow our companion to be taken away from us. All through the night I looked in vain for a suitable spot to lay her to rest [...]. Suddenly, at the sound of the bell ringing four o'clock in the morning, I thought I heard these words ringing in my ears: THE VAULT IS UNDER THE REUILLY CHAPEL.[c]

The words seemed to spring up by themselves. The architect had wanted to fill in the useless hollow in the middle of the house, but an earlier superior, Mother Mazin, had refused–the reason for it is not known. This cave seemed tailor-made for Catherine's tomb.

The Marshal's wife took it upon herself to pay for a triple coffin– pine (inner), lead, and oak (outer): a necessary precaution against putrefaction and in accordance with the hygienic regulations in force since the epidemics.[42] The hermetically sealed coffin would solve the problem occasioned by what turned out to be the three-month delay before definitive authorization came through and the fitting out of the tomb could begin. Workers were hastily hired to cement the floor in the cavern and prepare an opening large enough for the coffin to pass through.

Neither hearse nor ribbons

The funeral took place on Wednesday, January 3, feast of St. Genevieve–a saint dear to St. Vincent–and the ceremony began at 10:00. The chapel at Enghien was filled to the bursting point. Who should be singing the Mass but Fr. Chinchon! Catherine had said to the sisters, "He will come back to us." In fact, the following year he would once again take up his role as confessor at Reuilly.[f]

The poor of the locality had paid for a sheaf of flowers and the elderly had bought another. They were all anxious to be at the head of the procession accompanying Catherine to her last resting place–she who had looked after them so well! Yes, "No sister was loved as much as she!" But her gift, her presence was only noticed now when it was no longer with them.

Behind them came "the young people's banner leading the procession." The young people were followed by the Children of Mary, led by their own banner. Next were the "externs" who had "left their work" to be there and the orphan girls wearing white veils.[43] Finally came Catherine's body, carried on shoulders.[44] Thus, her prediction came about: "There'll be no need for a hearse. I shall go to Reuilly!"

Sr. Maria Thomas, the negligent nurse, suddenly understood that phrase which had disconcerted her. She remembered that Catherine had also said, "There'll be no need for ribbons." ("This is what for us corresponds to the pall-strings held by those accompanying the dead," Sr. Cosnard was to explain later on.)

A crazy idea, a gesture of defiance came into Sr. Maria's head. In her own words:

> As there were no ribbons, I was just going to seize one of the four corners of the pall with the secret idea of *making Sister Catherine tell a lie* when one of the bearers said to me, "Move back, Sister, you're getting in our way!"

She drew back. Using her authority as sacristan, she had signaled three others (including Sr. Cosnard) to hold the remaining corners. They, too, withdrew to the ranks. Despite "the solemnity" of the moment, Sr. Maria, flabbergasted, murmured loudly enough for Sr. Cosnard to hear, "Sr. Catherine, you haven't changed a bit!"[45] Her attempt had failed and the prediction was accomplished.

"We walked, my sister and I, immediately behind the coffin," Marthe Duhamel, Catherine's niece, tells us, "and we did not cry despite our grief at having lost her, for we did not see her except as someone blessed whose happiness was not a cause for grief."[46]

Procession

Following the coffin came the Sisters of Charity, about 250 strong, and the clergy, with a large number of Vincentians. Last of all there followed a huge crowd of people from all over the surrounding area. Young workers from the Faubourg St. Antoine were there, Miraculous Medals hanging from their buttonholes on blue ribbons,[47] and that discreet friend of the community, the wife of Marshal MacMahon.[48] Near the coffin was carried the magnificent wreath this good woman had bought, bearing these words of hers: *Respectful homage to Sr. Catherine.*[49]

From Enghien to Reuilly, the funeral procession took the main path across the garden that Catherine had fashioned in her own image during a period of forty-six years. The fruit trees she had planted, the shrubs and beds she had shaped, adapting her Burgundian experience to the soil of the Ile-de-France, were a living on of her peasant body. Long afterward, they would continue to bear the fruit she had prepared. The pigeons that had hovered over her childhood now hovered over her death.

The procession made its way slowly—partly due to the numbers of people and the restricted width of the path, but also through devotion.[50] Invocations and chants poured forth as if it were a feastday[51]— not funeral chants, but the *Benedictus* [Canticle of Zechariah], the *Magnificat,* the *Litany of the Blessed Virgin,* and, above all, the invocation inscribed on the medal: *O Mary, conceived without sin....*

The singing of the invocation grew in fervor. Arriving at Reuilly, those in front parted and crowded on both sides to leave room for the coffin to pass through their midst. The singing started again even more strongly at the moment when the four bearers took the coffin down through the narrow opening, constructed the previous day, and laid it down on the cool cemented floor of the vault.[52]

People had climbed up onto the roofs of neighboring houses.[53] Far from being a funeral cortège, the crowd was turning the occasion into a joyous spectacle.

Tears, however, were not totally absent—there were the elderly, who knew only too well what a great loss Catherine was; and then there was Léonie Labouré. "I cried," she admitted. People were amazed at this and tried to comfort her. "But I'm her niece...."

"All the same, you shouldn't be crying. She was a saint; she saw the Blessed Virgin!"[54]

Pilgrimage to Reuilly

During the days that followed, crowds continued to flock to the vault where the coffin had been placed on two trestles.[55] Among the visitors were the wife of Marshal MacMahon, the Countess of Eu, daughter of the ex-Emperor of Brazil, the wife of Senator Buffet—but above all, the poor people of the locality came.[56] Near the very beginning a poor woman brought a box on wheels containing her 12-year-old child, who "had come into the world with knotted legs," as she put it. Tearfully, she tried to take him down into the vault, but it was scarcely possible. There was only a very steep and narrow ladder. A sister quieted the child with sweets; then the family let him down with the help of ropes. All of a sudden he came up again by himself, his legs having become firm and strong. This was doubtless Catherine's first miracle for the poor; but the one who had received her gift disappeared before inquiries could be made, like so many other poor and anonymous people.[57]

One remarkable thing was how many children there were among the crowds.[58]

It was only after three months, in April 1877, after a critical inspection by an architect and a police inspector, that definitive authorization for the entombment came through. And here was a strange coincidence. Before her death, Catherine had said that, digging in the ground at Reuilly, "at a depth of 1m 50" "a *tombstone* will be seen [...] and there will be found the wherewithal to build [...] a church."

Sr. Dufès had thought that this was to do with come kind of buried treasure. Together with two successive Superiors General, she had dug—but in vain. So, Catherine must have been mistaken! She herself had agreed with this verdict. But here was the police inspector in fact ordering Catherine to be buried "at 1m 50."[59] *The vault was arranged accordingly,*[60] together with a *tombstone*.[61] Around 1896, a Spanish priest, Don Dadorda, came to France for the sake of Catherine and with the greatest difficulty obtained permission to re-order the vault as a chapel. He spent 3,000 gold francs on it; and an altar was set up there at the expense of Madame Gil Moreno de Mora.[62]

Now, one might think that these kinds of celebrations and pilgrimages to the tomb were anticipating the Church's judgment on the matter; and indeed, this was a cause for concern later on during the canonization process. But the impossible now became possible. Martyr-like, Catherine had suffered the refusals which for more than forty years had balked the requests of the Virgin, whose impotent messenger she was. She had regarded the year 1870 with some dread as a "dark" year, but caught a glimpse of hope fulfilled for 1880. In fact, the year before her death, she had included in one of her handwritten accounts the words, "10 years after—peace!"[g]

What had so far been refused her was granted that year. A commemorative altar and the statue of the Virgin with the globe were erected in the chapel of the apparitions by Fr. Fiat. The chapel was at long last opened up for pilgrimages, and the fiftieth anniversary was celebrated there. The two Holy Communions requested by Catherine for the anniversary days of the apparitions of St. Vincent's heart and the medal were also granted.[63] Catherine had said and written, "Ask Rome and more will be granted."[64]

This hope for the future, as caught sight of in 1880, soon ran into a snag, however. In 1881, the Congregation of Rites ordered the Virgin with the globe, erected less than a year before, to be removed. But four years later, Pope Leo XIII reinstated it. In 1894, Fr. Fiat, having had his fingers burnt once, put forward a very timorous request concerning the celebration of "votive Masses," without even mentioning the medal; he found that the Congregation of Rites granted him the Little Office of the Miraculous Medal, including readings relating the apparition and Catherine's life. The liturgical feast of the Manifestation of the Miraculous Medal was thus celebrated on November 27, 1894. Even this was not enough for Cardinal Aloïsi Masella, who had passed on the request. He claimed that he was "scandalized by the [excessive] modesty" of the Vincentians. "I censured them loudly," he wrote.[65]

The following year, he took to one side the Superior General of the Sisters of Charity on her arrival in Rome. "When are you going to introduce a canonization petition?" he asked her. And, getting a rather evasive answer, he energetically called her up on it: "What? She was an eminently saintly religious! If you won't do it, I will!"[66]

The objections brought about by the influx of pilgrims to Reuilly, which could have appeared to be anticipating the official cult, were swept aside. Similarly, objections that Catherine's life had been too *ordinary* were dealt with. The "scandal" of an everyday visionary who had not been touched in the slightest by any passing human glory meant a return to the very source–the Gospel. Here was the wellspring from which Catherine's disconcerting sanctity took its rise. Her sanctity, in fact, compelled the proper honoring of the Gospel itself. This was precisely what Sr. de Geoffre, Catherine's first biographer, did in order to try and reduce the considerable opposition that existed.

> Were not our Lord's contemporaries scandalized because his parents were poor, because he came from Nazareth, because he ate and drank like anyone else, because he talked with sinners?[67]

The criticisms were drowned and what emerged in their place was the frequent and unacknowledged holiness of the poor. This was Christ's point of departure: Blessed are the poor (Mt 5:1).

On July 27, 1947, in the presence of the Universal Church in St. Peter's Basilica in Rome, Pope Pius XII declared Catherine a saint.[68]

Seventy years previously, Sr. Dufès had already guessed what God's judgment might be in the matter. She had spent so much time trying to understand Catherine, and on January 4, 1877, the day after the burial, she had written to Philippe Meugniot (who had been unable to be present at this brightly shining point in time):

I regarded her as a blessing on the house, and now I like to think of her in heaven as a protector [...].

We are happy to have been able to keep her precious remains, and we like [...] to recall [...] the inestimable graces she received.... In her we learn again how the saints die, with what feelings of confidence and joy the arrival of this final moment is seen when one has been able to live for God and God alone.[69]

CHAPTER IX

Catherine's Sanctity

CATHERINE—MYTH AND REALITY

HOW MUCH DO WE REALLY KNOW ABOUT CATHERINE? Due to a lack of documentary evidence, she certainly did remain an unknown figure; but various discoveries, coupled with the use of an analytical methodology, have allowed us to scale down this lack of knowledge to an amazing extent and, in the final analysis, to follow her life in detail from one day to the next.

Two flattering myths, not wholly without foundation, contributed to a feeling of complacency when faced with such a lack of knowledge.

Firstly, there was a myth which has carried a lot of weight: the myth of Catherine's silence....[1] It is true that she was a silent sort of person and that her silences had a meaning. But her words and actions, insufficiently known hitherto, speak more eloquently than the "mist" surrounding her silence.

Secondly, there was the myth of Catherine's *secret*.[2] Again, it is true that she kept it hidden in an astounding manner, but there was nothing absolute about it: the seal was not hermetic. "A city placed on a mountain cannot be hidden." Catherine knew this from experience. The secret intended for her by God only too soon started to leak out. Catherine fought tenaciously to keep it hidden. This daily drama, mostly unrecognized, is also charged with significance.

There is also another way of looking at all this, and that is that both the apparitions and the medal, so often described as "miraculous," have resulted in people tending to forget about a more deeply hidden marvel–Catherine's sanctity itself.

What, then, is this sanctity? Let us begin answering that question by drawing attention to one of God's grand designs that has not been sufficiently perceived. In the nineteenth century, the Holy Spirit seemed to be leaving to one side the conventional sort of saintliness and saints who *did* things—martyrs or founders of orders, builders or doctors of the Church. Instead, the Spirit appeared to be provoking a saintliness devoid of the glory of human triumph and reduced to the very essentials of the Gospel message: charity and humbleness of heart, taken at their source (Jn 7), the giving up of self and the simplicity which inspired Catherine's confessor, Fr. Chinchon, to "define" Catherine as "a violet hidden in the grass."[3] In short, we are talking about the *sanctity of the poor,* of which St. Bernadette of Lourdes was also an example.

For Catherine, as for Bernadette, the apparitions were not a jumping-off point nor a wave of a magic wand but the momentary white heat of a sanctity already deeply formed from childhood. If Catherine had scaled the heights of Mount Tabor, she had straightaway come down again to return to the cross.

Catherine's *ordeals* have in a sense complicated matters as so far as a balanced appreciation of her life is concerned. Even the limited extent to which she referred to her "martyrdom" could be thought an exaggeration.

To illustrate the reaction against the diaphanous, stained-glass sort of sanctity that was well in accordance with the tastes of the day, our main prosecution witness is Fr. Coste. From the secret memoirs that he distributed among various archives, he was able to paint a caricature of an overrated woman: a poor girl, mediocre, gluttonous, riddled with faults, struggling in the midst of a morass of false predictions and confused imaginings. Fr. Aladel's only merit was to have released the initial spark and then to have swept out the refuse—"Catherine's autographs," "the Virgin with the globe, deceiving prophecies," and so on.

Going beyond both Misermont's biased account and Coste's demolition exercise, it is necessary to demonstrate the unvarnished truth in a serious and scientific—in other words, verifiable—manner. We have seen Catherine in her everyday life, so exaggerations at one end of the scale or the other can be left on one side. There is no point in attacking Catherine or defending her. Her sanctity no longer needs to be proved—her life has demonstrated it to us through its own transparency.

So, then, who was the Catherine that we have observed living so simply day by day? What was her secret and the meaning of her destiny? Let us try to answer the question by moving from the frequently discussed charisms toward the essential sanctity itself.

Charisms

If we take charisms as our starting point, it is because they are what have made Catherine glorious. Without the apparitions, she would have remained a saint unknown among many others.

By *charisms* we mean *free gifts* given by the Holy Spirit for the *edification* of the Church and its communities, through the manifestation of his presence, his strength, and even the blazing brilliance of his saving power.

A. Extraordinary Charisms

Opposition and mistrust

Such brilliance is sometimes overrated and sometimes contested.

Apparitions have long aroused mistrust, and not without reason. The exceptional nature of the supernatural does not always manage to shake off a certain ambiguity. There are risks of illusion, of deviation from the norm, of self-aggrandizement. A claim to have a direct line to God can put "official" power and knowledge into the shade.

More recently, there has been widespread concern for a Christianity devoid of myth, for a faith without religion, a reductionist and critical attitude anxious to explain everything only in terms of the narrow limits of vision of the human sciences—psychology, psychoanalysis, sociology. This concern has branded *apparitions* as *hallucinations,* as Abbé Marc Oraison is fond of putting it. Such prejudices have for nearly half a century paralyzed any official recognition of *apparition* in the Latin Church; and a certain type of *intelligentsia* has accordingly come to consider the visions that are found throughout the Bible as outmoded charisms or literary artifice, not just in relation to the prophets but also in the context of the early Church, beginning with Peter and Paul, who are firmly associated with the illumination of visions in the Acts of the Apostles— Peter at Antioch, Paul on the road to Damascus.

The excessive weight given to visions and charisms has provoked a severe reaction. We can of course see good reasons for this. It is true that *private revelations* are an ambiguous phenomenon, not to be confused with *Revelation,* given once and for all. But we should beware of going from one extreme to the other. Tangible signs that man as a rational animal is capable of grasping have always been a normal dimension of culture, as of Christianity. It is a *religious* dimension, in the etymological sense, whereby *religion* indicates a *link* which binds men to

God and thereby to each other also. Visions and apparitions are, among other signs, stimulating and fruitful gifts—far more than those theoreticians of a faith without religion are capable of realizing, for abstraction leads to asphyxiation. Faith lives by manifesting itself bodily through signs. Reductionist distrust, therefore, sterilizes the vitality of faith, sometimes even sterilizes its very life.

This sort of mistrust is on the wane, for the symbolic dimension of consciousness—which had been increasingly devalued from the time of Greek rationalism right up to the age of eighteenth-century philosophers and of the development of science—is showing itself today to be more radical than the rational dimension. The rationalist repression that has raged systematically throughout the Church has proved how excessive it really is. Today, symbols and signs reveal their importance. They appear as necessary, in the same way that soil is necessary for corn to grow and bear fruit. Today, apparitions are rediscovering their meaning and their value. The extraordinary wave of conversions and renewal signaled by the apparitions of the Miraculous Medal—and among that wave let us not forget Ozanam and Newman (the latter wore the medal for several months before his conversion)—encourage us to look positively at the matter. A peasant girl, illiterate until the age of 18 and chosen in 1830 as the prophetic instrument of renewal, is an illustration of a cause of joy to Christ: "I thank you, Father, for hiding these things from the wise and revealing them to little children" (Mt 11:25-27).

It is not by some lucky chance that the obvious meaning of the communion of saints reaches the poor—less intellectual, closer to the real world and the true nature of things, those for whom the *Gospel* is first and foremost intended. Too often we forget that Gospel means the *Good News proclaimed to the poor.*

Devalued medals[4]

However, the medals that have made Catherine illustrious have been the subject of special disparagement. They do not figure in the *Dictionnaire de théologie Catholique;* and the excellent *Dictionnaire d'archéologie chrétienne et de liturgie* only mentions them in passing under the heading "bangle." They are considered to be a form of popular superstition still hanging on, destined to disappear, and are relegated to the realms of primitive and private piety.

Abstraction and distrust have annihilated the life proper to holy pictures and have created a kind of wilderness out of the ruins of a disintegrated iconography. In this way Christians of the Latin tradition, cut off from their "icons," today are having recourse to those that the Eastern tradition has preserved more carefully. The increase in their use and the value attached to them is considerable in "prayerful" circles. Recent theology can see there the manifestation of a presence, a transparency of nourishment granted for the needs of man.

The medals are first and foremost an image: a visible expression of the invisible, a humble representation of the mystery, a miniature icon which, in monochrome bas-relief, does what icons do in color. The intention and the function are not fundamentally different. Miniaturization necessitates a concentration of the message.

The Miraculous Medal is not at all inflated, nor does it belong to a fantasy world. In a restrained fashion it provides a richly concentrated catechesis.

The essential is on the reverse side, the hidden side. At the top is the cross, appropriately. "When I am lifted up from the earth, I will draw all things to me," said Jesus (Jn 12:32). At the bottom is the hidden love which inspires the whole work of salvation, represented by two very simple (and biblical) signs—the heart of Christ, crowned with thorns, and the heart of Mary, pierced by the sword predicted by Simeon (Lk 2:35). The cross is inherent in love.

The light-filled obverse side shows how this divine love spreads out, diffused by the Holy Spirit. As a consequence of "the wonderful exchange in the incarnation," the Mother, called to produce God in human form and to make his human heart, radiates his glory throughout the great family of humanity. For the handmaid of the Lord all is grace, everything comes only from grace, right from the beginning. Thus she shows forth the light of the sun of justice.

We can also better understand the medal's humble function:

1) It is a *Bible for the poor,* a pictorial representation of the Gospel. This image is nothing in itself, but, in accordance with the authentic doctrine of the Church's Councils regarding idolatry, it refers to Something Else—in fact, to what it is representing. Thus, it is a modest launching pad for human prayer.

2) It is a memorial, a catalyst for anamnesis—i.e., the re-enacting of memories issuing from Christ himself with the object of stimulating confidence and generosity.

3) It is a link with Christ in the communion of saints, a support for hope and prayer.

After all that, is it necessary to present objections?

People have often denounced the exaggerations, preoccupation with material things, even the abuses, that can arise in the context of "popular religion"—in this case, for instance, distributing medals far and wide in places or to persons not familiar with faith, rather like trawling a fishing net through the sea. Such things are certainly both of only secondary importance and open to criticism, and one should also not forget the "might is right" fallacy; but at the same time neither should one forget that Christian hope has its unexpected pathways, its interior rationale, even its follies, which are often worth more than distrust. Indeed, certain contestable "impertinences"—e.g., Théodore de Bussière regarding Ratisbonne—are nothing less than a challenge to faith. Let us not be too quick to set up faith in opposition to the freely given signs by which faith is expressed and on which faith leans—sometimes a little too heavily, in its weakness and its boldness. Jesus was not offended when the woman with the issue of blood came up behind him, saying to herself, "If only I can touch the hem of his garment, I shall be cured!" He did not reprimand her for being superstitious, but said to her, "Your faith has saved you" (Mt 5:34; Lk 8:48).

Faith is not in opposition to discernable signs, any more than physical nourishment is to spiritual nourishment, even if fasting does have its value and its function, as Catherine discovered in her childhood.

Apparitions must be judged by their fruits. We have glimpsed some of those considerable fruits, both in the Church across the world and, more intensely, in St. Vincent's two families, with great fertility for Ozanam and Catherine herself. To set out all the details would go beyond the brief of the present life story, but one day these too-easily-misunderstood phenomena must be evaluated. Popular religion, the religion of the poor, the religion of signs, should not be looked at askance, as if from the heights of some ideology or other, but in the light of God's ways and their results.

Apparitions, visions, dreams[5]

We have encountered the apparitions to Catherine in the very midst of her daily life. They are both diverse and convergent.

The first apparitions—of St. Vincent's heart—were a great family benefit for the two communities he had founded. They acted as the catalyst for a renewal that had been searched for unsuccessfully and which benefited the work of the missions and indeed the whole

Church. Why should it be that the human person, in the area of the supernatural as elsewhere, had need of an often irrational sign or symbol to provoke him or her into movement?

After that, the eucharistic visions were something rather more personal nourishment to strengthen Catherine after her long march through the desert and the dark night of faith.

The three apparitions of our Lady first of all gave Catherine her mission by making her aware of the Lord's very simple wishes for his Church; then the medal acted to awaken fresh hope and thus stimulate the rebirth of the miracle in a Church debilitated by centuries of rationalism and suffering from loss of blood in persecutions.

Catherine's apparitions took place within a very limited time scale—scarcely the duration of her seminary years, from April to December 1830. Then she was warned by our Lady that she would *not see her any more* but instead would hear her in her prayers—an invisible form of revelation, more in conformity with the nature of faith, for faith comes through listening: *fides ex auditu* (Rom 10:17). Her inspiration was God's Word, God's illumination; and so the rest of her life was a pattern of long service fed by a secret dialogue.

She did not experience visions except in a very spasmodic manner at turning points in history during her lifetime—for the 1848 Revolution, a vision of the cross; then, during the Commune, the dream in which the Virgin promised to protect Reuilly. This "dream," more real than reality itself, tied in with Catherine's dream of St. Vincent when she found the path of her vocation.

Today, the humble sign shown forth by the medal for millions of Christians is a stimulus to humble and joyful hope, more fruitful than we can guess at.

Prophecies

Another of Catherine's charisms—her predictions—has also been contested.

They are just as "ambiguous" as the charisms we have been talking about. In general, where the gift of prediction is found to exist, we tend to contest it or exaggerate it, challenge it or take it out of context. As with Bernadette of Lourdes, large quantities of prophecies have been attributed to Catherine. Knowing both of them to have been visionaries, people have retrospectively looked for premonitory meanings in their words—words that were sometimes rather banal when the visionaries were talking about events or giving advice. Some of the predictions attributed to Catherine look more like answered prayers than anything else, or like the intuitiveness of hope. But hope stands on a foundation and could be a stimulus, illuminating for those able to benefit from it.

There are thirty-five predictions associated with Catherine over the course of her life, summarized in the documentary volume that accompanies the French edition of this book.[6] They sometimes go beyond the ordinary, though it is not actually easy to say to what extent.

A clouding factor over these prophecies has been the way people have tried to find in them a clear description of the future, when rather it has been a case of an unclear anticipation of those things that God's desires enkindle in human hope and human aspirations. Thus, every authentic prediction remains ambiguous up to the moment of its realization. The Old Testament prophets did not produce picture postcards of what Bethlehem would be like, or the cross, or Jesus, the carpenter from Nazareth. And the realizations of their prophecies were not without a certain surprise element which inquisitive people find especially disturbing. This is even true for those admirable prophecies in Isaiah chapter 35.

A whole movement that understood prophecies as a kind of magical foretelling of the future was responsible for Catherine's "predictions" being challenged even during her lifetime. We have seen how Sr. Dufès, who felt herself taken for a ride, said to Catherine, "You have got it wrong," and Catherine's humble agreement, "Yes, I'm certainly mistaken and I'm very glad that people can see the truth!" (This provided Fr. Coste with a sledgehammer argument. "She was never anything but mistaken," he generalized.[7])

The official biographies have passed lightly over this "failure," or have even suppressed it, saying in Catherine's defense that errors in this domain can even be found in the case of the saints. "Bernard of Clairvaux predicted the success of the Second Crusade, which actually collapsed," Misermont reminds us.[a]

But a proper methodological approach teaches us not to be so quick to attribute to Catherine the obvious mistakes that she acknowledged as such in her humility and obedience when appearances and those in authority were against her. In the Bible itself, the way in which prophecies were realized generally baffled the prophets as well as their contemporaries. And their enemies triumphed over them. In similar cases, the mistake is often in interpreting things that may be either clear or obscure in precise terms and with precise dates, instead of trying to discern the basic dimensions. If we read the prophecies in the context of Catherine's life and the life of her community, the evaluation is positive and the "stigmata" of being contradicted take their proper place as part of the usual lot of prophets in general.

In this area, Fr. Coste's contestations are more useful than Sr. Dufès' biased attempts to make things fit. If Catherine was mistaken, she humbly acknowledged the fact. It is rather Sr. Dufès and others who have rushed to interpret obscure prophecies according to their own lines of thought and have then branded them as errors after the subsequent and inevitable letdown.

In the course of six papers (1909–1933) in which he set out his objections, Coste severely criticized four prophecies, and only four–those that appeared to him the most obviously "erroneous."

1. The first is a laconic premonition regarding the year 1880: "peace." It is true that this prediction, received in 1830 and noted down in 1876,[b] gave rise to exaggerated expectations, mentioned by Sr. de Geoffre on January 1, 1878,[c] and thus to disappointment in proportion to the exaggeration. Misermont openly notes this failure, and his apologia attempts to get out of it by challenging the authenticity of the actual words, even though the unarguable evidence is present in an autograph document:[d] "ten [years] and afterward–peace."

However, as we have seen, *1880 was in fact the year in which Catherine's wishes,* refused during her lifetime of "martyrdom," *were realized:* the commemorative altar and the Virgin with the globe, the granting of a supplementary Communion on the anniversary days, and the opening up of the chapel for pilgrims.

The fact that 1880 was marked by a first wave of anticlerical interference, and 1881 by Rome's temporary action against the Virgin with the globe, provoked great disappointment among those who were expecting a peak of "glory."[e] And this produced misunderstanding of the importance attached by Catherine to these realizations. The statue of the Virgin with the globe, re-erected in 1885, on May 31, 1980, drew a special, silent prayer from Pope John Paul II during his visit to the Rue du Bac. Is that not a final sign that Catherine's prayer was well and truly answered?

2. The symbolic vision of a cross set up in the square in front of Notre Dame has been denounced as another of Catherine's mistakes. But here it is less a case of an *unrealized prediction* than *a request that was refused.*

This prophecy (in the biblical sense where the term signifies a word spoken in the name of God in the midst of the people) nevertheless ties in strikingly with a deep-seated, nineteenth-century aspiration concerning the cross of Christ. If Catherine's cross had been realized, it would doubtless have produced a wave of devotion and grace similar to that produced by the medal. It would have been a christological complement to and a crowning of the message, in the sense of that which is at the summit of the message: the cross which dominates the medal.

3. Fr. Coste took Catherine to task for having predicted to her nephew, Philippe Meugniot, that he would become "Superior General of the Vincentians"; but this is a caricature of Catherine's prophecy. The subject of the prediction himself was edified by it. He testified to it on oath twice in the course of the canonization process. The prediction lit up the unexpected path of his vocation. When he had still been chewing over his possible entry into the Vincentians, Catherine had said to him not, "You will be Superior General," as Fr. Coste gratuitously supposed, but, to quote the words as twice testified by Philippe himself on oath, "It's possible to become a superior soon" (no more than that), "then go to China, like Fr. Perboyre," and so on.

Now, this prediction came true. Philippe Meugniot was made superior at the age of 29, against his will, as we saw in chapter 7. Then he went off to the missions in China. Since Catherine did not in fact say to him that he would be Superior General, it is almost unnecessary to add that for many long years he agreed to shoulder the burden of a major superior's post—that of Director General of the Sisters of Charity.

When Coste says that "this prophecy only began to be talked about in 1900," after Fr. Meugniot's nomination as director, he is merely showing his ignorance of the normal process whereby Philippe Meugniot had already reported this prediction as early as October 20, 1899 (well before Fr. Coste began to talk about it), in terms which it would have repaid Coste to acquaint himself with.

4. The prediction that draws the most criticism is the one about the "tomb" buried "at a depth of 1m 50," whose discovery would be the foundation of a "church." Repeated searches were made in the hope of digging up...buried treasure! And these provoked bitter disappointments which were held against Catherine. Nevertheless, those companions of hers who received this statement were uplifted by its totally unexpected outcome: the tombstone of St. Catherine herself, who was buried at Reuilly, contrary to all the usual customs and regulations. It

was the police inspector who, knowing nothing of the prediction, gave the order for the body to be buried at a depth of precisely "1m 50."[f] Thus the vault at Reuilly became a chapel, a place of pilgrimage to which people came to invoke her intercession while awaiting her canonization, which would permit the dedication to her of (to date) twenty-three churches, basilicas, or chapels across the five continents, to say nothing of the 408–some going back considerably further–which are dedicated to our Lady of the Miraculous Medal.

The sort of rationalism that reduces prophecies to a clear expression of some material (and often mistaken) thing totally misunderstands the very nature of prophecy, which is an indistinct anticipation of God's vital work in the Church. Malraux said, "The prophet is not someone who predicts but someone who can express a word in which people can see their future." Looked at in this kind of perspective (which we must expand to include God himself), Catherine's prophecies were a source of enlightenment, support, and edification for her community. All through her life, they appear to us as being simple and unpretentious.

In the French volume of documentary evidence already mentioned, a summary of Catherine's thirty-five predictions can be found, together with cross-references to her life.[7] Catherine's predictions have to do with the protection of the Vincentians, of the Sisters of Charity, of France itself during the troubles of the nineteenth century, but above all they deal with the future of prayer and of the Church. Those who benefited from realizations of the predictions were amazed by them. Fr. Etienne, Superior General, and his successors publicly expressed their thanksgiving for the astonishing protection of St. Vincent's two families. The first criticism of this wonderful experience came from young Vincentians who felt that such protection had "prevented" them from carrying their cross or even from undergoing martyrdom.[g]

It is of course difficult to gauge just how far Catherine's *prophecies* incorporated extraordinary *predictions*. As is nearly always the case in these matters, they were not noted down until after they had come about–except for the one concerning the year 1880. But Catherine already had a certain track record in this area, and this was what prompted the three Superiors General to undertake exploratory excavations at Reuilly in order to find the tombstone mentioned by Catherine–who never dreamed that her own modest tomb would itself be the realization of the prophecy. Fr. Chinchon, her confessor, who had given Catherine a public dressing-down for the failure of a prediction (doubtless the one we are discussing), testified on oath (at the beatification process) to his admiration because of several predictions that had come to pass and of which he is furthermore the only source.

The important thing about the entire matter is that these uplifting charisms were able to stimulate hope, generosity, devotion, and initiative among those who related them or found themselves affected by them. This is thoroughly in conformity with the nature of such free gifts, destined for the spiritual uplifting of the Church.

Power of seeing and discernment

Catherine is also credited with supernatural intuitions regarding the distribution of the medal,[8] as well as the rapid launching of Lourdes and Notre Dame des Victoires in which she saw influxes of pilgrims compensating for those who could not go to the Rue du Bac, since the decision to open it had not been taken.[9] In addition, she is credited with inspired advice and actions that seem to suggest a kind of mind reading or spiritual science from which her companions were able to benefit.[10] There is a very blurred borderline between such intuitive acts or sayings, orientated to a greater or lesser extent toward the future, and those which appear more clearly as "predictions." We will not dwell on this any longer, as we have already given the details in Catherine's life story above. It is "in the flesh" that one can best see, without exaggeration, what it was that made these things so uplifting. The reader with access to the French documentary volume is invited to consult notes 6 and 10 of chapter 9, where one will find a listing of the relevant data.

Limited and modest charisms

In accordance with the Church's tradition, it is important to emphasize the "modest" character of these extraordinary charisms. Their function is more especially to awaken hope rather than faith itself. They can add nothing to the perfect Revelation of Christ. Their status is a modest one. Even St. Vincent de Paul mistrusted his own visions as he did those of others. The Bible itself tells us that one cannot see God without dying. Moses and Elijah, the two Old Testament characters who seem to have had the most formal meetings with God, encountered him through the medium of *mysterious signs:* the burning bush or the cloud over Mount Sinai in the one case, the "voice of a gentle silence" in the other. (I do not care for the senseless modern translation "the sound of a gentle breeze," however correct it may be. The biblical expression in 1 Kings 19:12 presents a negative theology in which the *silent and invisible* passing of God is contrasted with the thunderous din of the signs that acted as forerunners—storm and earthquake.) Does this mean that the recipients of God's gifts *only see subjective signs* and do not communicate with God himself?

That would be a simplistic conclusion to draw. No, *the function of a sign is to announce what it signifies*. God's signs announce God himself. If God gives a sign to people, it is as a means that he has adopted in order to announce himself in accordance with earthly people's capabilities. All our knowledge comes to us through *signs,* and those signs have no function other than to refer us to a reality. It was with analogous humility that Catherine experienced her encounters with Light.

B. Ordinary Charisms[11]

It would therefore be a serious mistake to concentrate only on Catherine's extraordinary charisms: visions, apparitions, predictions, intuitions, or the reading of minds, which in any case are both sober and only occasionally met with during her life. Charisms are free gifts given for the edification of the Church. Furthermore, *the extraordinary is not the basic requirement for edification*. It is only a stimulus. The Church is above all built on acts of humble daily service inspired by charity—especially acts of service for the poor. More than it might appear, these acts are themselves charisms—free gifts of the Holy Spirit at the service of the Church.

So, Catherine's life was above all one of "daily charisms." For her, the important thing was serving the poor. Similarly, she showed herself strictly accountable for the time and money that were available to her. In the same way, she took upon herself unpleasant and thankless tasks and tiresome or mistrustful people, as we have already seen. One of her charisms involved putting first those most in need, both materially and spiritually; it was the preferential treatment she gave to the poverty stricken and the suffering whom others turned away or got rid of—in other words, those who were the most forsaken. There was no category of poor person known to her with which she was not thoroughly familiar. She was a refuge and a defense for such individuals as Blaisine Lafosse and others, whose superiors had mercilessly recorded them as being "intolerable characters." Catherine was a calming influence and a safety valve for Sr. Tranchemer. Last but not least, she had an acknowledged gift for "liberating sinners"—not by autosuggestion but through constantly going back to the one true source. "The Spirit blows where he will," but above all in the direction of the poor; and Catherine was well able to receive a great variety of breaths of the Spirit, beginning with that particular one.

The most important thing is that her visions did not deflect her from faith, and her extraordinary charisms did not deflect her from the humblest and most ordinary service. Quite the reverse; they encouraged her along this dual pathway. This is one of the most striking features of her life.

We still have not looked beyond those charisms accomplishing God's work to her sanctity as such. We do not need to dissect it in minute detail but to grasp its concrete reality, taking physical and mental data as our starting point (for grace does not short-circuit nature but fulfills it).

A Portrait of Catherine: Roots and nature

Who, then, was Catherine?

A. Physical Description[12]

The Photographs

On the physical side of things, our information is much more scanty than it is for Bernadette, who was photographed no less than seventy-five times during the period 1861–1879–from the age of 17 right up to the time of her death at a very young 35.

Catherine was only photographed once during her lifetime, at the age of 70, and twice on the day after her death. We only have a faint image of what she must have been like. The "photos of Catherine, aged 26" that were published at the time of her beatification were in fact of another sister, a century younger, who was thought to look somewhat like her.[13]

One thing which Catherine and Bernadette had in common was the *look* in their eyes—most striking in Catherine's case. It seemed to radiate goodness, a sense of the ascendant, but also a very clear reference to "the beyond."[14]

Another point in common with Bernadette: Catherine's body did not putrefy in the tomb. It was recovered intact, just as it had been on the day of her death.[15] Dr. Didier, in charge of the exhumation of March 21–23, 1933, recorded the details in astonishment.

> Perfect suppleness of arms and legs; muscles preserved after more than half a century. They could be easily dissected as with an anatomical specimen [...]. The gray-blue coloring of the iris is still there.

Only the removal of relics, injections of formaldehyde, and other treatments wrought damage to the body, which was still intact when it was exhumed. It is now preserved in a shrine in the chapel at the Rue du Bac, the site of the apparitions. Duly authenticated as a result of painstaking procedures, Catherine's body retains a fundamental documentary value, taking into account a covering of wax and the difference between a body and a corpse more than a hundred years after death. The descriptions furnished by Catherine's contemporaries are an encouragement to invest her with fresh life: she was quite the opposite of inert—"smiling and joyful," "energetic and lively."

She was also said to be "rather tall." In fact, she was scarcely 1m 60" [5 feet 3 inches],[16] but this was a respectable height for a woman of the period. For the rest, she had a high forehead, a rather pronounced nose, a large, firm mouth, and the large hips of a peasant woman.[17]

Prosopology

The state of Catherine's body, coupled with the mediocrity of the photographs, create difficulties in the field of study of the character from looking at the face—an undertaking which can be worked at using two recently begun academic disciplines: *prosopology,* which deals with muscular contractions and the direction in which a person looks, and *morphopsychology,* first developed by Dr. Corman, which looks at the forms of faces and evaluates their correlations with character using as parameters the contrasted aspects of dilation and retraction worked on by Claude Sigaud.

Catherine, in her seventies and not far from death, appears dignified, if a little cold—perhaps already a little detached from this world that she was soon to leave for good. Shyness in front of the camera seems to have combined with a certain drowsiness that took away all sense of expression from her. It is rather like a winter photograph of a lifeless tree.

Dr. Ermaine, the first practitioner of prosopology, who had been fascinated by the photos of Bernadette, did not want to pass judgment on Catherine's. He confined himself to noting, "She must have been energetic, but a bad judge of herself."[18]

Such brevity demonstrates one of the difficulties with prosopology, which is really only at home with people who are alive and encounters problems when dealing with poor photographs. As far as the above diagnosis is concerned, it seems to me to indicate that Catherine was the opposite of introspective—she concentrated on her work and her plans. In any case, at the age she was when the picture was taken, she was well beyond any delving inside herself and trying to find out about herself. The 1876 photo, as far as prosopology goes, is only a chrysalis. The look in her eyes only betrays waiting in patience for the revelation that God would soon give her when she met him face-to-face.

Morphopsychology

Morphopsychology is better placed to analyze this picture of an older woman, since it is based on *the study of static forms*.

From this point of view, the first things that spring to one's notice are (despite the sort of weakening that one would expect at the age of 70) strength, energy, and equilibrium between the three areas of the face: a powerful jaw, denoting strength and activity; a substantial nose, indicating contact with the world; and the forehead that, although not of an intellectual, is still by no means small. These three areas possess a similarity of size and a very balanced development, which implies an understanding both of life and of its realities.

I showed the photographs to Madame Courtin, who for many years has been a practitioner of the study of the human face. When she saw them, she said to me straight away, "If I saw someone like that arriving at my home, I would say 'There is somebody to whom one can turn for support.'"

At that age Catherine did not have the engaging charm which comes across so strongly in the photos of Bernadette, but she did have the "superiority" of being an active, organized woman who knew how to conduct her own life.

Before my visit, Madame Courtin had already produced a preliminary "diagnosis" based only on the deathbed photograph of Catherine and so with no expression in her eyes. This first report is interesting because it is based purely on morphology, extinguished by death.

> The face, with eyes closed, is only three-quarters visible, the forehead being partially hidden by the bonnet. It is a powerful face, well developed in all areas: the cheek bones are large, the nose is substantial, the mouth is big. In the stillness of death, the face expresses intense vitality

of a virile kind, such as one often finds in old women who have suffered much, fought much, and conquered much. The upper lip is hidden by a shadow which looks like a moustache. If we ignore this blemish, the face, which basically is permeated with a certain virile energy, becomes more feminine. The rounded aspect of the facial characteristics betrays a certain gentleness. But the most noticeable thing, once again, is energy well above the average, a readiness for action of any kind, a tremendous openness to communication, and a rich and powerful emotional life, but a well-controlled one. Catherine is direct, uncomplicated, a bit trenchant, and without superfluous refinement. Efficiently, she goes straight to the heart of things. She has a presence, an impact on people and events; she has the power and the serenity of a woman who solves problems by action.

Those over whom she was in authority (the sick and the elderly) sensed within her a strength of mind against which there was no question of rebelling.

"What does a photograph of Catherine when she was alive add to that judgment?" I then asked her.

First of all, it eliminates some deathbed "distortions" which I had had difficulty with: the nose was a little deformed after death and a shadow hid the lips and masked her femininity. Next, the lifetime photo of Catherine confirms that she had very strong emotional appetites, with a passionate side to her personality, but also with the capacity to filter those appetites and control them. Looked at from a *morphopsychological* point of view, this photograph tends to confirm that Catherine belonged to the category of lateral retraction, with a hint of interior retraction on a dilating base.

"In other words?"

The differentiation which appears on the face, like the work of a refined sculptor in which can be read subtleties of sensitivity, is not present on the vigorous nose, which is very little differentiated (without proper lighting, etc.). This indicates a simplicity in her emotional relationships. To put it another way, her contacts with people and the world were imprinted with a great simplicity. She could be lively, even cutting, unlike more refined characters. The root of the nose testifies especially to great vitality.

It is here that we need to notice, from one part of the nose to another, what is called latero-nasal retractions in which we can read reactions to the shocks that life brings. These retractions can be seen on each side of the nose, from the eye down to the corner of the mouth. The anterior line of junction of the cheeks in Catherine's case is much more "differentiated" than the rest of the face. These light undulations that "furrow the hill" betray an interiorized sensitivity on the emotional level. From her nose, with not much differentiation, Catherine could appear to be a bit brusque, but sensitivity *is something that goes on at a certain depth*. In Catherine's case, the differentiation is clear, subtle, and not exaggerated. Her emotions are passionate, but well under control, an aspect accentuated by the vitality of cheekbones and cheeks (the latter less chubby in the photo taken when she was older than they were when she was young). From the emotional point of view, Catherine's had "interiorized affectivity." The downward movement of the mouth is due to old age–it is often to be found at this age. The fold in the skin is actually moderate, with no trace of bitterness, and denotes a bodily weakening in the approach of death.

This retraction is not accentuated but normal. It shows her patient side, her resignation in the face of the problems she took on. But her lips, pressed firmly against each other, show a victorious struggle against disappointments. Catherine overcame her disappointments.

The most striking thing on this lifetime photo is the eyes (open): *her look is extraordinary. There is a deep intensity there, a presence*. Some faces show depth without presence–the intimate side of life remains inaccessible. Others have a presence, but superficial, with no depth. In the case of Catherine, these two characteristics are, extraordinarily, combined. She is both *deep* and *present*. She communicates. This look confirms the dominant characteristic that I had glimpsed in the deathbed photograph.

Then Madame Courtin looked in turn at each eye, covering the opposite side of the face.

The left eye shows seriousness which examines and overcomes difficulty, efficient willingness, imperiousness. The right eye is sad, far away, perhaps even grief-stricken. A cry for help can be discerned in it, almost as if she could do no more.

"In an astonishing fashion you have brought together the two linked aspects of Catherine's personality–on the one hand the realism and efficiency which is confirmed by the ministering which she carried out so well right up to the end, according to the demanding and generally severe testimony of her superior; on the other hand, what Catherine herself (but still in moderation, in her language) called her 'martyrdom.' But which characteristic is the deepest, the most significant in her face?"

First of all, great energy, capable of an impact on people and realities; certainly a dominant characteristic. However, going beyond her well-ordered efficiency, she had in the midst of her problems (even her times of distress) a remarkable power of resistance, being able to call on deep resources within herself that she was totally sure of. She had an amazing capacity for going back to bathe herself again in the sources within her, of finding in them the power to go beyond the shocks that had shaken her, the power of resilience, of bounding back up to the surface again with efficiency and serenity.

This conversation and consultation took place without Madame Courtin having read a single word of my work on Catherine. I was tremendously struck by the accuracy she showed in double-checking (and in detail) what I had laboriously extracted from the (sometimes very acute) observations and testimony of those who had known Catherine. Madame Courtin's objective analysis confirmed several points which might have appeared exaggerated in one set of depositions or another–particularly regarding the very noticeable look in Catherine's eyes which had fascinated so many of the sisters and had aroused in Sr. Jeanne Maurel the desire to go and pray in Catherine's habitual place in order to "obtain access to" Catherine's way of looking at God. For a long time, such pieces of evidence had seemed to me to be very peripheral. But they were trying to express something that is not expressible and so one should try to preserve only the heart of the matter, not the surface trappings.

The analysis, deriving as it does from the body and what it must have been able to express in life, sends us back to basics. For Catherine, grace was not like the wave of a magic wand turning Cinderella's pumpkin into a gorgeous carriage; it was the fulfillment of a resource-filled person's character. This is by way of illustrating one of the great truths–that grace does not destroy nature, it liberates it by realizing all its hidden potential virtues. By looking at the question in what might seem to be this roundabout way, we are already coming into contact with St. Catherine's deepest secret.

B. Character[19]

Looking at morphopsychology has bridged the gap for us between the exterior and the interior.

How could Fr. Aladel have described Catherine as "cold and apathetic"? This testimony, given at the *Procès Quentin,* is rather overdoing things in order to emphasize that Catherine was not subject to trances. That is certainly true, but it is a very coarse way of putting across Catherine's self-control, which bottled up her own vitality to such an extent that it even led people astray. Many sisters assure us that the opposite was the case: Catherine was lively, even "a pretty strong mixture," as Sr. Dufès put it.[h]

Her reactions were strong, even explosive. Her Burgundy blood rushed easily to her face, but immediately she would regain control of herself. Her spontaneous initial movements were not followed up. "I don't know how she managed instantaneously to regain absolute calm," said Sr. Dufès (quoted by Sr. Tanguy).[i]

Her first reactions ("sizzling" was Sr. Tanguy's description) had the effect of releasing her from any bottling-up that could have been unhealthy for her. Her ability to get quickly back to normal came from the hidden depths within her and this was also responsible for her efficiency. She was able to control not only her normal aggressiveness but also her peasant woman's second nature.

Sr. Dufès said, "If there is a difference between Sister Catherine and me, it is that although we are both very animated characters, she is quick to control herself, whereas with me things last longer."

Passionately concerned about things, Catherine avoided becoming polarized on those that were dear to her heart. She channeled her vital powers by taking on many things at once–jobs, plans, all mixed together in an orderly and logical fashion. Though overburdened, she worked steadily without rushing, but also without letting up. Her peasant upbringing had taught her how to work on another field while waiting for the first one to ripen, in order to gather "each fruit in due season."

Above all, she knew the secret of transcending overwork or worry in deep prayer. She went to the foot of the altar in her "troubles"–sometimes severe–as our Lady had told her to. There she found true repose in God–the deep rest of the seventh day of creation where God was her model and her inspiration. This grace was a fulfillment of an already inherent characteristic in her.

In her relationships with others, the witnesses emphasize Catherine's straightforwardness and honesty. She was not a gossip and was often silent–not one for spreading rumors about others or scandal mongering. But she still had plenty to say for herself and expressed herself in a picturesque fashion when talking to people she knew. For those dear to her, her speech was animated. But here she also had the unexpected knack of saying things impulsively without thinking if someone touched one of her sensitive spots.

Catherine was as generous as she could be, simple and accessible, although discreet and reserved and without ostentation. Beneath the rough hide she had developed to protect herself from indiscretion or futile familiarity, she radiated a transparent goodness. It would be a mistake to stress her severity from the evidence of a single photograph that shows her very much on the defensive. She smiled often, and gaiety was her predominant characteristic according to the records of her seminary days—and nothing subsequently happened to change that.

She had neither the inclination nor the education for speculative analysis and was indeed rather suspicious of a certain intellectual superstructure which she saw in the formation of the Sisters of Charity. "There are some sisters who have never tended a sick person in their life. They would not know where to begin if it came to rendering the most basic service," she regretted.[j]

Her intelligence was totally oriented toward people and the efficiency of her daily ministering to them and has, therefore, been underestimated. A laconic note from the end of her seminary records: "Mental powers and sense of judgment not outstanding." What has gone unrecognized in Catherine's case is her intuition, her understanding of people and situations, with a sensitivity illuminated by God that sometimes was nothing short of sheer genius. Insofar as intelligence is defined as the capacity for adaptation to things as they are, Catherine's intelligence showed itself to be exceptional in unexpected or difficult situations, notably during the Commune. Her intelligence consisted in knowing how life works, being able to keep to whatever disciplines are demanded of one (including accountability) while never losing touch with things as they really are.

Catherine was formed by the ancestral demands of the land—the Burgundy soil,[20] its culture and its cultivation—and she knew how to accommodate the impulsiveness of her lively nature with the demands of her service, her mission, her charity. She was exemplary from the point of view of orderliness, punctuality, and moderation—not for nothing was she referred to as the "regular" sister.

And now we must look into the shadows without which light will have no meaning. The shadows are those of "faults" and "ordeals."

C. Catherine's Faults[21]

Examination of "faults" is very important in canonization processes—for if only a single one be found, even though not at all serious but persisting uncorrected to the end of one's life, then the cause is lost. In

Catherine's case, the investigating judges in the apostolic process were extremely insistent on this point; and the Devil's Advocate played his part with great enthusiasm.

The principal accusation was one of gluttony.[22] Fr. Hamard, a Vincentian, had said, "several weeks after her death":

> Sr. Catherine was a good girl, but when she was ill she allowed herself to drift into a certain amount of sensuality. When sisters were present, she made herself out to be more ill than she actually was, and when they were absent she used to get up to go and find little delicacies and bring them to the infirmary where she was confined to bed.[k]

Sr. Lenormand was concerned that no "objections" should be omitted. When she was invited to, she cited this statement, but corrected it.

> I think that in the matter of delicacies, this actually means a few grapes in this case. I should add that in other situations Fr. Hamard has come across to me as someone inclined to exaggeration and I think that in the present case he has exaggerated somewhat. I was all the more surprised by his statement in that every time that I had the occasion to see Sr. Dufès at the time referred to, she always had nothing but praise for the virtues of the Servant of God.[l]

We have looked at the basis of Fr. Coste's accusation, here clearly inflated. There is very little to discover. During her final illness, Catherine was concerned to keep up her strength in order still to be of as much service as she could be, right up to the end, and because of this she made use of very modest means of alleviating her pain: one pastille, a small lump of sugar, a cup of milk or of clear soup, an apple cooked in the embers—whatever was available, without ever asking for anything special.[m]

Such little assuagements as these were demanded by her age and her infirmity, and it appears that she took them instead of dinner on the days when she had to go without meals in the community—she could not rely on her "negligent" nurse, for whom carrying a meal up to her was like climbing the Matterhorn. Catherine had courage but she was certainly not a stoic. She took a *just* pity on herself. These seeming lapses on Catherine's part were the pride and joy of the file of evidence against her. But the witnesses on the subject, who were absolutely grilled by the investigators, tried to outdo each other in emphasizing how much such "assuagements" were in conformity with the Rules established by St. Vincent de Paul, actually practiced in the community. They went to great lengths to justify Catherine's conduct.

Indeed, the evidence was abundantly in the other direction—it testified to her sobriety. Here is an example:

> In 1848, when Fr. Etienne, Superior General, "gave permission for two ounces of bread on fast days" and confirmed "the use of wine by reason of diminishing strength of health," Catherine was "the last person to do so, and only when she saw all the other sisters doing it," and even then she only took "the tiniest amount of wine."

This, according to Sr. Tanguy (in authority over Catherine during the last years of her life).[23]

Catherine did not aspire to the sort of ascetic performance that in those days one expected from a saint. If she was able to go beyond normal limits in facing up to repeated vigils or the dramas of the Commune, she hid the fact well and "never went to sleep in her prayers." In the ordinary way of things, "she avoided anything which could have weakened her in carrying out her work," one of the witnesses makes clear. She looked after her body to be able to serve others the better.[24]

Any asceticism that she practiced was based on a well-ordered sense of charity. Her fairness had been the reason for her being chosen to be in charge of the distribution of food to the sisters in the refectory. She served in order. First, the best bits went to the sick and to the superior; the rest went to everyone else; finally, she would say, "This is for me, if that is all right with you,"[25] and give herself the worst pieces.

When she received sweets, she always gave them to her nieces or to the poor. She had acquired this habit in childhood.[26]

The Process was less concerned with other points of suspicion for which evidence was available. Catherine's natural vivacity was healthy and well controlled.[27] "Her dominating character" (as Sr. Dufès put it in 1877), which had been forged by the exercise of authority in her youth, was no less the subject of a counterweight to balance it: she "struggled to comply graciously," and turned down the task of being a superior—a task that would have been well suited to her. If she was occasionally gruff in the recreation room, this was in order to defend her orders…or her secret. Her abruptness and outbursts happened promptly and without premeditation—but they were never wounding. Apart from these minor details, the witnesses said that she was amiable, affable, and kind. Furthermore, they were surprised that she had never given cause for complaints, even when doing difficult work with the elderly and at the door where such things were two a penny.

Catherine's entire character was the other side of the coin from her honesty: her "stubbornness," an essential and well-controlled resource for carrying out her mission.[28] She was well endowed with tenacity, like Bernadette, and she certainly needed it.

Briefly, like Bernadette, she too had the faults that go with her qualities. It is therefore not possible in this case to make use of St. Bernadette's dictum:

> People talk too much about the visions and miracles of the saints. That serves no useful purpose. What you need to know is their faults and how they managed to control them.[29]

Catherine does not reveal great faults and, therefore, nothing in the way of good improvements, but rather a good mastery of herself, not through voluntarism but by calling deeply upon her rich natural resources and even more upon those of grace. This deepening evolved into a transfiguration which irradiated the peacefulness of her old age. Like Bernadette, she could have said, "I have never wanted to offend God."

This maxim is written in filigree lettering running through the whole of Catherine's life. It subtends the whole of her being and her "efficiency" at doing good.

Her apparent faults and mediocrity were for her a protection that she cultivated for the good of a secret that was so difficult to keep. This is why the sisters' desire for admiration of a stained-glass sort of figure alighted upon an older sister: Vincent Bergerault, the parsimonious cook who played that kind of role better than Catherine, and was even thought at one time to have been the visionary herself. Catherine aided this diversionary tactic which helped her service of the poor and her secret.

Ordeals

Was Catherine heroic? This was called into question in the Process on the virtues, for canonization requires proof of heroic sanctity. And heroism in daily life is more difficult to identify than the heroism of martyrs or the founders of great works. The same problem was very acute in the case of Thérèse of Lisieux. There is no question as to whether Catherine was heroic. She was so, as we have seen, in her everyday life, and the Process judges acknowledged this. It is rather a question of knowing *in what sense* she was heroic.

Her ordeals did not attain the tragic proportions of Bernadette, who went from destructive hunger to permanent illness (tuberculosis) and a dark night of the soul, both of which were totally dizzying in their effect. Nor did Catherine's ordeals compare with those of Thérèse of Lisieux, involved in the conflicts of a community torn apart, struck down in her youth by tuberculosis, plunged, too, into a dark night of the soul where she found herself "seated at the table of sinners."[30] Catherine's ordeals sprang rather from the lot of common folk, but with "a full measure, shaken down, running over," like a great peasant basket, filled to the very limits of her strength to carry it, constantly on the point of falling and upsetting, borne valiantly to the very end.

Bereavement in childhood

Catherine's ordeal began when she was 9 with the greatest trauma that a child can undergo: the death of her mother. We have seen how she overcame it by taking Mary as her mother and, at her tender age, taking on the role of mother of the household.

Thwarted vocation

Catherine's special links with her father, in which she found fulfillment over a period of twelve years, were broken by her vocation. She accepted this "death to her father" (a psychological death) by strengthening her ties to God to a very great depth. But the wound remained. In 1844, the physical death of her father reawoke that death within Catherine's soul, and wrenched a heartfelt cry from her: "That sacrifice cost me dearly...only God and Mary know how much. And how this grief is renewing itself again!..."[31]

But in this loss she acquired a new freedom, a strength sunk deep in God himself, which, like Abraham, called her to give everything. And without finding any kind of substitute, but simply by dint of patience, prudence, and genuine love, she resolved this crisis. Through reconciliation, she was able to find a new sense of distance and accept it. "A man must leave his father and mother...."

All her life, Catherine kept up family ties. Above all, like a kind of Good Samaritan she was present at all the dramatic scenes of distress, of which there were many. There was the departure from the community of her calumnied sister Marie-Louise, whom she was able to bring back to the Sisters of Charity after ten years of prayer. There was Marie-Antoinette, abandoned by her husband, in a state of neo-widow's distress, pitted against harsh financial problems. There were the illnesses and the deaths of her brothers, not to mention their drifting away from their religion in the tow of the bourgeois society and ideas of the era. We have seen how Catherine was present—almost omnipresent in proportion to the size of the family. She was able to do all this thanks to a knowledge of how to avoid (with one single exception, as we have already seen) the anxiety that sometimes gets entangled in family relationships. Always, Catherine went back to the same source which allowed her to take on even bereavements in a strong and enlivening way.

Problems living in community

However, we should not let this section of ordeals present an artificially black picture. Catherine's vocation was basically a happy one. The beginnings were so brilliant as to prompt her to write, "My feet no longer touched the ground," but a vocation is realized in the cross. Catherine had met St. Vincent in a "celestial fashion," under the filmy appearance of a dream, and she was soon suffering from the gulf between the ideal and the reality that she found in the relative decadence that followed the Revolution. Her praying about this was all the more ardent, her hope all the stronger. She soon had the joy of seeing a new springtime of fervor in the spirit of the origins of the community and an expansion without precedent—an expansion in quantity and also a geographical one, but above all an expansion in quality. Catherine was able to enjoy the extraordinary bursting-forth which at that time was a characteristic of St. Vincent's two families.

Catherine's great suffering was the continuous and strained refusals on the part of her confessor.[31]

As the proverb has it, it is better to go to the good Lord than to his saints. Catherine knew this from experience. The more her relationship with heavenly things was filled with light, the more the dissuasions of God's representative filled her with grief. The confessional became a dark night and an opaque wall for she who begged, reduced to being nothing more than a "blasted wasp." These things need to be placed in the context of the era—a time when there was a great insistence on obedience, a time when the subordination of women went uncontested throughout family, civil, and religious life. Catherine accepted the rules of the game, but (and remember how carefully she weighed her words) it was here that (she tells us) she found her "torment" and her "martyrdom." From her point of view, this was not an outrageous description, for it was the very light of God, whose messenger she was, that was being rejected. In her distress, she found comfort in deep prayer at the foot of the altar, as the Virgin herself had told her. The wonderful thing is that through this medium she was able to dissolve tensions and the risk of neurosis and to leave "the torment" on the surface of her spiritual being. Her prayer was answered after a wait of two years for the medal, forty years for the statue of the Virgin with the globe (realized "privately"). As far as everything else went, her prayers were only answered after her death. She had had to bear her "martyrdom" for the whole of her life.

The torment experienced by rejected visionaries is much worse than it might appear, for the "light" received appears to them like the command of God. Worse, any impossibility of achievement seems to them to be attributable to some fault in themselves. Humble Catherine did not try to lay the blame at God's door, nor at that of his representative. She took it on herself and not without risking destroying herself in the process.

More than we could know before now, Catherine was also familiar with the other ordeal that is the fate of visionaries, one which demolished Mélanie and tortured Bernadette: being, as it were, constantly under siege by those who hovered with their traps around her, as if around a curious animal. She underwent this ordeal daily from her fifties onward—the sisters and the servants, the elderly people and the visitors (two of the latter came directly from the Archbishop), not to mention Marshal MacMahon's wife, who brought her guest, the Shah of Persia, to Reuilly.... It was a situation where the slightest weakness on the part of the besieged would have placed her at their mercy.º

But as far as the superiors are concerned, we must not be overdramatic. Catherine began in happy conditions with the kind Sr. Sévart, friend of the poor. Sr. Mettavent and Sr. Guez were sufficiently appreciative of Catherine's qualities to propose her as a superior despite her lack of education. But Sr. Dufès, who ruled during more than one-third of Catherine's religious life (the last 17 years) herself acknowledged that she felt impelled to neglect Catherine and treat her harshly.[32] The odd thing is that during the Process she seemed to have forgotten some of that severity, which in any case had softened in the final months after Catherine had imparted her confidences in 1876. But Sr. Cosnard had been scandalized, to the point of protesting about it, even though she was only young. The "tension" between Sr. Dufès and Catherine is even more amazing when one remembers that it was Catherine who had saved Sr. Dufès' "bacon" in the stormy reception after her arrival: Catherine had rallied the community and brought them together. She did not only take on the entire ordeal with humble patience, but without stiffness. Here again, she arranged things in a responsible way, like the business of the farm. Once the storm of abuse had passed, she re-established contact herself, going to ask whether her superior would have the "goodness" to grant her some harmless permission or other. This was an appeal to her superior's better nature, and it worked. Catherine was thus able to avoid both the build up of layers of bitterness and drama-filled situations. It is incredible that her pride allowed her to lower herself to such an extent. Bernadette had not been able to cross this psychological bridge with Mother Marie-Thérèse Vauzou.

Now, the Labouré sense of pride was in no way inferior to that of the Soubirous. But Catherine had an upsetting grace of humility in every sense of the word, which explains the inexhaustible capacity for reconciliation that we find in her from childhood onward. So it was that Catherine made this superior, who had been hostile toward her for so long, the confidant and recipient of her last wishes in the spring of 1876.

Sr. Tanguy extended Catherine's ordeal. As a young assistant superior, still unsure of her own authority, secretly embarrassed by the shadow cast by Catherine's status in the house, and less equipped than Catherine to deal with certain difficult situations, she demonstrated a starchy and aggressive behavior that astounded Catherine right up to her deathbed, at which time (as we have already seen) she said without bitterness, "She hasn't been to see me all day, and look how she treats me!"

It was in this context that Catherine was provided with a negligent nurse. She suffered the repercussions of this right up to Fr. Hamard's accusations regarding self-indulgence in her old age. Catherine, numb with cold and without a fire at the beginning of her last winter, had to do the best she could for provisions for her upset stomach with whatever was at hand...rather than make a fuss.

During the years when she was in charge of the hospice, Catherine was the first to weather the attacks resulting from the unease that existed between the two houses of Enghien and Reuilly: recriminations from the elderly who were frustrated or frightened by the invasion of "young bloods," and the anxiety of the administrator and the d'Orléans family, who were affected by the elderly people's complaints.

The principal Reuilly sisters–those who had a voice in the Chapter–followed Sr. Dufès' example and kept a remoteness from the aging Catherine. Her ambiguous position as a secret visionary irritated them. They got this out of their systems by the use of scorn. One of them went so far as to treat her as an "idiot" and "simpleton," Sr. Clavel assures us.[p] Thus under attack, Catherine "held her tongue and kept smiling." These sisters preferred a different sort of sanctity, another type of visionary.

Catherine, in charge of operations, always took on herself the hard or despicable chores; this brought her no great recognition, but only the usual disparagement: "She likes it—it's up to her!" and they piled up her burdens even more.[33]

Catherine's ordeals also consisted in the sheer weight of her task of service—from 4:00 A.M. to 9:00 P.M., not to mention all the times when she would regularly stay up and keep watch with the sick and the dying. There was the nonstop round of things to do in her different roles as a peasant in the milking parlor and the garden, as an infirmarian, and as a laundry woman constantly setting the pace on the days of the great washes. There was also the care of the elderly categorized as "wicked." Catherine looked after them with especial kindness when they were unable to fend for themselves. Then there were waifs and strays like Blaisine, whom Catherine "rescued" and defended against those who wanted to be rid of her. If Catherine was able to stand all of this, it was not through insensitivity but quite the opposite—by dint of knowing when to retreat, when to be patient, when to return to her own sources of inspiration.

It was Catherine's job to welcome the flood of poor people without, however, having the means proportionate to the dramatic situation in this deprived suburb. She took on the ordeal without any sentimental weakness. She knew how to give, but also how to advise or even to reprimand in case of error. Her suffering at not being able to do more than she did was transformed into an active concern for seeking out solutions for the insoluble.

If Catherine was able to find God's peace, it was not through mere facility. She had her fair share of exceptional ordeals. She showed not the slightest problem during the Commune, even though she was in charge of the house during the most tragic phase of it. Finding herself at the "hot spot" between service of the House of Orléans and the ideology of the Commune, she extricated herself according to Gospel principles, with "the simplicity of a dove" and a quiet courage that enabled her to confront people and situations as they were, without drama.

Health[34]

It has often been thought that Catherine's natural vigor meant that she mostly avoided the normal pattern of suffering during her life. This is not precisely the case.

Catherine was a peasant woman, brought up to make use of physical strength. Apparently solidly built, she was given heavy manual work ("courtyard work") from the time of her seminary and subsequently at Reuilly. But since her youth she had had problems with arthritis, which was sufficiently bad to put her into the hospital in 1841, in spite of her tremendous courage. Nevertheless, we see her still refusing the use of a cushion during her final retreat (November 1876) and kneeling with her 70-year-old swollen legs on the hard wooden kneeler. Her heart was giving out; she had to put up with respiratory problems and coughing fits. Despite all that, she kept on with the heavy jobs right up to her last months, including the to-and-fro of the heavy polisher (aptly named the "galley-slaver") across the elderly people's floors, which she kept as brightly shining as those of the palaces in the days of the former servants' glory.... In January 1876, Sr. Dufès, who was aware of Catherine's "very bad health," added that she "fulfills all her duties very well indeed"—a contrast that speaks for itself. We have seen how, right up to the final weeks, she persisted assiduously with those smaller (and less savory) tasks that she was still strong enough to undertake, such as cleaning out commodes a month before her death.

Here is a disconcerting detail: Catherine herself noticed that accidents happened to her on the feastdays of the Blessed Virgin that she celebrated so well—right up to the final one, December 8, in the year of her death. On this feast of the Immaculate Conception, she had to bind up her own dislocated wrist, accepting it as a feastday "bouquet of flowers." The humor with which she accepted these upsetting penances not only runs counter to any idea of Catherine being subject to mystical suffering or to pseudomystical dramatization, but also eliminates any suspicion of "magic." Catherine knew very well that the medal was not some kind of lucky charm, that it suppressed neither cross nor sufferings. Her faith could move mountains, but was not of the millenarist variety. She did not fight against death, but accepted it as a gift.

Yes, Catherine's ordeals were "a full measure, shaken down, running over" (Lk 6:38). They were extraordinarily varied but nearly always ordinary. All this is both simple and imitable, not forgetting (as one of her companions noted) that Catherine was able to accept this "ordinary" life with "extraordinary love."

The amazing thing is that her death itself seems to have been an exception to her suffering condition. She went to her death as one might depart on a happy journey. Although there is certainly no such thing as a painless death, anymore than a pain-free birth, Catherine's long wait for death had given her the power to accept her final bodily cataclysm in joy and peace, without any superfluous convulsive movements, in order to launch her body toward its meeting with God, like a rocket whose entire power is bent toward the victorious upward leap. This was the triumphing of a rare sanctity; Catherine had glimpsed it in her retreat notes as early as 1834.[q]

In an admirable manner, Catherine illustrated the discoveries made recently by Dr. Elizabeth Kubler-Ross. This American doctor has exposed both the false "dramas" of death and the normal phases of a death that is properly accepted. Catherine scorched straight past the normal stages of anxiety and conflict to enter directly upon the final phases of peace and light.

VIRTUES

Now that we have looked at the shadows in Catherine's life—faults and ordeals—how can we best approach the crux of the matter? It is difficult, because her sanctity was of an extreme simplicity. Light is transparent—you cannot photograph light itself, but only whatever is lit up by light.

One possible way of grasping Catherine's life might be the use of analytical grids like the ones adopted in the two beatification processes: the observance of commandments, vows, and virtues.[35] Misermont, vice postulator of the cause, gave a very good exposition of these criteria. To do the same thing would be a duplication and not sufficient to bring us to the gist of things.

Commandments and vows

It is also true that Catherine—"the regular sister," as she was called[36]—faithfully observed both the commandments and her vows of poverty, chastity, obedience, and service of the poor—the fourth vow added by St. Vincent, not specifically examined as such by the canonization process.

Cardinal and theological virtues

It is also true that Catherine gave satisfaction in the examination of her virtues—which was indeed the very core of the process. She gave ample proof of the four "cardinal virtues" so dear to Péguy.

Prudence, in the best sense of the word: retentive intelligence; use of means at the service of well-chosen projects.

Justice: good order in all things, fairness, impartiality, exact accounts.

Fortitude: which enabled her to accept interior and exterior difficulties without panicking: those of the community and those of the Commune—with a courage that knew no fear of death.

Temperance: fully acknowledged at the canonization process, despite spurious and niggling objections.

Catherine also gave ample proof of the theological virtues: faith, hope, and charity.[37] But these three virtues were combined in a sort of symbiosis—they were but three aspects of a single life, a life given by God and oriented toward him. The witnesses in the processes sometimes used one and the same fact to illustrate now one, now another of the virtues.

Catherine was more concerned about God than about virtues as such. This latter word was not in her vocabulary. She did not shine as a "virtuous" person. But she was virtuous in the way that one should be—without realizing it, in the same way that a musician in the grip of inspiration becomes a virtuoso in order to fulfill the impulse of the music.

"Virtues" according to St. Vincent[38]

Perhaps we can get closer to the unique quality in Catherine, the resilience in her sanctity, through the medium of what are called "the Vincentian virtues," the five virtues extolled by St. Vincent himself: *simplicity, humility, mortification, gentleness,* and *zeal.* It is less a question of virtues than of the atmosphere of full bloom that is the mark of an authentic Christian life. Philippe Meugniot also attributed to St. Vincent "the respectful cordiality" that Catherine was such a good example of, for with her everything came from the heart, with a correct distance from people and respect for them.[r] Catherine certainly practiced these counsels. Her unfailing humility was not flabby or debasing. She was unfathomable. Like Misermont, we could dizzily explore the degrees of this virtue, following the subtle scale of values established by mystical theology—accept unmerited reproaches without a word; sincerely believe oneself incapable of any important work; rejoice to see one's faults made known; hide whenever possible the good that one does, etc., etc. This analysis, and many others, has been exhaustively carried out, and it is unnecessary to do it again. The same is true for mortification, gentleness, and zeal.

It is, however, the first of these virtues that seems to be significant and capable of throwing light on the matter: *simplicity* as defined by St. Vincent—"gazing into God," seeing everything in him. It is *that* which corresponds best with Catherine's life from the inside: the saintliness of the poor she exhibited, so simple that we narrowly miss passing over it without seeing the essential thing. Catherine's saintliness has no history, for it is devoid of fuss and provides no documentary evidence. Nevertheless, it existed. We must root it out by looking at how Catherine went about her personal relationships, both earthly and heavenly. (The heavenly side of things was in no way a form of escapism but rather the quintessence of the incarnation itself.)

HUMAN RELATIONSHIPS

A relationship with God, relationships with others, all illuminated by simplicity—this was what Catherine lived out, from one day to the next.

The world of the nineteenth century

She lived out her human relationships within the social and cultural world of her century. She inhabited the traditional and hierarchical order—a model whose apex was the Pope in Rome, the King of France, the father at home,[39] the pyramid of superiors in her religious family where women were strictly subordinated to men. If she accepted this world as it was, it was not through a blind belief in the established way of things but through a closeness to the people and the human communities that she served and edified.

Her father, who had been an officer of the civil state in the administration of the Revolution without giving up his traditions, was doubtless a model for Catherine. He had been able to see God in his priestly vocation shattered by the Revolution, and subsequently in his family responsibilities. He passed on to her an extraordinary scope for meeting people of all kinds on an equal footing—including the communards who were hostile to the "Enghien House"—rather than in a superior or inferior capacity.

As a young mistress of the farm, she had while still a child exercised authority over the day laborers, men included. One of her particular merits was that of living out what her niece Marie-Antoinette Duhamel described as a "subjugated position."[40] Catherine had accepted this form of humility so well that she turned down a superior's power when it was offered to her well before the 1870 war.

Responsibility, but in *humility*—these are the two features that characterize all her human relationships.

Family[41]

Family ties hold an important and misunderstood place in Catherine's life. The first roots are not very clear. The extant documents leave us almost totally in the dark concerning the character of her mother. Catherine saw her disappear like some kind of weary shadow. At the age of 12, she took over her mother's place in order to return to the house and the father she loved and admired. For her, he was the earthly image of God. With him she had a strong relationship that needed few words; it was a robust relationship, not servile—a daily collaboration. She drank in his advice and held in great esteem the individual peasant wisdom that he inculcated in her by example more than by words. She would speak about him with admiration and pride for the rest of her life. This was the reason for her terrible suffering at having to resist him in order to realize her vocation, then at having seen him abandoned in his old age in his own house, whose subsequent passing into other hands tore at her heartstrings.[42] Despite his bluntness and his misunderstandings, he was not a possessive father. He allowed the eldest son, Hubert, to enlist in Napoleon's army at the age of 17, and the others to leave the family home when they were still young in order to seek their fortunes in the capital. There were more Labourés in Paris than in Fain les Moutiers.

We already know to what extent Catherine "remained present" to the members of this large family.

"She loved us with great sincerity," said Fr. Meugniot.[s]

"She was always very discreet with me [...], even though I was her favorite niece and though she showed friendship toward me," said Marie-Antoinette Duhamel.[t]

Community life

At the age of 23, Catherine's family relationship was transferred to the family of St. Vincent, the light of her vocation.

Thus, in admiration and friendship, she took upon herself her confessors, her hostile superior, her community (partly ill-disposed toward her because of her secret)—all through the medium of the ordeals we have been examining. Her secret was being able to "gaze into God"— which affected difficult relationships for the better.

"Without obedience, no possible life in common,"[43] she used to say. Her obedience in accordance with the Spirit of God was neither unthinking nor excessive. "She never went beyond what was asked of her," said Sr. Olalde[44]—a measure of Christianity in the Burgundian fashion.

With her companions she was apparently gentle, affable, and considerate, and those same companions testify that she took on herself the heaviest burdens—floor-polishing, washing, ironing—or the most repulsive ones, such as commode cleaning and looking after the personal hygiene of the elderly residents. She was both available and benevolent beneath her slightly rough exterior, and above all, she was not a scandal monger.

"Whoever it was, she would not pass judgment on them," said Sr. Charvier. "If she was asked to express an opinion on a person, she would invariable say, 'Leave me alone. That's not my business.'"[u]

Sr. Tranchemer would sometimes venture to criticize or utter indiscreet remarks about other members of the community in the course of the "garden walks" that Catherine granted her in her role of Good Samaritan. On these occasions, Sr. Tranchemer, who was occasionally a little bitter, would hear Catherine say, "They [the sisters in question] are perfectly good. Don't be uncharitable. The Blessed Virgin would not be pleased! We ought to know how to see the positive qualities in others!"[v]

Thus, Catherine kept herself ignorant of gossip and sometimes of news, too; but she kept her ear to the ground when the running of the community was involved, or the kingdom of God. She could discern and foster each person's qualities and knew how to defeat evil with good.

Friendships[45]

Did Catherine have any friendships at a time when this virtue was viewed with suspicion?

"No special friendships," Sr. Mauche stated.

Bernadette of Lourdes blossomed with her fellow countrywomen and other open and natural companions—even if they were a little rough. Pleasing to all women, she gave more of herself to this type of person. Was this also the case with Catherine?

She seems to have had an understanding with her fellow-Burgundian womenfolk—Jeanne Léger and Sr. Séjole, who initiated her into the Sisters of Charity at Châtillon. Their rare visits to Enghien were occasions for celebrations on both sides, but Catherine's "secret garden" was nevertheless not opened up.

Among Catherine's companions at Reuilly, Sr. Tranchemer (the only one to have written her "Intimate Memoirs") presented herself as "the sister that Catherine seemed most affectionate toward."[w] But this confidential information itself allows us to perceive that her excitable partiality for Catherine was a sore trial for her whose friendship helped her peripheral companion to moderate her hot-headedness.... She got her own back in her "haloed" memoir on Sr. Catherine.

Sr. Cosnard had many affinities with Catherine, who exercised a deep influence on her. Sr. Cosnard received confidences from Catherine, even to the extent of details of the apparitions themselves. This was thanks to her tact, which allowed Catherine to talk to her about them without revealing herself, in the third person—"the sister 'who saw' and did such-and-such," as if it were someone else altogether.

More discreet, Sr. Henriot and Sr. Charvier, to whom Catherine confided her family problems, were close to her in a simple way and on an equal footing; but we do not have enough information to speak of *friendship* in these cases, such as had existed between Bernadette and her compatriot Sisters Bernard Dalias or Julie Garros.

This could be because of the advanced age at which Catherine died. The sisters who gave evidence at the process were all much younger than Catherine—Sr. Cosnard and Sr. Hariot, thirty-four years younger; Sr. Charvier, thirty-two years younger. Among possible friends, only Sr. Pineau was of Catherine's own generation (she was four years younger), but her testimony on the visionary tells us nothing of their relationship, except some conversations touching on "the glory of God and the good of the community."[x]

What, then, does Sr. Tranchemer mean when she writes that Catherine, "like our Lord, had her little 'Johns,' her favorites"? She clarifies it immediately: "Her favorites were not those that people speak highly of, inquire about, or put well up on the list of probables, but quite the opposite."y

Here, Catherine's admirer is very perceptive, and this explains Catherine's friendship for Sr. Tranchemer herself. The best testimony regarding her preferences indicates that these were for sisters in difficulty. The strong points in her relationships spring less from the lively intuitions of a young Bernadette or from her innate gifts in psychotherapy than from a strong maternal or grandmotherly character, welcoming all kinds of weakness. She was a discreet, strong, and comforting presence, rather than being good at disentangling things. Quite simply, Catherine was there. She did good by her very presence, calming and pacifying. She listened, gave encouragement, and brought peacefulness, looking after the daily "transferences" that make up the psychological health of a group or community.

She had a gift for communicating peace and reawakening hearts far outside the community, with the elderly, the dying whom she led toward the light, or the convict Siron whom she converted at the height of the Commune.

Young newcomers

Catherine's most obvious preferences were for the young newcomers among the sisters. She "initiated" them and consoled them when they had their first shock at how things really were.

"Come along, my dear. It's the good Lord who allows things like that to happen. Do not be discouraged. Go and find Sister Superior; tell her what's troubling you."[46]

"She always gave us good advice," said Sr. Cabanes.[47]

So, when Sr. Maurel got angry because the sister relieving her was always late and thus prevented her from arriving in time for the beginning of Mass, she was given this sound advice: "Give everything to the good Lord and don't go around grumbling."[48]

When Sr. Charvier was tried beyond the limits of her strength, Catherine shared with her the "oracle" she had received from our Lady for overcoming her own troubles. One day, when the young sister was coming out of Sr. Dufès' office, overwhelmed by the storm that had broken over her head, Catherine said to her, "Go to the foot of the tabernacle and say what you have to say to the good Lord. He will not repeat it and you will have the grace to put up with it."[49]

At the time when her being reputed to be a visionary had circulated around the seminary and given her a certain prestige among some of the young sisters, she avoided these "bees" from concentrating on her "honey pot" by telling them, "Go and ask Sister Superior."[50]

The witnesses at the Process did not tire of mentioning her tact and her kindness. The youngest sisters sometimes took separation from their families rather badly and Catherine reserved "motherly attention" for them, Sr. Cosnard and several others testified.[51]

In 1868, at the age of 25, Sr. Lestrade was sent to the Eugène Napoléon house (very near Enghien-Reuilly). She retained a glowing memory of her welcome.

> For my part, when I went on some errand to our sisters [in Enghien], I felt a great happiness at meeting her. She always welcomed us with such kindness and affability. It was simple, natural, and gracious, all at the same time. She would ask for news of our sisters and of the children, and would busy herself in getting what we wanted.[52]

Her prayer life was a radiant source. To see her pray was to pray oneself and to discover the presence that lived within her.

But above all, she knew how to succor those who were totally overwhelmed. Thus we have seen her procuring a flannel vest for Sr. Combes, soaked as a result of laundry work,[53] and getting a new job for Sr. Henriot, totally overcome with the one she had.[54]

In community crises, she exercised a calming influence, even rallying the young sisters together in 1860 to the side of the new superior who had received a hostile reception, reminding them: "God's work is at the superior's side."[55]

Faced with some misfortune or other, the tone of voice, the calmness and serene acquiescence with which she would say, "Don't get upset,"[56] were quite inimitable.

Sometimes her advice was out of the ordinary run of things and indicated some kind of premonitory intuition—as testified by Sisters Fouquet and Combes in particular.[57]

On the eve of a Communion day (for Communion was not authorized for every day of the week), she would say with infectious joy: "Come along, my little ones, we must do something for the good Lord!"[58]

She left behind her the memory of "a great old lady"—indulgent, charitable, affable, concerned with cultivating a sense of poverty.[59]

"[We should use without] abuse," she said. "We should be economical [...] with our habits. They do not belong to us. We will have to account for them to God."[z] Here she was echoing St. Vincent, who used to say, "It belongs to the poor."[aa] But Catherine's example went far beyond her own advice.[60]

"She did not hold anything to be her own," confined herself to what was strictly necessary, and left nothing behind her at her death–neither trinkets nor books, nor even pious objects: just "a little statue of the Virgin, of no artistic merit..." and the medals and rosaries that she gave away generously. She patched up clothes to the utmost, but with a sense of art. She made her own clothes last and wore them to the bitter end, but kept them always very clean. She left such a wretchedly small amount of clothes when she died that Sr. Dufès reproached herself for it. But how was one to know, when "she never complained"? That was a recurring refrain among the witnesses–Sr. Darlin even going so far as to say, "There was never a religious as poor as she was."[b]

Servants and helpers[61]

The same characteristics endeared Catherine to the servants, who loved and admired her simple holiness–the old serving woman at Châtillon, who had noticed the quality of her prayer life, and Jeanne Léger in Burgundy. At Reuilly there were Blaisine Lafosse and Cécile Delaporte, the little laundress to whom Catherine took "an eiderdown and some cordial" in the great freeze of the tragic winter of 1879, and whose twenty years under Catherine left her a memory with no shadow cast over it.

Orphans and Children of Mary[62]

The same kind of empathy existed between Catherine and the young orphans, whose numbers increased from the 1860s onward. The girls liked to greet Catherine and hid themselves in order to "watch her praying" for, as they put it, "you could see very clearly that she was talking to a real person." They had recourse to her prayers "for success in exams," and several of them got "truly miraculous" results according to one of them.

Catherine was interested in them and they were her favorite topic of conversation with Sr. Tranchemer, who was responsible for teaching them drawing and needlework.

She also had a relationship with the "externs"–"young working boys and girls" for whom a center had been set up in the house. They made it their business to escort her to her place of burial, medals in their buttonholes.

We have seen Catherine's predilection for the Children of Mary, founded by Fr. Aladel in accordance with the message Catherine had received.

> She made the most of every opportunity to do good for them. Some of them told me that they received the wisest advice from her before leaving the house at Reuilly.

What sort of advice? Crapez collected the details:

> When they left the house at the age of 21, Catherine recommended them to recite the *Memorare,* "bent so low as almost to fall down." To one of them, Catherine said when she was received as a Child of Mary, "The Blessed Virgin will never forsake you."

She taught them prayers like this one:

> O Mary Immaculate, cover me with thy virginal mantle, that I may emerge from it purified; and present me to Jesus, thy beloved Son. O Mary Immaculate, [...] lead all thy children to heaven.

When one of the orphans wept buckets because she was refused entry to the community, Catherine comforted her and said, "Don't cry. Sisters of Charity are needed in the world, too. You'll do much more good in the world."

Children[63]

Catherine had a great attraction for children. She remained not far from her own childhood–not childish, but honest and simple. Her childhood companions remembered how she used to be the peacemaker in their quarrels.[64] This was a very pronounced characteristic of her life. When still very young, she had learned how to care for an infant in all his weakness in the person of her little brother Auguste–mentally and physically handicapped. This was his "schooling."[65]

She loved very small children and derived much pleasure from them. Sr. Tranchemer tells us:

> When she crossed the courtyards to go to Enghien, the children from the refuge surrounded her, smiling. They linked their arms with those of the good sister [...]. The poor little ones had to be restrained in order

to restore her freedom to good Sister Catherine, who gave them her sweetest look, her most captivating smile.[66]

Catherine took an interest in the little wretches, whose needs were catered for in the locality on a greatly increased scale under Sr. Dufès– there were the child workers ("winders") and the backward children for whom an evening catechism class had been set up.[67/cc]

We have seen Catherine's circumspect affection for her nieces: Léonie Labouré and especially the little Duhamel girls, Marthe and Jeanne. She used to welcome them with the kind of presents and goodies that children like, but also made them love the noble art of "making amends to the poor or visiting a sick person." Her seemingly fanciful desire to have sixty-three children praying at her deathbed was due to the fact that right up to the decline in her lucid old age she had remained a child.[dd]

The elderly at Enghien[68]

However, the center of Catherine's life was the elderly to whom she dedicated forty years of tireless service. In no way was she one of those who find merit and importance in doing good works. What mattered to her was her duty toward people in their position.

They were always served first. One day Sr. Thomas asked her if she could try some fruit. "Oh no, my dear," replied Catherine, "this fruit is for the old people. If there is any left, you can have it [...]." Sr. Thomas adds: "There was none left!"[69]

Catherine liked to give big helpings and always asked, "Do you have enough?"[70]–a considerateness rare in others, and one which alleviated everyone's fear of missing out. Her principle was a simple one: "What is necessary is necessary."[71]

"For her, her duties were everything," said her companions.[72]

Punctual and regular in her habits, she was above everything else available and generous; hence "no one was loved so much," as we have already seen.[73] And this was because she loved them, quietly, without using fine words, but by deeds and a thoughtful presence. Her smile, which was not forced, could hide behind a gruff attitude and take some time in appearing when things were not going well. Instinctively, Catherine found the right pitch for all long-term human relationships– an extraordinary combination of self-giving and discretion, of openness and strength of purpose.

She respected her elderly charges, and they respected her in their turn, for she was fair-minded and held her own against those who tried to take advantage of her kindness to the disadvantage of others. She was no fool, and her authority was reassuring.

Although Catherine was remote when it came to those elderly men whose conduct was out of place,[74] she was lenient with those who got drunk.[75] She enforced the penalty demanded by the rules—three days of confinement—but was wise enough to wait until the next day before carrying it out. This she did without humor, but she tempered the humiliation of the confinement (such a bitter pill for those former servants of the nobility) by keeping them in bed as if they were ill. Then she had to bring them their meals—one more task among thousands, but one which she made use of to listen to them on familiar terms and give them advice. When they made excuses, moved by her kindness, she would tell them, "It's not me you should be asking pardon from but God."[76]

Her gentleness was not of the dominating or intimidating variety. One day, an old man got angry. Catherine had given him a shirt that he needed, but he did not find it sufficiently elegant—perhaps it had been darned! The old palace servant threatened Catherine: "I'll make a complaint to the administration!" This meant ultimately to Queen Amélie, who concerned herself that everything should run smoothly. This was a real threat then, but Catherine merely replied calmly: "Very well, my dear man, off you go and make your complaint!"[77] Which of course he did not do.

Here we can see a reappearance of her childhood steadfastness when Tonine threatened to tell her father about Catherine's untimely fasting. "Go on, then; tell him!"[78]

Catherine's humility had no weak points. But her kindness could become gruff. If an elderly man tackled her about one of the "new girls," she would say, "Get out of here!"[ee] or "That's not my business."[ff]

Her manner of speaking had retained its strong Burgundy flavor. Those who knew her had difficulty in adequately describing her kindness, "her gentleness," "her straightforwardness." "Her manner touched all hearts and won them over."[79]

Catherine was there, ready for all the little acts of service that nobody else ever thought of, with her country woman's knack of not losing a single minute nor wasting a single crumb, never getting restless, tireless in repairing what had been broken, picking up what had been dropped, mending what had been torn.

She initiated Sr. Thomas and many others of her companions (not to mention her nieces) into the last-mentioned job. For Catherine, mending clothes was in no way a demeaning activity but rather an enduring service. She patched up her own things to the last thread, just as much as she did for the poor. In this, she was living out Jesus' words: "I was naked and you clothed me" (Mt 25:36). Surely Mary mended Jesus' clothes in the same way....

Her attentiveness to mundane realities—bodily needs, food and clothing—went hand in hand with her concern for the basic necessities of grace and God himself. For Catherine, material and spiritual possessions went together, as they did in the incarnation. She distributed them in equal shares, simply and without separating them.

We have seen her special care for the sick[80] and the dying[81] with whom she regularly kept watch. "Not a single one died without being reconciled, and often they made a holy death," Sr. Dufès and other witnesses stated in amazement. This was a grace that was Catherine's own. She did not forget the dead and had Masses celebrated for the repose of their souls, while she herself continued to pray for them.

When any kind of outing or excursion was organized—for example, to celebrate the feast day of a neighboring community (and such celebrations were a very welcome diversion in the midst of an austere life)—Catherine used to give up her place to one of the young sisters. She actually preferred to stay behind and look after the poor. This was not due to asceticism or mere affectation, but because she felt that this was her *proper place,* in line with God's choice for her and her own choice. The only exception to this was a "heavenly" outing when it was a question of going to the Rue du Bac,[82] where she could steep herself once again in this wellspring of grace which she wanted to share so widely—so says Sr. Desmoulins.[gg] "An infirmary sister could not have found a better model."

One of the most striking things was her particular care for the most difficult and most awkward among the elderly,[83] including one who was "an absolute devil who didn't believe in anything." When she was criticized for her leniency, she would say, with tears in her eyes, "Pray for him!"[84]

Her earnest and sharp character became very indignant when faced with sinfulness,[hh] but nevertheless she had a great love of sinners—the first to be wounded by their own failings. This was the secret of her radiant and steadfast appearance when dealing with the communards.[85]

The poor

In charge of the door, Catherine efficiently welcomed all callers without superfluous chitchat, and was able to get rid of intruders who were trying to sniff out her secret, even if they were prelates sent by the Bishop! But she did this with tact and *never hurt anyone nor gave cause for any complaints.*

For Catherine, the important thing was being open to the poor–a difficult task in such a wretched suburb where the imperative alleviation of human misery was quite impossible to carry out. This was where she preferred to be. She gave as much as she could and was almost scarred by requests that she was unable to fulfill. She sometimes realized the impossible through skill or through grace–for example, the 60 gold francs given by Marshal MacMahon's wife.[ii]

We should consider well the convergent opinions of several of Catherine's companions (notably Sr. Combes and Sr. Darlin) that she was "*especially* good with the poor."

"HEAVENLY" RELATIONSHIPS

Catherine's attentiveness to the realities of earthly life did not mean that she was caught in a terrestrial quicksand. She was indeed only able to carry so many burdens because her heart lived in a "heavenly dimension."

Prayer[86]

The great wellspring of her life was prayer. Here she found strength, patience, and light. Although from the time of her childhood she had been as it were dogged by work, she had nevertheless always managed to find time for God–a time that she would throw herself into completely. Her companions learned a lot from watching her pray. Sr. Cosnard wrote:

> Whenever possible, she would make for the chapel, put down her apron outside, go in and make a deep bow of extreme respect for the tabernacle (at this time women did not genuflect); then she would cast a glance of filial piety toward the statue of the Blessed Virgin, kneel down, and, a moment later, leave the chapel with her face lit up, pick

up her apron, and return to her work. It was extremely striking. A few times I saw her enter the chapel with tears in her eyes, and when she came out again [...] her face was all lit up.[87]

Sr. Tranchemer tells us that she received the following reply when one day she complained to Catherine that she did not know how to formulate her prayers:

> Oh, it's very easy. I go to the chapel and I talk to God. He answers me. He knows that I am there [...]. I wait for whatever I have to wait for, whatever he wants to give me; and, whatever it is, it always makes me happy. Listen to God, talk to him, sort yourself out. It's all there—that is prayer. Go and do the same and you'll see![jj]

Catherine herself summed up this oneness to the things of heaven in the names of the three persons who dwelt in her life: *our Lord, our Lady,* and *St. Vincent*.[kk]

These were indeed the subjects of Catherine's visions, but made manifest in the opposite order, as if she had arranged them in ascending order of dignity.

St. Vincent[88]

St. Vincent had been the first to call upon her in a dream, with his passion and his humor: "You may be running away from me now, but one day you'll be happy to come to me!" Step by step, she discovered his "look," his heart, his customs, learned with the Sisters of Charity that she might serve "our masters, the poor."

This was not as it were an academic study of St. Vincent, but merely the kind of attitude that he appreciated above all in "good village girls" who knew how "to love God to the last drop of sweat on their foreheads and the last ounce of strength in their arms."

The witnesses at the Process summed up Catherine as "a true daughter of St. Vincent."

Mary[89]

As an orphan, Catherine had entrusted herself to Mary. Although still very young, in so doing she had received the grace of an adult's peace and strength. This deep tie was linked to a tradition coming down from St. Vincent. It was on the eve of his feast that Sr. Marthe, preaching on the piety of the Founder, had with her ardor awoken in Catherine that crazy desire to see our Lady herself. It was a very long time since she had begun to pray, like a good Catholic, in the parish church before the statue in the Labouré chapel. The first visible meeting was a decisive light in her life. There she received the mission and the broad outlines for the future that would be clothed in detail in the two apparitions of the medal. This light continued for Catherine in a more discreet fashion, in the form of inspiration and an interior voice. Quite simply, Catherine was living out Mary's presence in the communion of saints.

The way Catherine looked when she was at prayer was deeply edifying. Certain sisters felt urged to interpret it along the lines of a trance-like state.[ll] Her "look" is doubtless not without its importance, since according to St. Vincent it was this which defined simplicity.

Catherine was not too fond of statues. As far as we can tell, she was not satisfied with what was done in 1876 at the Froc-Robert workshop. She certainly did not like the "little old ladies" that people produced in the guise of the Blessed Virgin. Questions were asked about Catherine's apparent preference (according to Sr. Tranchemer) for our Lady of Good News in the garden at Reuilly. "It's the most beautiful in the house."[mm] According to that same witness, she preferred it because of a certain smile; but perhaps she also loved it because of its natural surroundings under the vault of the sky.... At any rate, it was this statue that she chose for making her final invocation before leaving Reuilly at the height of the Commune.[90]

Her retreat notes–notable for their brevity–harked upon the theme of Mary at the foot of the cross and Mary at Pentecost. Catherine desired to imitate Mary,[91] especially in her care for the poor. Following her example, she wanted to reconcile the two elements of Martha and Mary.

We do not have many of her sayings on our Lady, but they were simple, deeply felt, and filled with warmth. "Do not be afraid; pray and place yourself under the Blessed Virgin's protection," she would say with a hope that was almost tangible.[92]

The way she recited her rosary was positively glowing.[93] Said Sr. Dufès: "We were always struck, when we said it together, by the serious and pious way in which she pronounced the words." [94]

Sr. Maurel relates:

> I recited the rosary with her virtually every day. There was something in her eyes, as if she had seen the Blessed Virgin. She pronounced the words very deliberately, without exaggerating them. It was a simple and genuine piety that thought about what it was saying. She made several observations to me because I used to go too fast and trip over my words a bit. I was in the habit of going too fast in everything I did. She

mentioned this to me as well. "Don't get so excited!" she said to me. "Don't get so excited!"[95]

If she happened to see other people praying the rosary in a mechanical fashion, she showed herself to be very hurt by it, Sr. Vignancour tells us.[96]

> When the sisters recited the rosary in the course of work requiring concentration, such as ironing or washing, [Catherine] responded with the same attentiveness and the same recollection. In spite of her normal reserve, she could not stop herself from reproving—even a little severely—the young sisters who recited it too negligently.[nn]
>
> One day a sister came to Enghien with her superior. The latter had business to do with Sr. Dufès and she told her companion to wait for her in the parlor. The companion began to recite the rosary, but at the same time she walked around the room, stopping at each picture hanging on the walls and examining it. When Sr. Catherine noticed this, she remonstrated with the sister, and the sister told me that the remonstrance was a very salutary one for her.[oo]

Catherine recommended the recitation of the rosary, and taught others to love it.[97]

We have seen how she used to distribute medals generously as a sign of hope, enjoying a paradoxical success with the communards.

Catherine wanted the chapel at the Rue du Bac to become a widely accessible place of pilgrimage.[98] In this desire we can recognize her generosity, her concern that everyone should "have enough" of that font of living water, as with bodily nourishment. From this sprang her wish for an altar, a statue, and annual special Communions to commemorate the giving of these graces.[99]

She loved the feasts of the Blessed Virgin, but without any sort of sentimental facility. The accidents which marked out these days for her were welcomed by her as a "bouquet of flowers," a gift, up to and including the last one: the broken wrist on December 8, 1876.[100]

Catherine, the silent one, would talk quite willingly about the Blessed Virgin, not at length but "from the depth of her heart," Sr. Vignancour tells us.[101] In such cases it was "as if she were outside herself, even though remaining calm and self-possessed," says Sr. Cosnard,[102] who adds, "Her devotion to the Most Holy Virgin was so great that I cannot find words adequate to express it."

But Catherine's words, like her prayers (contrary to Sr. Tranchemer's predictions), were sober and without affectation.

She would willingly emerge from her silence in order to urge people to "pray much to the Blessed Virgin," but she would close up again rapidly if they tried to ensnare her by asking her for edifying words so that she might betray the secret of her apparitions.[103]

In 1876, two sisters who tried to get her to talk about the Blessed Virgin before going into the seminary only got these words out of her: "Young women, MAKE A GOOD SEMINARY!"[104]

They got the message: piety regarding the Blessed Virgin was really a question of DOING, following her example. That is what Catherine wrote down in her retreat notes. The happiness and glory of our Lady were to be found in "*Doing* God's Word" (to use the very strong Gospel expression of Mark 3:35 and Luke 11:28), and Mary's only piece of advice to the servants at Cana was to indicate Christ to them, saying, "Do whatever he tells you" (John 2:4).

Faced with a companion's trick question, "Do you love the Blessed Virgin a lot?" Catherine was unable to dodge it, but she restricted herself to answering, "Well, Sister, who could fail to love her?"[105] That said everything and any indiscretion was thus avoided.

Catherine loved the prayer inscribed on the medal: *"O Mary, conceived without sin...."*[pp] These words had been dulled by gynecological discussions in the Middle Ages, but Catherine saw them inscribed in letters of light in the apparition of November 27. For her, they signified quite simply the triumph of grace alone in a human creature for whom everything is grace, the transparency of God, the radiance of his merciful love.

Christ[106]

Catherine's first apparitions of Christ preceded those of the Virgin. They were the eucharistic visions. For Catherine, Christ held pride of place—he was everything. The cross, which is prominent on the reverse side of the medal and which dominated the whole of Catherine's life, was the subject of her last apparition in 1848. But it is by approaching from a different angle that we can find the essential place that Jesus' humanity held for Catherine—a place in action.

GOD IN ALL THINGS[107]

God

Catherine's human relationships, earthly and heavenly, derived their inspiration from a simple insight that can be summed up in four words: *God in all things.* Yes, *all things* were present for Catherine, beyond the meaning of words.

As far as she was concerned, God was not an abstract idea but a living presence. She was well aware of the importance of this concept—hence her stereotyped self-accusation during the Conference of Faults: "I missed making the acts of the presence of God."[108] (The Rule stipulated that every hour a prayer should be recited to revitalize that presence.) Catherine's concern went beyond mere ritual formula. Her superior, Sr. Dufès, was able to testify that Catherine "did not normally lose her sense of the presence of God."[109]

Sr. Olalde confirmed that, adding: "Her actions in themselves were quite ordinary, but she carried them out in an extraordinary manner."[110]

Fr. Chinchon, Catherine's confessor, depicted her life by the phrase: "a great intimacy with God."[111]

God in all things, but also *all things in God*[112] and *all things for God*—these were equally important in Catherine's life and followed the thread of those words repeated daily by her in which the direction and the "color" of her life were expressed: "One must put one's trust only in God and hope for nothing except from him."

She saw God in the saints—both heavenly ones, beginning with the Virgin Mary, imbued with his light, but also those on an unenlightened earth: even sinners, called by God to holiness through a conversion that Catherine was able to glimpse against all hope and obtained so often.

She saw God in events both happy and unhappy[113] and in ordeals.[114]

She saw him in a special way in the poor,[115] in the elderly (including those who were described as "wicked"),[116] but also in priests (representatives of God)[117] and in her superiors.[118] She said it many times in different ways: "Do not grumble! Our superiors represent God!"[qq] or "Do not rebel! The superior is the good Lord!"[rr]

To Sr. d'Aragon (aged 21) she one day confided that "to see God in our superiors is the secret of happiness in religious life." Thus she avoided all dilemmas.

When it came to events in public life over which she had no control or influence, she would widen the horizon by saying: "Let the good Lord look after it. He knows better than we what we need." Annoyances in community life were, in this way, totally transformed.[ss]

When she was put to the test, Catherine would have recourse to God alone, at the floor of the altar, as our Lady had told her, and she would come out "radiant." Blushes that had mounted to her easily reddening Burgundian cheeks would have disappeared.[tt] Peace and serenity would have silently risen from the depths. This was God's triumph. This was how she managed to get herself under control so quickly, even when she was scoffed at (as one of her companions put it), saying, "It's that much more for the good Lord."[119]

In the same way, when events overtook her, she would say, "My God, you see everything, you can see what it's all about."[uu]

It was God's eye on her that enabled her to emerge from being overwrought or even from seething with anger on a human level. "It's God's will, don't be so upset,"[120] she would say, using once again a familiar formula that was an expression of her peacefulness, lost and refound.

Catherine could see God even in her own failings or errors of perspective, without needing to defend her ideas. Thus she was able innocently to admit that she was mistaken when taken to task over predictions that had apparently not come true.

"I am relieved that the truth is known."[121]

"God is always on the side of truth." She would also say: "Let us work for the good Lord!"[122]

"You never get bored when you're doing God's will." [123]

Witnesses who tried to discern Catherine's secret put it in terms like these: "She looked for no one but God and relied on no one but God."[124] For her, "love of God was everything."[125]

Her companion, Sr. Mauche, wrote:

> It was love which led her to community life, which made her choose our community as the source and model of all charity and pour out the ardors of her devotion on her neighbor without exception.[vv]

Sr. Vignancour summed it up as "a life of love."[126] Looking and loving were inseparable for Catherine.

According to Sr. de la Haye St. Hilaire, a companion during the last two years of Catherine's life, it was this ability to look into God—what St. Vincent called simplicity—which really defined her.

> She gave me the impression of being a person who, while accomplishing on this earth all that she was given to do, never considered what people thought of her but contemplated God as it were face-to-face. In fact, she was always united to God, and sought his will in all things. God's gaze on her was sufficient for her.[127]

So, there was a reciprocal gazing from one to the other. Sr. Eugéni Mauche put it in similar terms: "Her pure and limpid gaze, like a dove's, looked for God alone."[128]

This young sister had been with Catherine through the tempestuous times of the Commune (at the age of 16) and would later become Superior General. Her admiring memories of Catherine were summed up in three words: REPOSE IN GOD. This terminology tied in with the deepest definition that Thomas Aquinas gave of sanctity at the end of his life,[129] when he referred to God's example of rest on the Sabbath day at the end of the work of creation. Catherine had reached this consummation, in the humility of her endless tasks—"united to God in the least of her actions," as Sr. Hannezo put it.[130]

Such was the depth of Catherine's heart, which gave meaning to her in her apparitions, in her service of others, and in their harmonious overlapping; and this explains how she came to die in peace with no trace of a shadow.

Jesus Christ[131]

For Catherine, God was not a remote, faceless mystery, but Jesus Christ, God-made-man among men, among the poor. Even when he appeared to her as a king, in her eucharistic vision of June 6, 1830, he was stripped of his garments and his crown, placed in a position of poverty and humiliation. Her last vision relating to Christ, during the unrest of 1848, was that of the cross, already engraved on the medal above the two hearts—symbols of love. Thus were the different parts of the messages Catherine received tied together at a deep level.

It was no accident that the apparitions of Christ were given to Catherine in the sacrament of the Real Presence by a sort of unveiling process. The Eucharist[132] had captured her heart from the time of her First Communion. This hunger had grown deep in her, before the empty tabernacle in her village church where she prayed, alone but filled with desire for the Lord. She lived out the Eucharist in the austere context of the nineteenth century. At that time a certain distance was maintained; the eucharistic fast was cultivated in order to make sure that the sacrament was not debased. Reception of Communion was infrequent and the Eucharist could never be received on three consecutive days.[133] Certain of Catherine's companions hesitated to approach the Lord's table as often as they were allowed to. If anything, virtue tended toward abstention from the Eucharist.

Catherine, however, never missed a Communion. Indeed, she obtained supplementary ones for herself from 1850 onward—which shows how highly her superiors thought of her. From 1841 on, she requested the same thing for her community on the anniversary day of the apparitions of the medal and St. Vincent's heart.

The way Catherine gazed on the Eucharist edified many of those who saw it—there were dozens, among whom we may cite as an example Sr. Maurel:

> I cannot say that on her way to and from the holy table Sister Catherine was in an ecstatic state; but it was striking how recollected she was. It was the same thing during thanksgiving. I don't think a cannonball would have made her turn her head, she was so bound up in the good Lord. In church, [she] held herself upright, scarcely ever leaning on her hands. Normally she looked at the tabernacle.

The look in Catherine's eyes also struck many onlookers who were unable to find words for their clear impressions.

"You'd have said that she was seeing [what wasn't there]."[ww]

"She appeared as if in an ecstatic state."[xx]

"She saw with her bodily eyes what her companions could only see with the eyes of faith."[yy]

"It seemed that a veil had been dawn back"[zz]

"You'd have thought she was above the earth, talking to God."[aaa]

Perhaps there is an excess in those descriptions, but how else to proceed when faced with expressing a transparency whose radiance goes beyond all expression?

For Catherine, Communion was an act requiring *movement,* and she encouraged the young sisters to *do* it. "We need to do something...."[bbb]

Following our Lady's example, Catherine did not dissociate *doing* from *contemplation,* actions from faith, Martha from Mary. St. Vincent and Fr. Aladel had taught her. Receiving Communion is a practice which commits one's life to Christ but also to men and women—and first of all to the poor. It was through her meditation of the God-man—the suffering, humiliated man with no other crown than a crown of thorns—that Catherine acquired her knowledge of the unity of God and humanity, beginning with those who suffered most, who were the most deprived. Thus she maintained great respect for the elderly who would not normally have merited it by reason of the deprivation of their old age, and sometimes by their drunkenness. When taken to task for her leniency, she would say: "What do you expect? I see our Lord in them."[134]

It was a cry from the heart and an echo of St. Vincent, whose words Catherine also borrowed, according to Philippe Meugniot, her nephew: "What a fine thing it is to see the poor in God and in the esteem that Jesus Christ had for them."[ccc]

Yes, Catherine was one who had *seen* Jesus Christ as he was in the Gospel, not only in the brilliance of the visions but in the darker world of earthly relationships, of daily service at the very table of sinners. There is no more important vision, nor one more worth sharing: "I was hungry and you gave me food; I was naked and you clothed me; I was in prison and you visited me" (Mt 25:36); "whatsoever you do to the least of my brothers you do to me."

This sums up Catherine's outlook on life perfectly.

Calendar

1806 *May 2 (Friday), 6 P.M.:* Birth of Catherine Labouré (called "Zoe" within family) at Fain-les-Moutiers, Côte-d'Or. Birth certificate filled out immediately.[1]

May 3 (Saturday): Baptism of Catherine by Fr. Georges Mamert, priest in charge of chapel-of-ease of Fain.[2]

1807 *March 14:* Abbé Hyacinthe-Louis de Quélen, future Archbishop of Paris, ordained priest at St. Brieuc.

1808 *October 21:* Birth of Marie-Antoinette Labouré, known as Tonine, at Fain.

1809 *November 19:* Birth of Auguste Labouré, youngest brother of Catherine, at Fain.

1810 *June 30:* Death at Fain of Hubert (III) Labouré, paternal grandfather of Catherine.

1811 Pierre Labouré elected Mayor of Fain, a position he will hold until September 1815.

1814 *April 20:* Napoléon abdicates at Fontainebleau and is exiled to the Isle of Elba.

1815 *March 20:* Napoleon, having escaped from Elba, enters the Tuileries, vacated by Louis XVIII the day before.

July 8: Second Restoration under Louis XVIII.

July 24: Fouché Ordinance, transforming 18 generals and officers implicated in return from Elba into Council of War. 12 later executed, including Marshal Ney.

July–September: White Terror against Bonapartists and Republicans.

October 9: Death at Fain of Louise-Madeleine Labouré, née Gontard, mother of Catherine, at 5 A.M.[3]

1818 *January 25:* First Communion of Catherine at Moutiers-St. Jean, after which, according to her sister, she becomes more "mystical." Several weeks later she becomes "farmer's wife," replacing Marie-Louise who leaves to be a postulant with the Sisters of Charity at Langres.

June 22: Entry of Marie-Louise Labouré into the Sisters of Charity.[4]

1819 *September 24:* Msgr. Hyacinthe-Louis de Quélen nominated Coadjutor Bishop of the Archbishop of Paris. Installation takes place the following February 12.

Foundation in Rue de Varenne of Enghien Hospice by the Duchess of Bourbon in memory of her son, the Duc d'Enghien. (Transferral to Reuilly in 1828.)

1820 *February 13:* Assassination of the Duc de Berry.

October 4: Jean-Baptiste Etienne, future Superior General, received into the Congregation of the Mission.

Between 1820 and 1828, creation of an *Association of Children of Mary* at the *Providence Orphanage*, 3 Rue Oudinot, by Fr. Dufriche-Desgenettes, founder of the orphanage and curé of the parish of Notre Dame des Victories.

1821 *November 12:* Entry of Jean-Marie Aladel, future spiritual director of Catherine, into the St. Lazare seminary.

November 21: Msgr. de Quélen nominated Archbishop of Paris.

1822: *May 23:* Birth of Sr. Dufès, future superior of Catherine.

1823 *August 20:* Death of Pope Pius VII.

September 28: Election of Pope Leo XII.

1824 *June 12:* J. M. Aladel ordained priest by Msgr. de Quélen.

September 16: Death of Louis XVIII. Accession of Charles X, last brother of Louis XVI.

November 25: Msgr. de Quélen elected to the Académie Française.

1825 *September 24:* J. B. Etienne ordained priest.

1826 *April 3:* Msgr. de Quélen signs the declaration of the 68 cardinals, archbishops and bishops on the independence of temporal power.

July 20: Marriage of Charles Labouré (brother of Catherine) to Jeanne Pommelet in Paris.

1827 *May 2:* Catherine, aged 21, asks to enter the Sisters of Charity. Her father refuses.

June 4: Sr. Antoinette Beaucourt elected Superior General of the Sisters of Charity.

1828 *February 21:* Death in Paris (second *arrondissement*) of Jeanne Pommelet, spouse of Charles Labouré, restauranteur. Arrival shortly after of Catherine at her brother's house, 20 Rue de l'Echiquier.

September 23: Death of Jean Gailhac, curé of Châtillon-sur-Seine from 1781.

December 15: At Châtillon-sur-Seine, marriage of Hubert Labouré (brother of Catherine) to Jeanne-Antoinette Gontard.

Transferral of the Engien Hospice from Rue de Varenne to Rue de Picpus at the request of Mme. Adélaïde d'Orléans, heiress of the Duchess of Bourbon.

1829 At Semur, marriage of Charles Labouré (brother of Catherine) to Marie-Virginie Gontard.

February 10: Death of Pope Leo XII.

March 31: Election of Pope Pius VIII.

May 18: Election of Dominique Salhorgne as Superior General of the Vincentians and the Sisters of Charity (position held until August 15, 1835).

September 10: Birth of Paul Labouré, son of Hubert, at Châtillon-sur-Seine.[5] Catherine leaves for her sister-in-law's, Châtillon-sur-Seine.

1830 *January 14:* Catherine proposed as candidate by Sr. Cany, begins her postulancy at the Sisters of Charity, Châtillon-sur-Seine.

April 6: "Recognition" of body of St. Vincent by the Superiors of the two families founded by him.

April 21: Arrival of Catherine at the Sisters of Charity, Rue du Bac.

April 24: Solemn transferral of the relics of St. Vincent de Paul from the Archbishop's palace to Notre Dame.

April 25 (Sunday): Transferral from Notre Dame to St. Lazare, 95 Rue de Sèvres. Catherine takes part in procession of the people.[6]

April 26–May 1: The heart of St. Vincent appears to Catherine in the chapel at the Rue du Bac.

May 25: Catherine makes her first full retreat over the period Ascension–Pentecost.

June 6: Feast of the Trinity: vision of Christ the King, during Mass, at the Gospel.

July 5: The taking of Algiers.

July 18–19: (11 P.M. to 2 A.M.): First apparition of the Virgin to Catherine Labouré in the chapel of the Rue du Bac: apparition in the chair.

July 25: Fall of Charles X following promulgation of the "July Ordinances."

July 27–29: The "Three Glorious Days": Revolution with sacking of the Archbishop's palace on the 29th.

July 30: The Duc d'Orléans becomes Lieutenant General of the Realm.

August 2: Charles X proposes his abdication in favor of his grandson, but the rebels summon Louis-Philippe I, Duc d'Orléans, to the throne of France. Charles X (his cousin) takes ship for England.

August 7: Accession of Louis-Philippe, who is to reign until 1848.

October 23: Calumnious public notice attacking Msgr. de Quélen. He replies, "I shall seek a way of getting my own back by doing good."[7]

November 27: (Saturday): first apparition of the Miraculous Medal.

November 30: (Tuesday): Death of Pope Pius VIII.[8]

The same year, J. M. Aladel is nominated chaplain, confessor and conférencier at the Motherhouse of the Sisters of Charity.

December: Third apparition of the Virgin to Catherine (second apparition of the Medal).

1831 *January 30:* Catherine receives the habit.

January 3–February 5: Catherine in transit in a "house in Paris" is involved in a conversation on the apparition of the heart of St. Vincent, in the presence of Aladel.[9]

February 5: Catherine arrives at the Enghien Hospice where the community numbers four. Sr. Savart, the superior, assigns her to the kitchen where she will work for two years, at the same time looking after the garden.

February 14: Sack of the Church of St. Germain-l'Auxerrois.

February 15: Sack of the Paris Archbishop's palace. Msgr. de Quélen takes refuge with the Dames of St. Michael, and then with the Caffarellis.

February 18: Pillaging of Msgr. de Quélen's second residence at Conflans.

Lent: Msgr. de Quélen's Pastoral Letter on the schism of Châtel.[10]

May 3: Letter from Msgr. de Quélan to the Abbé Grégoire.[11]

May 9: Without authorization, Lacordaire and de Coux open a primary school and teach there themselves. They are thrown out by the public.

In the same year, at Lyon, uprising of the silk weavers who remain masters of the city for several days.

Publication of Victor Hugo's book, *Notre Dame de Paris*.

1832 *March 26:* Epidemic of cholera, of Russian origin, bursts upon Paris in mid-carnival. 100 deaths by the end of the month.

April 2: Msgr. de Quélen visits the Hôtel-Dieu where the cholera epidemic is rife. This is his first public appearance [since taking refuge].

April 9: 861 deaths in a single day.

April 18: Msgr. de Quélen orders prayers for the cessation of the cholera epidemic.

May 6: Letter of Msgr. de Quélen founding the Cholera Orphans Fund.

End of May: J. M. Aladel receives the first 1,500 medals. He sends some to the Reuilly community where Catherine receives one.

Second half of June: The epidemic starts up again.

Towards the end of this year, Jean-Baptiste Etienne and Jean-Marie Aladel visit Msgr. de Quélen and speak to him about the apparitions of the Medal.

1833 *May 27:* Election of Sr. Marie Boulet as Superior General of the Sisters of Charity (1833–39).

This year, Msgr. de Quélen brings together the Superior General (Mother Boulet) and the Council of the Sisters of Charity to discuss the apparitions of the Miraculous Medal.[12]

Guizot has a law passed granting freedom in primary education.

Ozanam founds the *Conferences of St. Vincent de Paul*.

In England, beginning of the *Oxford Movement*.

1834 *April 26:* Marie-Louise Labouré leaves the Sisters of Charity.

December 25: Birth of Antoine-Ernest Labouré, son of Charles the restaurateur, now living at 11 Rue de l'Echiquier.

This year, a fresh uprising in Paris and the massacre of the Rue Transnonian.

Lamennais publishes *Les Paroles d'un croyant,* condemned by the Encyclical *Singulari vos.*

Circulation of Medals reaches 8 million. They have reached China.

1835 *January 24:* Marriage of Joseph Labouré (brother of Catherine) to Victoire Naudin in the second *arrondissement* of Paris.

March 20: Installation of the two Lecerf paintings: vision of the heart of St. Vincent and vision of the Virgin.

May 3, Good Shepherd Sunday: At Enghien, Sr. Catherine makes her vows for the first time.

July 18: Marriage of Jacques Labouré (brother of Catherine) to Adélaïde Donon in Paris.

July 28: The Fieschi outrage.

August 15: Fr. Salhorgne, Superior General, resigns.

August 17: Apparition of the Miraculous Medal to a female religious at Einsiedeln.

August 20: Fr. Jean-Baptiste Nozo elected Superior General.

September 3: According to the newspaper *La France* (July 28), King Louis-Philippe and his two children agree to wear the Medal.

September: Repressive laws against *La France*.

In the course of this year, Fr. Aladel asks to go on the missions, but the Assembly nominates him assistant to the new Superior General in Paris.

1836 *February 16:* Opening of the Quentin inquiry into the 1830 apparitions.[13]

February 21: Birth of Louise Adèle Labouré, daughter of Jacques, in the twelfth *arrondissement* of Paris.

May 1: The Curé d'Ars blesses in his church a statue commemorating the apparition of the Miraculous Medal and consecrates his parish to the Blessed Virgin.

June 18: Marriage of Pierre-Charles Labouré to Gabrielle Loichemol in Paris.

July 13: End of the Quentin inquiry.

July 19: Death in Paris of Jean-François Richenet, spiritual director of the Sisters of Charity since 1829. Fr. Grappin succeeds him.

August 27: A decree of the Congregation of Rites forbids the Vincentians in Naples to place a painting of the Miraculous Medal on the altar in their chapel (dedicated to St. Nicholas).[14]

December 3: Fr. Dufriche-Desgenettes, while celebrating Mass at the Lady Altar, after the *Sanctus* distinctly hears the words, "Consecrate your parish to the Most Holy and Immaculate Heart of Mary." At this moment, he rediscovers peace and fulfillment in his priestly ministry.

December 16: Msgr. de Quélen erects the Congregation of the Most Holy and Immaculate Heart of the Blessed Virgin Mary in the Church of Notre Dame des Victoires.

Catherine is assigned to the old people's quarters where she will spend the rest of her life.

Children of Mary associations spread rapidly.

1837 *August 14:* The Virgin of the Miraculous Medal is exposed for the veneration of the faithful in the parishes of Paris.

August 15: The painting of the Miraculous Medal by Victor-Joseph Vibert is blessed at the Church of St. Gervais, where it had been installed the previous day.

1838: *March 25:* Catherine makes a retreat conducted by Fr. Grappin. Her autograph retreat notes have been preserved.

June 11: Gregory XVI promotes to an Archconfraternity the Congregation in honor of the Immaculate Heart established at Notre Dame des Victoires.

June 24: Pope Gregory XVI adds to the Litany of Loreto the invocation "Queen conceived without sin."

September 11: Marriage of Tonine Labouré (sister of Catherine) to Claude Meugniot at Fain-les-Moutiers.

December 8: A rescript from Gregory XVI grants Msgr. de Quélen the permission requested to solemnize the feast of the Immaculate Conception.

1839 *January 1:* Pastoral Letter from Msgr. de Quélen, solemnizing the feast of the Immaculate Conception.[15]

Boulet, Superior General of the Sisters of Charity, officially recommends for the first time the invocation "O Mary, conceived without sin..."

May 17: Catherine takes part in the retreat conducted by Fr. Aladel. Her autograph retreat notes have been preserved.[16]

May 21: Sr. Marie Carrère elected Superior General of the Sisters of Charity. She will hold this position until May 12, 1845.

June 14: Birth of Marie-Antoinette Meugniot, daughter of Tonine, at Viserny (Coête-d'Or).

December 31: Death of Msgr. de Quélen, 37 years before Catherine.

This year, Lacordaire re-establishes the Dominicans in France.

1840 *January 18:* First apparition of the Virgin to Sr. Bisqueyburu (1817–1903), Sister of Charity, in the retreat room, then situated over the chapel in the Rue du Bac. She receives the green scapular under the sign of the Immaculate Heart. Its success will be considerable. Sr. Bisqueyburu had been brought from Pau (where she did her postulancy) to Paris by Fr. Aladel on November 27, 1839. He resisted her visions for a time and accused her of being "mad." Wasn't all this leading to an epidemic of visions?[17]

May 23: Birth of Charles Meugniot, son of Tonine, at Viserny (Côte-d'Or).

1841 *February 2:* Catherine takes part in the retreat conducted by Fr. Etienne. Her autograph retreat notes have been preserved.

March 22: Laws forbidding children under the age of 8 to work and restricting the working hours of children less than 12 years old.

May 1: Jules-August Chinchon is received into the Congregation of the Mission.

June 11: Letter from Sr. Cany to Catherine mentioning the sciatic pains Catherine was suffering from.

August 15: For the first time Catherine sets down the account of the apparition of November 27, 1830.[18]

This year Letaille produces a first sketch of the Virgin with the globe.

The construction of nine main railway lines is decided upon.

1842 *January 20 (Monday):* In Rome, conversion of Alphonse Ratisbonne in the church of Sant' Andrea delle Fratte.

February 2: Catherine takes part in the retreat conducted by Fr. Etienne (her autograph retreat notes have been preserved).

February 15–April 1: In Rome, Ratisbonne conversion process.

June 3: Cardinal Patrizzi, Vicar of Rome, recognizes the conversion.[19]

June 7: Birth of Léonie-Victoire Labouré, daughter of Jacques, in Paris. She will be a future witness at the Process.

August 2: Resignation of Fr. Jean-Baptiste Nozo, Superior General.

1843 *March 22:* The Superior General of the Sisters of Charity writes to the Minister of Worship (who is also Guardian of the Seals) for permission to construct the seminary building on the site of the Hôtel de la Vallière, occupied by the Sisters of Charity since 1815.

April 13: Request for permission granted.

May 25: Catherine takes part in the retreat conducted by Fr. Aladel (her autograph retreat notes have been preserved).

June 10: Jules Chinchon, future confessor of Catherine (1851–1875) ordained priest.

August 4 (Friday): Jean-Baptiste Etienne elected Superior General.

December: Brother François Carbonnier paints the picture of the Miraculous Medal, still hanging in St. Lazare, 95 Rue de Sèvres, Paris.[20]

This year, J. M. Aladel becomes assistant to Fr. Etienne.

The Vincentians receive from the Baroness of Lupé a house situated close to Dax, at the birthplace of St. Vincent de Paul.

1844 *March 19:* Death of Pierre Labouré, father of Catherine, at Fain-les-Moutiers.[21]

March 22: Letter from Joseph Labouré giving news of this death.[22]

End of March: A requiem Mass celebrated in Paris for Pierre Labouré, to which Catherine is invited.[23]

May 15: Birth of Philippe Meugniot, son of Tonine, at Viserny (Côte-d'Or). Future spiritual director of the Sisters of Charity.

July 28: Catherine takes part in the retreat conducted by Fr. Grappin (her autograph retreat notes have been preserved).

September 15: Catherine writes to her sister Marie-Louise who is looking for a path through life outside the community.[24]

September 29: Another letter from Catherine to her sister Marie-Louise.[25]

December 26: Death of Sr. Savart, first superior of Sr. Catherine at the Enghien Hospice.[26]

1845 *May 12:* Election of Sr. Marie Mazin as Superior General of the Sisters of Charity.

June 26: Marie-Louise Labouré (having left the community in 1834) is authorized to take the habit again at Enghien.

July 2: Sr. Marie-Louise Labouré posted to Turin.

August 22: "On this day I decided to put a Medal around my neck," wrote Newman on August 22, 1867. He had already visited the Abbé Desgenettes at Notre Dames des Victoires on Friday, September 11, 1844.[27]

October 1: Jules Chevalier (future historian of Catherine) received into the Congregation of the Mission.

November 10: Catherine takes part in the retreat conducted by Fr. Grappin (her autograph retreat notes have been preserved).

December 16: J. M. Aladel, director of the first Parisian Association of Children of Mary, erected the same day at St. Louis-en-l'Île. Associations would spread to other parishes during the following year—St. Vincent de Paul, St. Roch, St. Paul, St. Louis, etc.

1846 *March 19:* Catherine purchases her first cow for the cowshed at Reuilly which she is now in charge of.

June 1: Death of Pope Gregory XVI.

June 16: Election of Pope Pius IX.

July 26: In Paris, vision of Christ to Sr. Apolline Andriveau, a Sister of Charity, who receives the model of the Red Scapular of the Passion.[28]

September 19: Apparition of the Blessed Virgin at La Salette.

November 21: J. M. Aladel nominated Director General of the Sisters of Charity. He will occupy this position until his death, April 25, 1865.

1847 *June 20:* Rescript of Pius IX granting to the Children of Mary associations erected under the auspices of the Sisters of Charity, for young girls of the ordinary people, the same privileges as the *Prima Primaria* of the Jesuits.

July 9: Campagne des Banquets against the King and his minister.

This year, the center of the Associations of Children of Mary set up at St. Lazare, 95 Rue de Sèvres. It will stay there until 1914 when it moves to 140 Rue du Bac.

This year in London the first Communist congress as a follow-up to the manifesto published in January.

1848 *February 22:* The government forbids a reformist banquet by opposition members of parliament.

February 23: Demonstration by the National Guard which announces itself against the régime. The King sends Minister Guizot to intervene. That evening, under the lights of Paris, the officials responsible for law and order fire on the republicans. Barricades are set up during the night.

February 24: Marshall Bugeaud abandons the center of Paris to the rioters. Louis-Philippe abdicates in favor of his grandson, the Comte de Paris, and designates the Duchess of Orléans as Regent.

The Republic is proclaimed.

February 25: Inauguration of the Second Republic and universal suffrage. Abolition of the death penalty and slavery.

February 26: Opening of national workshops to give employment to the unemployed.

March 2: Decree reducing the working day: 10 hours in Paris, 11 hours in the provinces.

March 3: Revolution in Budapest.

March 4: Riot in Turin. In Paris, proclamation of freedom to meet and freedom of the press.

March 10: Riot in Rome.

March 12: Uprising in Prague.

March 13: Riot in Vienna.

March 19: Upheaval in Milan.

June 17: Jules Chevalier ordained deacon.

June 23: Workers' Revolt.

June 25: Msgr. Affre wounded on a barricade.

June 26: Cavaignac puts down the revolt. The Faubourg St. Antoine surrenders.

June 27: Death of Msgr. Affre, wounded two days previously.

July 30: Letter from Catherine about the vision of a cross.[29]

September 23: Jules Chevalier ordained priest at St. Lazare, 95 Rue de Sèvres.

November: Constitution of the Second Republic.

December 10: Louis-Napoléon Bonaparte elected President of the Republic.

This year, Fr. J. M. Aladel publishes a *Manual of the Children of Mary,* of which 25,000 copies will be printed by 1857.

Local authority changes street numbers in the Rue du Bac, 132 (Motherhouse of the Sisters of Charity) becomes 140.

1849 *August 16:* Catherine takes part in retreat (preacher's name not known). (Her autograph retreat notes have been preserved.)

This year at Reuilly, installation of classrooms, refuge and catechism classes for the children of this deprived area, under the title *Providence Ste Marie.*

1850 *April 7:* Eugène Boré (future Superior General) ordained priest at Constantinople.

May 15: The Falloux Law on education.

June 17: Birth of Emile-Hubert Labouré, son of Joseph, in Paris.

June 30: Fresh outbreak of cholera in Paris.

July 19: Rescript from Pius IX gives the Sisters of Charity and Vincentians the possibility of entering the Associations of Children of Mary.[30]

This year, expansion of the boarding school founded by the Archbishop for cholera orphans; it is moved to 79 Rue de Reuilly, further away from the old people. Queen Marie-Amélie requested this after the boys had set up a barricade in the Rue de Picpus.[31]

This year, Léonie-Victoire Labouré meets her Aunt Catherine.[32]

Setting up of an old-age pension system.

Amalgamation with the Sisters of Charity of the community founded in the U.S. by Mother Elizabeth Seton.[33]

1851 *June 9:* Election of Sr. Gilberte-Elise Montcellet as Superior General of the Sisters of Charity. She will fill this position until 1857.

November 21: A Children of Mary association erected in the Rue de Reuilly.

December 2 (Tuesday): Coup d'état by Louis-Napoleon Bonaparte, aged 44.

This year Catherine obtains permission from the superiors for one more Communion than that allowed by the Rule.[34]

Sr. Léopoldine de Brandis and her community at Gratz (Austria) are joined to the community of the Sisters of Charity.

1852 *June 2:* Sr. Jacquette Randier nominated superior at Reuilly, where she will stay till September 10, 1855.

November 21: Louis-Napoléon Bonaparte becomes Emperor, taking the name Napoléon III.

1853 *June 26:* Death of Marguerite Labouré, widow of Antoine Jeanrot, at St. Rémy (Côte-d'Or), aunt of Catherine who took her in after the death of her mother.

1854 *January 16:* Félicité-Robert Lamennais makes his will.

February 27: He dies.

December 8: Pius IX defines the dogma of the Immaculate Conception.

This year, the Crimea War begins.

1855 *April 17:* Jacques Labouré dies in Paris (twelfth *arrondissement*); Catherine had visited him.[35]

October 17: Sr. Guez nominated superior at Enghien where she will remain until 1860.

First Universal Exhibition.

1856 *February 7 (Thursday):* Death of Sr. Rosalie Rendu, a Sister of Charity and apostle of the Mouffetard area.

This year, Sr. Catherine sets down the account of her first apparitions: those of April–July 1830.[36]

Installation of marble statue of the Virgin with rays coming from her hands, above the main altar in the chapel, replacing a plaster statue.

Catherine initiates Sr. Charvier into the work of the chicken-run.

1857 *January 3:* Assassination of Msgr. Sibour by a madman as he comes out of the church of St. Etienne-du-Mont.

June 1: Sr. Eulalie Devos elected Superior General of the Sisters of Charity (she will fulfill this office until 1860).

July 28: Death of Claudine Labouré (spinster), sister of Pierre Labouré, aunt of Catherine, at Flavigny-sur-Ozerain.

This year Tonine comes to live in Paris.[37] Her husband, Claude Meugniot, works on the railways. They live with their children, Marie-Antoinette and Charles, in the Rue des Charbonniers, near the Gare de Lyon.

1858 *January 14:* The Orsini coup.

February 11: First Lourdes apparition, followed by a fortnight of apparitions *(February 18–March 4).*

March 15: Sr. Catherine welcomes to Enghien Sr. Clavel, who will later be a witness at the canonization process.

July: Sr. Marie-Louise Labouré leaves Turin for the Motherhouse.

This year Catherine has her nephew Philippe Meugniot, son of Tonine, brought to Paris. She takes him to the Montdidier college run by the Vincentians.[38]

Marie-Antoinette Meugniot, daughter of Tonine, is received as a Child of Mary by Fr. Aladel, to Catherine's great joy.

First treaty of Tien-Tsin.

1860 *April 25:* Death in Paris of Fr. Charles-Eléonore Dufriche-Desgenettes, curé of Notre Dames des Victoires.

May 28: Sr. Gilberte-Elise Montcellet, former superior at Enghien, elected Superior General of the Sisters of Charity (second term of office).

October 18: Sr. Dufès installed as Sister Servant at Reuilly. She will be Catherine's superior until her death. Catherine supports her, despite difficult beginnings, by rallying the young sisters.[39]

1861 *January 14:* Antoine-Ernest Labouré, nephew of Catherine, marries Claire-Marie Letort at Puligny-Montrachet (Côte-d'Or).

October 30: Catherine sells her thirtieth and last cow on Sr. Dufès' orders.

1862 This year Claude Meugniot, husband of Tonine, seriously ill, is given no hope of recovery by the doctors. Catherine visits him often and prays for his conversion. He has a reprieve lasting a year.[40]

1863 *February 17:* Fire in the wallpaper factory next to the house at Reuilly threatens the house, on the day before Ash Wednesday, about 4 A.M.; it goes out without causing damage.[41]

August 9: Catherine accompanies her nephew Philippe Meugniot to the St. Lazare novitiate.[42]

August 25: Death of Sr. Elisabeth de Brioys at Enghien. She had asked for Catherine to watch with her from 11 o'clock the previous evening.[43]

October 26: Death of Claude Meugniot, husband of Tonine, in Paris at 14 Impasse de Châlon.

Sr. Tanguy posted to Enghien where she will remain until her death on December 7, 1916. Straightaway she is informed that Catherine is the visionary of the Miraculous Medal.

1864 *January 23:* The Marchioness of Lépri, a Child of Mary in the *Prima Primaria* at Paris, sets up for the young country children in her school an association which will be canonically erected the following September 30.

August 26: Death of Antoine Labouré at Fain. A little while before, Catherine had visited him at the Lariboisière hospital. She broke her arm getting off the bus.[44]

This year, according to Sr. Cosnard, Catherine predicts that the Enghien house will move to a "great château."[45]

October 15: Marie-Antoinette Meugniot, daughter of Tonine, marries Eugène Duhamel in Paris.

This year, a law recognizes the right to strike. Karl Marx founds the first Internationale.

1865 *April 23:* Last conference of J. M. Aladel.

April 25: Death of J. M. Aladel at the Motherhouse of the Congregation of the Mission, 95 Rue de Sèvres, Paris.

April 27: Burial of J. M. Aladel. Catherine is present at the burial. Philippe Meugniot is "struck" by the radiant expression on her face.[46]

May: Fr. Vicart is nominated Director General of the Company.

July 17: Hubert Labouré, eldest brother of Catherine, dies at Nuits-St. Georges (Côte-d'Or).

August 4: Birth of Marthe-Marie-Eugénie Duhamel, granddaughter of Tonine, in Paris (twelfth *arrondissement*).

1866 *May 31:* Sr. Félicité Lequette elected Superior General of the Sisters of Charity. She will hold this position until 1872.

December: Eugéne Duhamel, son-in-law of Tonine, leaves home without warning and goes to America.

This year, Sr. de Geoffre de Chabrignac, future biographer of Catherine, is posted to the secretariat at the Motherhouse.

1867 *January 22:* Birth of Jeanne-Caroline Duhamel, granddaughter of Tonine, in Paris (twelfth *arrondissement*).

Sr. Eugénie Mauche, future Superior General (1910–1912) is posted to Enghien where she will stay until 1872.

Community activities transferred from Enghien to Reuilly. The month of St. Joseph is celebrated for the first time at the Motherhouse.

Second Universal Exhibition.

1868 *December:* Publication of the first issue of the *Annals of the Children of Mary.*[47]

Sr. Cantel posted to Reuilly where she finds Catherine busy with the door and the old men.[48]

Following a difference of opinion with the "royal foundress" of the Enghien Hospice, Sr. Dufès, superior, together with 25 sisters, transfers from Enghien to Reuilly.[49] Catherine is put in charge of the Enghien Hospice where 7 sisters stay on.

1869 *February 2:* Charles Meugniot, son of Tonine, marries Philiberte Neugniot at Montbard (Côte-d'Or).

May 22: Philippe Meugniot, nephew of Catherine, ordained priest at St. Lazar, 95 Rue de Sèvres.

November 17: Opening of the Suez Canal.

1870 *April 10:* Birth of Lenin.

July 19: France declares war on Prussia.

July 21: Sister Bursar at the Rue du Bac leaves for Metz to organize military medical units.[50]

July 30: The Mayor of Metz asks for 30 sisters to run a 2,000-bed medical unit.

July 31: Community appeal to the Sister Servants in Paris for help and medical units.

August 3: Renewed appeal to the Sisters of Charity for organization of medical units. A reinforcement of 6 sisters is sent.

August 4: Circular letter of Fr. Etienne.[51]

September 2: Disaster at Sedan. Collapse of the Empire.

September 4: Proclamation of the Republic. Foundation of a Government of National Defense: Thiers, Favre, Picard, etc.[52]

Fr. Etienne leaves for Belgium on the advice of his Council.

September 11: Fr. Director grants daily Communion to the sisters: exceptional favor.

September 13–14: 30 houses from the suburbs withdraw into Paris, sometimes accompanied by their poor, in preparation for siege.

September 14: Installation of medical unit at the Motherhouse for 50 wounded.

September 18: Beginning of the siege, which lasts for 4 months and 10 days until January 29.

September 22: The Central Committee of the 20 Paris *arrondissements* (a federation of committees of vigilance that had sprung up spontaneously) together with the commandants of the National Guard calls for the election of a Commune [municipality].

September: Fr. Chinchon joins the Vincentian students at the birthplace of St. Vincent de Paul, Dax.

October 27: Metz capitulates.

November 14: 30 sisters receive the habit to replace those going to Bicêtre to look after 1,600 smallpox cases.

November 28: 23 others take the habit and take over the smallpox cases in the Alfort medical unit.

December 8: Dogma of papal infallibility defined in Rome.

December 17: 33 more sisters receive the habit. Mobilization on all fronts! A medical unit organized at Ivry-Incurables for 1,800 wounded soldiers.

Winter 1870–1871: Intense cold and famine. The sisters at Reuilly run a "cook-house" which turns out 1,200 portions of food daily.

1871 *January 5:* Beginning of the German bombardment.

January 7: J. Vallès' red poster calls for a general offensive, free rationing and government by the people.

January 17: Apparition of the Virgin at Pontmain.

January 19: Futile and bloody Buzenval sortie. Trochue replaced by General Vignoy, Jules Favre negotiates with Bismarck.

January 22: In front of the Hotel de Ville the National Guards call for war to the bitter end. Breton militiamen fire on the crowd.

January 26: 72 bombs fall on the military hospital of Val-de-Grâce that the sisters and their 200 wounded are evacuating.[53]

January 27: Only 8 days' bread left, rationed to 300 grams.[54]

January 28: Surrender of Paris. During this month a national vow made to build the Sacré-Coeur Basilica.

February 3: P. Meugniot leaves for Arcueil.[55]

February 5: Sr. Mettavent enters Paris.

February 12: Fr. Chinchon returns to Paris.

February 20: 1,400 cannons surrendered to the Prussians.[56]

February 26: The armistice is prolonged.

February 27: Violent upheavals. 30,000–40,000 National Guards mobilized.

February 28: Demonstrations.[57]

March 1: The Germans enter Paris.

March 2: They leave again. Newspapers are suspended. Thiers Proclamation.

March 3: Republican Federation of the National Guard constitutes itself to take power.

March 10: The Assembly moves to Versailles, designated as the new capital.

March 18: Uprising of the Commune. Soldiers join the rioters and shoot Generals Le Comte and Thomas.

March 19: The Central Committee of the National Guard prepares Paris elections for 229,000 voters.

March 21: Fr. Cinchon goes to Reuilly, then into hiding in the Rue St. Guillaume, where Sr. Nathalie Nariskime[58] is Sister Servant.

March 22: Elections. Commune proclaimed at Lyon.

March 23: Commune proclaimed at Marseille.

March 24: Commune proclaimed at Toulouse, Narbonne and St. Etienne.

March 26: Commune proclaimed at Le Creusot. In Paris, elections to the Commune Council.

March 28: Commune proclaimed in Paris.

End of March: Dr. Marjolin, seeing the difficult situation of the Enghien-Reuilly sisters, spontaneously proposes to take 30 orphan girls into his convalescent home at Epinay-sous-Bois (Seine-et-Marne). Sr. Millon escorts them there at the beginning of April, "sheltered from all danger."[59]

April 2: Decree of separation of Church and State.

First Versaillist shells fall on Paris. The rebels attempt to take Versailles but are repulsed.

April 3: Communard sortie blocked.

April 4: End of the Marseille Commune.

April 7: Sr. Dufès, superior at Reuilly, refuses to hand over two gendarmes that the communards want to shoot.

April 9, Easter Day: Fr. Chinchon celebrates Mass at Reuilly and leaves the house. The premises are searched twice. Sr. Dufès threatened with an arrest warrant after the second.

April 10 (Easter Monday, 11 A.M.): Sr. Dufès leaves with Sr. Tanguy. Federals occupy the Reuilly house. Sr. Catherine goes to the seat of the Reuilly Commune to plead Sr. Dufès' cause.

April 11: Barricades in Paris: Place de le Concorde, Place Vendôme, etc.

April 14: Anticlerical poster at Montmartre.

April 15: P. Meugniot leaves for Les Invalides as chaplain to the sisters.[60]

April 17: Around this date, Sr. Tanguy is sent back to Reuilly by Sr. Dufès and sends Sr. Claire in her place to accompany Sr. Dufès to Toulouse: Catherine's prediction thus realized.

April 19: Fr. Chinchon leaves for Brussels.[61]

April 22: Two "citizennes" replace the sisters in the classes at Reuilly.[62] Death of Antoinette Gontard, widow of Hubert Labouré (sister-in-law of Catherine), at Nuits-St. Georges (Côtes-d'Or).

April 24: Fr. Mailly comes to celebrate Mass at Reuilly—the first Mass since Easter. Immediately after his departure, the premises are searched.[63] Communards attempt to replace the sisters in the distribution of the provisions sent by the English, but withdraw in the face of the crowd's protests.

April 25: Fresh expulsions of sisters from St. Jacques-du-Haut-Pas, St. Etienne-du-Mont, St. Séverin.

April 28: The fourteen sisters remaining at Reuilly are accused of thefts and even more serious crimes. About the same date, Sr. Catherine summoned as witness against excessive female communard ("la Valentin"): Catherine gets her acquitted.

April 29: Catherine "escorted" by two soldiers to appear before impromptu tribunal.[64]

April 30 (Sunday, about 6 P.M.): Departure of the last sisters from Reuilly. Catherine arrives at St. Denis about 7 P.M. Before leaving Reuilly, she removes the crown from the Virgin in the garden and announces a return before the end of the month of May.

May 11: Occupation of the Church of St. Sulpice.

May 16: The Vendôme column pulled down.

May 18 (Ascension Day): A detachment of the batallion of Avengers of the Republic surrounds the Church of Notre Dames des Victoires and scatters Fr. Desgenettes' ashes. Other churches occupied, including Notre Dame.

May 19: Fr. Chinchon, back from Brussels at Fr. Etienne's side, returns to Dax, to the birthplace of St. Vincent de Paul.

May 21: The Versaillists enter Paris. Beginning of the Bloody Week.

May 24: Execution of hostages, including Msgr. Darboy, in La Roquette prison.

May 25: At Ballainvilliers Sr. Catherine hears a newsboy shouting for sales of *Le Petit Journal.* She has a copy bought and thus learns of Msgr. Darboy's death.[65] In Delescluze's office an order to shoot priests and religious is found.

May 27: "Paris burns." Catherine reassures the sisters.

May 28 (Pentecost Sunday): Last bouts of fighting at Père-Lachaise, by the Federals' wall. End of the Commune.

May 30: Sr. Dufès, recalled, arrives at Versailles where Sr. Catherine joins her from Ballainvilliers.

May 31: Sr. Dufès and the sisters return to Enghien. After attending Mass at 5 A.M., Catherine replaces the crown on the head of the statue of the Virgin.

June: Celebration of the month of the Sacred Heart.[66]

1872 *May 20:* Election of Sr. Louise Lequette, Superior General of the Sisters of Charity. She will hold this office until 1878.

June: Sr. Tanquy summoned to testify before a council of war of the army at Versailles. Another summons in July.

October: Tonine falls ill.[67] Catherine had dreamed of her death not long before.

1873 *March 20:* Death of Brother François Carbonnier, painter of the apparition.

May 24: MacMahon becomes President of the Republic.

June 8–July 8: Apparitions of the Virgin at St. Bauzille-de-la-Sylve (Hérault).

July 18: At the invitation of the wife of Marshal MacMahon, the Shah of Persia visits the community at Reuilly.[68]

July 23: Law passed taking on the national vow for the Montmartre basilica.

October 6: Death of Fr. Vicart, Director of the Sisters of Charity.

1874 *January 18:* Catherine's last visit to Tonine, who wakes from a four-day coma.[69]

January 20 (4 A.M.): Death of Tonine, at 5 Rue Crozatier, Paris 12. She is buried in the Père-Lachaise cemetery.

March 12: Death of J. B. Etienne, Superior General of the Vincentians and of the Sisters of Charity.

June 6: Execution of the last communard.

September 11: Eugène Boré elected Superior General of the Vincentians and of the Sisters of Charity. He will fill this office until May 3, 1878.

This year the major superiors interrogate Sr. Catherine on her revelations, according to Fr. Chinchon.[70]

December: Sr. Tanguy nominated assistant to Sr. Dufès and directress of the Enghien house in Catherine's place.

1875 *January 9:* Death of Virginie Gontard, wife of Charles Labouré and sister-in-law of Catherine, at Puligny-Montrachet (Côte-d'Or).

July 24: Death of Victoire Naudin, wife of Joseph Labouré and sister-in-law of Catherine, in Paris (twelfth *arrondissement*).

In France, opening of Catholic universities.

At the end of the year, due to Fr. Chinchon being overburdened by work, Fr. Boré relieves him of being confessor at Reuilly.

1876 *January 1:* Sr. Dufès notes the "very bad health" of Catherine.[71]

April 10: Catherine writes down two accounts of the vision of the Virgin with the globe.[72]

End of May/beginning of June: Visit of Catherine to Fr. Boré to ask if she can continue to have Fr. Chinchon as confessor. Request refused. The following day, after praying about it, she confides her message to Sr. Dufès.

June 24: Sr. Grand's reply to Sr. Dufès, who had consulted her about Catherine's revelations regarding the Virgin with the globe. Sr. Dufès immediately orders the first statue of the Virgin with the globe from the sculptor Froc-Robert.

August 15: Catherine visited by Marie-Antoinette Duhamel and her two daughters Marthe (11) and Jeanne (9). Catherine gives them a picture and medals, and tells them, "Next year I shan't be here."[73]

September 8: P. Meugniot's last visit to Catherine.[74]

September 10: The Association of Children of Mary is opened to young people outside the houses of the Sisters of Charity and the Vincentians.[75]

October 30: Fresh autograph accounts by Catherine of the Virgin's message of the night of July 18–19, 1830.[76]

November 5–14: Catherine's last retreat at the Motherhouse.

November 24: Catherine's feastday. Children come to wish her a happy feast while she is cleaning out commodes.

November 30: Death of Auguste Labouré, youngest brother of Catherine, at the age of 65, in the Chartreuse hospital at Dijon.[77]

December 8: Feast of the Immaculate Conception. Catherine goes to the Motherhouse for the last time and sprains her wrist.

December 18: Visit by Sr. Cessac. "I am on my way to heaven," Catherine says to her.[78]

December 30: Visit by Sr. Cosnard.

December 31: Last visit by M.-A. Duhamel and her children.[79]

A few hours before her death, Catherine has several visits; she dies in a state of serenity at 7 P.M. The secret is disclosed. A procession begins as her body is laid out "in state."

1877 *January 3 (Wednesday):* Burial of Catherine in the vault at Reuilly.

April 18: Definitive authorization to bury Catherine at Reuilly.[80] Following that decision, the coffin which has been resting on two trestles, is buried underground in the same vault.

July 25: Death of Marie-Louise Labouré at the Motherhouse.

1880 Celebration of the half century of the apparitions. Installations in the chapel at the Rue du Bac of the statue of the Virgin with the globe and the altar. For the first time, the chapel is opened to pilgrims.

1894 *August 19:* Cardinal Aloïsi-Masella writes a peremptory letter to Fr. Emile Miel CM, asking him to introduce the cause for the canonization of Catherine Labouré.[81]

October 25: Letter from Sr. Dufès about Catherine and Lourdes.[82]

November 27: Liturgical feast of the Manifestation of the Miraculous Medal celebrated for the first time.

1895 Visit by Sr. Lamartinie, Superior General of the Sisters of Charity, to Cardinal Aloïsi-Masella, who tells her, "If you do not introduce Sr. Catherine's cause, I will do it myself!"[83]

1896 *April 6:* Cardinal Aloïsi-Masella informs Mother Lamartinie that the informatory process on the cause of Catherine Labouré will soon begin.

April 13: First session of the ordinary process at Paris.

1900 *June 11:* End of the ordinary process (first stage with a view to canonization).

1905 *June 22–August 9:* Parisian process of non-cult.

1907 *December 12:* Pius X signs the Introduction of the cause.

1908 *July 8:* Verification of the absence of cult.

1909 *May 26:* Opening of the apostolic process *in specie*.

December 13: Opening of the apostolic process *in genere*.

1910 *February 24:* 82nd and final session of the apostolic process *in specie*.

March 15: 24th and final session of the apostolic process *in genere*.

1912 *May 17–November 22:* Apostolic process on the virtues of Catherine (43 sessions).

1927 *August 2:* Antepreparatory congregation on the heroicity of Catherine's virtues: 12 affirmative votes, 7 abstentions among the consultors.[84]

1928 *June 5:* Preparatory congregation on the heroicity of Catherine's virtues: 14 affirmative votes, 9 abstentions among the consultors.[85]

1929 *June 28:* Catherine's cause taken up again.

1931 *March 17:* Second preparatory congregation on the heroicity of Catherine's virtues: 21 affirmative votes, 3 abstentions, 1 negative vote among the consultors.[86]

1932 Recognition of two miracles by three successive congregations, the last in the presence of Pius XI (February 7), who accepts two miracles on the 13th.

1933 *February 15:* The general congregation replies to the question: Can Catherine safely be declared a saint? The affirmative reply is unanimous.

March 12: Pius XI signs the decree *De tuto*.

March 16: Instruction from the Congregation of Rites to Cardinal Verdier, Archbishop of Paris, for Catherine's exhumation.

March 21, 9 A.M.: Exhumation takes place at Reuilly with Doctors Didier and Auboux. Transportation of the body in a small van to the Rue du Bac. Processional reception of the body, which is placed in the retreat room.

March 22: Opening of the coffin in the presence of Cardinal Verdier. 300 sisters file past the coffin. Recognition and removal of relics by the two doctors together with Doctor Lesourd.

May 27: Petition to the Pope for beatification.

May 28: Beatification of Catherine,[87] followed by Triduum and celebrations until December 3.[88]

1938 *April 23:* Apostolic process on the two further miracles required for the final stage.

1944 *July 18:* Second process on the miracles.

1945 *June 26:* Voting on the miracles.

1946 *May 26:* Decree *De tuto* on the miracles.

December 8: Decree *De tuto* taking the decision that procedure to canonization can be undertaken in complete safety.

1947 *July 27:* Canonization by Pius XII in the Basilica of St. Peter: "We declare that the Blessed Catherine Labouré is a saint, and We inscribe her name in the catalogue of saints."

1980 *May 31:* Visit by Pope John Paul II to 140 Rue du Bac. He officially inaugurates "resumption of the cult" in the newly restored chapel.

November 27: 150th anniversary of the Apparition of the Miraculous Medal.

ABBREVIATIONS USED IN THE NOTES

An Fr *Annales de la Congrégation de le Mission* (Vincentians) *et des Filles de la Charité,* Paris, 95 Rue de Sèvres: 1884–1963.

CLM 1 R. Laurentin and P. Roche, *Catherine Labouré et la Medaille Miraculeuse,* Paris, Lethielleux, 1976, 400 pp.

CLM 2 R. Laurentin, *Catherine Labouré et la Medaille Miraculeuse. Procès de Catherine,* Paris, Lethielleux, 1979, 330 pp.

Crapez, Vie Edmond Crapez, *La Vénérable Labouré,* P. Lecoffre, 1910. Later editions are given appropriate dates.

Crapez, Message Edmond Crapez, *Le Message du Coeur de Marie à Sainte Catherine Labouré,* Paris, Spes, 1947.

Misermont, Ame Lucien Misermont, *L'âme de la Bienheureuse Catherine Labouré,* Paris, Gabalda, 1933.

Misermont, Graces Lucien Misermont, *Les grâces extraordinaires de la Beinheureuse Catherine Labouré,* Paris, Gabalda, 1934.

Misermont, Vie Lucien Misermont, *Soeur Catherine Labouré et la Medaille Miraculeuse,* Paris, Gabalda, 1931. Later editions were revised (p. 119).

No A reference to the basic chronological documentary dossier (1806–1980) in the archives of the Vincentians and the Sisters of Charity.

PA *Procès apostolique pour la beatification de Catherine Labouré* (1909–1912).

Paspec *Processus apostolicus...super virtutibus et miraculis in specie inchoativus* (pp. 1–1170k) *et continuativus* (pp. 1171–1713), 125 sessions, (May 26, 1909–November 22, 1912).

PNC *Procès de non-culte (Parisiensis Processus ordinaria auctoritatae constructus super cultu nunquam exhibito eidem Servae Dei),* manuscript in the archives of the Sisters of Charity, 195, p. 1905.

PO *Procès informatif de béatification de Catherine Labouré.* Original (without title) preserved in the archives of the Sisters of Charity, 102 sessions (April 13, 1896–June 18, 1900).

Notes to the Calendar

1. Birth certificate extant.
2. Baptism certificate extant.
3. Death certificate extant.
4. Cf. Records of the community.
5. Birth certificate extant.
6. CLM 1, p. 173.
7. No. 520a, Baron Henrion, *Vie de Msgr. de Quélen,* Paris, Périssé, 1842, p. 249.
8. CLM 1, p. 182.
9. Cf. chapter 3, note 127.
10. No. 520a, p. 338.
11. No. 520a, p. 345.
12. PO 34, CLM 2, p. 253.
13. No. 297, CLM 1, p. 234.
14. No. 356, CLM 1, p. 257.
15. No. 427, CLM 1, p. 283.
16. Crapez, *Message,* p. 238.
17. E. Mott, *Le scapulaire vert et ses prodiges,* Paris, Mother House, 140 Rue du Bac, 1923; Crapez, *Message,* p. 209.
18. No. 455, CLM 1, p. 286.
19. No. 506, CLM 1, p. 313.
20. No. 527a, CLM 1, p. 316.
21. Death certificate extant.
22. No. 528.
23. No. 528 and cf. chapter 5.
24. No. 531.
25. No. 532, CLM 1, p. 318.
26. *Livre des Circulaires,* 1846, vol. 4, pp. 3–5.
27. From his travel diary.
28. Crapez, 1947, p. 210.
29. No. 544, CLM 1, pp. 321–325.
30. Misermont, *Vie,* p.187.
31. Communicated by Sr. Dufès.
32. No. 1280, Paspec, p. 496.
33. No. 522a.
34. Fr. Chinchon's testimony, CLM 2, p. 221.

35. No. 876, CLM 2, p. 193.
36. No. 564, CLM 1, pp. 334–338.
37. CLM 2, p. 244.
38. No. 1336, Paspec, p. 1051.
39. CLM 2, p. 327.
40. No. 925, CLM 2, p. 245.
41. No. 1297, Paspec, p. 722.
42. No. 1336, Paspec 75, p. 1051.
43. CLM 2, p. 346.
44. No. 1280, Paspec, p. 499.
45. No. 1291, Paspec, p. 654.
46. No. 1338, Paspec, p. 1080.
47. No. 615.
48. CLM 2, p. 308.
49. No. 1360, circular of January 1, 1910.
50. An Fr. 36, pp. 1–13.
51. No. 619.
52. An Fr. 36, p. 7.
53. An Fr. 36, p. 288.
54. An Fr. 36, p. 310.
55. An Fr. 36, p. 314.
56. An Fr. 36, p. 336.
57. An Fr. 37, p. 340.
58. No. 1382, Paspec, p. 1112.
59. No. 966, Sr. Millon, CLM 2, p. 293.
60. An Fr. 36, p. 340.
61. No. 1382, Paspec, p. 1112.
62. An Fr. 36, p. 423.
63. An Fr. 36, p. 423.
64. According to Crapez, *Vie,* p. 182.
65. Testimony of Sr. Tranchemer.
66. No. 655, CLM 2, p. 98.
67. CLM 2, p. 249.
68. An Fr. 38, p. 520.
69. No. 928, M.-A. Duhamel, PO 31, CLM 2, p. 249; No. 1336, P. Meugniot, Paspec 75, p. 1049.
70. No. 895, CLM 2, p. 223.

71. No. 630.
72. Nos. 635–636, CLM 1, pp. 351–352.
73. No. 928, CLM 2, p. 246.
74. No. 1338, Paspec 77, p. 1077.
75. Misermont, *Vie,* p. 87.
76. Nos. 637–638.
77. Death certificate extant.
78. No. 1258, Paspec, p. 260.
79. No. 928, CLM 2, p. 247.
80. No. 649, CLM 2, p. 63.
81. No. 751, CLM 2, pp. 134–135.
82. Crapez, *Message,* p. 213.
83. No. 1278.
84. No. 1526.
85. No. 1531.
86. No. 1645.
87. Misermont, *Grâces,* pp. 214–239.
88. Ibid., pp. 240–257.

Notes

PREFACE

    a.   Deposition of December 21, 1897, PO 33, p. 349.

CHAPTER II: VOCATION

    a.   Letter to Marie-Louise, September 15, 1844.
    b.   Misermont, *Vie,* pp. 50–51.

CHAPTER III: SEMINARY

    a.   No. IX, CLM 1, p. 180.
    b.   No. 564, CLM 1, p. 336.
    c.   A synopsis of the two versions is to be found in CLM 1, pp. 352–357.
    d.   No. 619, CLM 1, p. 340.
    e.   No. 52, CLM 1, p. 220.
    f.   CLM 2. pp. 57–58.

CHAPTER IV: FIRST SETPS AT THE ENGHIEN HOSPICE

    a.   No. 626, p. 33.
    b.   Page 5; CLM 1, p. 218, note 3.
    c.   No. 368, CLM 1, p. 264.
    d.   Cf. p. 83 above.
    e.   CLM 1, p. 264.

CHAPTER V: TIME OF FRUITION

    a.   No. 1013, December 22, 1899, CLM 2, p. 345.
    b.   No. 988, Sr. Levacher, PO 68, CLM 2, p. 319.
    c.   Detail from the archives of the Orléans family.

d. No. 873, CLM 2, p. 183.
e. Cf. chapter 9, note 83, below.
f. Cf. chapter 9, note 77, below.
g. No. 947, February 15, 1898, PO 41, CLM 2, p. 268.
h. No. 1018, CLM 2, p. 350.
i. Sr. Patrissey, no. 1286, Paspec 40, p. 608; Misermont, *Ame,* p. 156.
j. Cf. Misermont, *Ame,* p. 152.
k. No. 1300, Paspec 53, p. 758.
l. No. 982, CLM 2, p. 314.
m. No. 979, CLM 2, p. 310.
n. No. 1018.
o. Cf. p. 45 above.
p. No. 532, CLM 1, p. 319.
q. No. 961, Léonie Labouré, CLM 2, p. 283.
r. CLM 2, p. 284.
s. CLM 2, p. 282.
t. Cf. p. 75 above.
u. Retreat notes, p. 74.
v. *Ibid.,* p. 76.
w. *Ibid.*
x. No. 655, CLM 2, p. 101.
y. No. 993, and cf. chapter 9 below.
z. No. 983, CLM 2, p. 316.
aa. No. 1012, CLM 2, p. 344.
bb. CLM 2, p. 258.
cc. No. 969, CLM 2, p. 296.
dd. No. 969, CLM 2, p. 259.
ee. Evidence from Sr. Lenormand, no. 956, PO 45, CLM 2, p. 275; no. 957, CLM 2, p. 276; no. 1268, Paspec, p. 363; cf. p. 825.
ff. No. 1297, July 20, 1909, Paspec, p. 725.
gg. No. 1360, pp. 17–18.
hh. Crapez, *Vie,* 1911, p. 167.
ii. No. 1291, Paspec 44, p. 652 and no. 937, CLM 2, p. 256.
jj. Nos. 970 and 972, CLM 2, pp. 298–300.
kk. No. 1018, PO 85, CLM 2, p. 348.
ll. No. 1072, postulatory letter of June 30, 1903.
mm. No. 1410.

nn. No. 1330.
oo. No. 960.
pp. CLM 2, p. 297.
qq. No. 870.
rr. CLM 2, p. 326.
ss. No. 1296.
tt. No. 904.
uu. No. 908; cf. nos. 956 and 970.
vv. No. 908, CLM 2, p. 234.
ww. No. 1014.
xx. No. 1014.
yy. No. 1717a.
zz. Nos. 455–457, CLM 1, p. 293.
aaa. Nos. 455–457, CLM 1, p. 293; cf. nos. 632–633, CLM 1, pp. 344–346.
bbb. Nos. 631–32, CLM 1, pp.344–346.
ccc. No. 461.
ddd. Autograph, July 30, 1848.
eee. Nos. 637–638.
fff. *Ami de la Religion,* February 29, 1848, p. 497; CLM 1, p. 321.
ggg. No. 1315.
hhh. No. 937, Sr. Cosnard, CLM 2, p. 255.
iii. No. 564, CLM 1, p. 335.
jjj. No. 604, CLM 1, p. 339.
kkk. No. 604, CLM 1, p. 338.

CHAPTER VI: THE WAR AND THE COMMUNE

a. No. 630.
b. An Fr. 1871, p. 221.
c. Ibid., p. 226.
d. CLM 2, p. 147.
e. Communicated by Marthe Duhamel, p. 4.
f. *Journal,* in An Fr. 1871, p. 264.
g. Ibid., p. 395.
h. No. 966, June 10, 1898, CLM 2, p. 293.
i. Cf. note 26 above.
j. Cf. note 50 above.
k. No. 1256, cited in note 53.

CHAPTER VII: DECLINING YEARS–ASCENDING LIFE

- a. No. 920, Sr. Tanguy, CLM 2, p. 236.
- b. No. 1283.
- c. No. 1280, Léonie-Victoire Labouré, July 2, 1909, Paspec 34, p. 497.
- d. Cf. chapter 2, note 65, above.
- e. No. 1453a, Marthe Duhamel, reminiscence dating from shortly before 1914, p. 10.
- f. *Vie de Monsieur Etienne,* Paris 1881, pp. 348–50.
- g. No. 942, Sr. Cosnard, CLM 2, p. 266.
- h. No. 978, CLM 2, p. 308.
- i. No. 1336, P. Meugniot, Paspec 75, p. 1052.
- j. No. 1299, Paspec 52, p. 746.
- k. Ibid., p. 745; cf. p. 746.
- l. *Notice* (no. 52).
- m. No. 1285, Sr. de Montesquiou, July 7, 1909, Paspec 39, p. 577.
- n. Cf. p. 144, above.
- o. Nos. 937, 1291.
- p. No. 1291, Sr. Cosnard, July 10, 1909, PA 44, p. 653.
- q. Nos. 635–636.
- r. Cf. chapter 5 above.
- s. No. 699, CLM 2, p. 120.
- t. No. 645, CLM 2, p. 48.
- u. No. 460.
- v. No. 674, CLM 2, p. 111.
- w. CLM 2, p. 92.
- x. Nos. 635–636, CLM 1, p. 351.
- y. No. 1251, Paspec 7, p. 180.
- z. CLM 2, pp. 118–132.
- aa. Cf. note 39, above.
- bb. July 3, 1905, PNC 5, p. 81.
- cc. No. 1257, Paspec, p. 237, cf. note 39.
- dd. No. 892; cf. nos. 1278, 1660; Misermont, *Vie,* 1931, p. 227 (1933 ed.: p. 229).
- ee. No. 961, Léonie Labouré, May 10, 1898, CLM 2, p. 283.
- ff. No. 961.
- gg. No. 939, cited in note 60, above.
- hh. No. 976, CLM 2, p. 307.

ii. No. 979, Sr. Cantel, CLM 2, p. 310.
jj. René Laurentin, *Thérèse de Lisieux,* Paris, 1973, p. 125.
kk. No. 892.
ll. No. 645, CLM 2, p. 50.

Chapter VIII: Catherine's Death

a. No. 524, Aladel retreat notes, *Cahier des Autographes,* pp. 76–78.
b. No. 637.
c. No. 1254, Sr. Tanguy, Paspec 10, p. 208.
d. No. 644, CLM 2, p. 53.
e. No. 645, Sr. Dufès, CLM 2, p. 53.
f. No. 898, CLM 2, p. 224.
g. No. 639, CLM 2, p. 357.

Chapter IX: Catherine's Sanctity

a. Misermont, *Ame,* p. 204.
b. No. 638, CLM 1, p. 357.
c. CLM 2, p. 85.
d. No. 638.
e. CLM 2, p. 85.
f. No. 649.
g. Cf. Chapter 6, note 91, above.
h. No. 1253.
i. No. 1253, June 8, 1909, Paspec, p. 195.
j. No. 1406, Villette, p. 20.
k. No. 957, March 24, 1898, PO 46, CLM 2, p. 277.
l. Ibid.
m. No. 819, CLM 2, p. 141.
n. No. 531.
o. Chapter 5, note 89, and chapter 7, section 2.
p. No. 970.
q. Chapter 8, above.
r. No. 999, CLM 2, p. 334.
s. Ibid.
t. No. 1277, June 30, 1909, Paspec 31, p. 461.
u. No. 990, CLM 2, p. 322.
v. No. 819, CLM 2, p. 145.

w. CLM 2, p. 143.
x. CLM 2, p. 210.
y. CLM 2, p. 143.
z. No. 1291, Sr. Cosnard, July 10, 1909, Paspec 44, p. 651.
aa. No. 1317, Sr. Hannezo.
bb. No. 1263.
cc. No. 1299.
dd. Chapter 8, above.
ee. No. 976, Sr. Charvier, December 2, 1898, CLM 2, p. 306.
ff. No. 990, Sr. Charvier, CLM, p. 322.
gg. No. 1304, Paspec, p. 821.
hh. No. 894.
ii. No. 1262.
jj. No. 819, CLM 2, pp. 141–142.
kk. Chapter 7, note 84, above.
ll. No. 1263, Sr. Darlin, Paspec, p. 298.
mm. No. 819, CLM 2, p. 159.
nn. No. 1315, Sr. Hannezo, October 25, 1909, Paspec 64, p. 919.
oo. No. 1264, June 18, 1909, Paspec 18, p. 324.
pp. No. 1363, Paspec, p. 139.
qq. No. 976.
rr. No. 964.
ss. No. 937.
tt. No. 982.
uu. Cf. note 86, above.
vv. No. 1279, Paspec 33, p. 485.
ww. No. 1264.
xx. No. 873, Sr. Dufès; no. 1259.
yy. No. 1281.
zz. No. 1286.
aaa. No. 1289.
bbb. Cf. note 58, above.
ccc. No. 1336, Paspec, p. 1057.

BOOKS & MEDIA

The Daughters of St. Paul operate book and media centers at the following addresses. Visit, call or write the one nearest you today, or find us on the World Wide Web, www.pauline.org

CALIFORNIA
   3908 Sepulveda Blvd, Culver City, CA 90230   310-397-8676
   5945 Balboa Avenue, San Diego, CA 92111   858-565-9181
   2640 Broadway Street, Redwood City, CA 94063   650-369-4230

FLORIDA
   145 S.W. 107th Avenue, Miami, FL 33174   305-559-6715

HAWAII
   1143 Bishop Street, Honolulu, HI 96813   808-521-2731
   Neighbor Islands call: 866-521-2731

ILLINOIS
   172 North Michigan Avenue, Chicago, IL 60601   312-346-4228

LOUISIANA
   4403 Veterans Memorial Blvd, Metairie, LA 70006   504-887-7631

MASSACHUSETTS
   885 Providence Hwy, Dedham, MA 02026   781-326-5385

MISSOURI
   9804 Watson Road, St. Louis, MO 63126   314-965-3512

NEW JERSEY
   561 U.S. Route 1, Wick Plaza, Edison, NJ 08817   732-572-1200

NEW YORK
   150 East 52nd Street, New York, NY 10022   212-754-1110

PENNSYLVANIA
   9171-A Roosevelt Blvd, Philadelphia, PA 19114   215-676-9494

SOUTH CAROLINA
   243 King Street, Charleston, SC 29401   843-577-0175

TENNESSEE
   4811 Poplar Avenue, Memphis, TN 38117   901-761-2987

TEXAS
   114 Main Plaza, San Antonio, TX 78205   210-224-8101

VIRGINIA
   1025 King Street, Alexandria, VA 22314   703-549-3806

CANADA
   3022 Dufferin Street, Toronto, ON M6B 3T5   416-781-9131

¡También somos su fuente para libros, videos y música en español!